Tiffany Blue

The True Story of Turquoise,
Tiffany & James P. McNulty
in Territorial New Mexico
⚜ 1892 – 1933 ⚜

Patricia McGraw

Lone Butte Press
Santa Fe, New Mexico
2006

Marketing & Distribution:
South Valley Ink
PMB 209
1625 Rio Bravo Boulevard SW
Albuquerque, NM 87105
(505) 873-4904
www.SouthValleyInk.com

© 2006 Patricia McCraw

All rights reserved

Cover Design: Lone Beaut

ISBN-13: 978-0-9666860-5-0
ISBN-10: 0-9666860-5-5
Library of Congress Control Number: 2006922523

Printed in the United States of America

CONTENTS

Prologue v

Leading Characters vi

Acknowledegments vii

Area Maps viii

1   1892 - 1899   Turquoise Fever 1

2   1899 - 1900   Plots and Rattlesnakes 37

3   1900 - 1901   Perfect Blue 67

4   1902 - 1903   The New Mexican's Peculiar Temperament .. 105

5   The Devil and Mariano F. Sena 131

6   1904 - 1907   A Judicial Shell Game 143

7   1908 - 1909   More Politics & Corruption 185

8   1910 - 1911   It is the Decision of This Court 231

9   1912 - 1915   A Telephone Might Help 257

10   1916 - 1921   The Protection of the Law 293

11   1922 - 1933   The End of the Turquoise Trail 327

About the Author 378

This book is dedicated to the memory of
James Patrick McNulty

PROLOGUE

It is only because my great grandfather, James Patrick McNulty, assiduously kept all his correspondence — all of it — and because my grandmother, Fannie, in her turn carefully preserved that archive, and my father, James, after her, that this story can be told. It has been my pleasure to assemble this true history of an extraordinary man from a nearly forgotten time. McNulty's letters show the connections that ran from New York City, the center of banking in the United States, to the little known town of Cerrillos, New Mexico. The Tiffany and Castilian Mines produced the rare, perfect blue turquoise that Charles Lewis Tiffany desired for his jewelry, and consequently the mines attracted the attention of politicians and land manipulators who endeavored to wrest control of those mines from the New Yorkers.

Our family tradition, supported by written recollections, says that McNulty supplied the Pueblo Indians in the area with turquoise upon request, and while they were camped at the mines McNulty and Emma gave them sugar and coffee. McNulty counted among his friends many Puebloans. And the same was true for his daughter Fannie, who became known in the area as "The Turquoise Lady".

This history is offered to the Santo Domingo Indians who still tell the tales of the Devil-possessed man at the blue stone hill. It is offered to the spirit of Charles Lewis Tiffany who could not have known the maelstrom he would create in his quest for perfect blue. It is offered to the many historians who have heretofore known only rumors of the American Turquoise Company. And I offer it to the curious who have no idea of the Tiffany-turquoise world in the heart of New Mexico that flashed so brilliantly a mere hundred years ago, and then slowly faded away.

The Leading Characters of TIFFANY BLUE

The McNultys
James Patrick McNulty – Irish immigrant, served in U.S. Army in the West, now the superintendent of the American Turquoise Company mines (the Tiffany Mines) at Turquesa, New Mexico.
Emma Hawley McNulty – his second wife.
Fannie, Eddie (E.J.), Agnes – his children, by his first marriage.

The New Yorkers
John Rutt Andrews - former jewelry manufacturer at Tiffany & Co. and a major stockholder in that company; the first president of the American Turquoise Company.
George F. Kunz - Tiffany & Co. gemologist; World-renowned arbiter of the value of gems and impetus behind the late-19th century fashion for turquoise.
Robert A. Parker – banker, second President of the American Turquoise Company.
Allan Pinkerton - principal owner of Pinkerton Detective Agency, and son of its founder Allan Pinkerton; ATC bond holder, financier.
James Stillman – President and Chairman of the National City Bank of New York, depository for the United States Government; the major ATC bond holder, financier.
Charles Lewis Tiffany – since 1837 a New York jeweler of note, whose company received the entire output of the Tiffany Mines in New Mexico; ATC bond holder, financier.

The New Mexicans
Charles Clossen - sheriff of Santa Fe County, stalled and refused to investigate the troubles at the mines.
Isidore Lazard, known as "The Jew" – Cerrillos merchant, formerly of Santo Domingo; participated (in disguise) in the nighttime raids, and later was a reluctant informant.
Mariano F. Sena — of the powerful Sena family; the son of the former Santa Fe County sheriff, and brother of the clerk of the Supreme Court; involved in land speculation and forgery.
The Santo Domingos - the nearby Native American Pueblo whose people had been using turquoise from the Turquoise Hill for more than a thousand years.

ACKNOWLEDGEMENTS

Tiffany Blue is the product of many people over many years, all of them looking to the day when this book would see the light. Truly, this could not have been done without you.

Deena Lewis helped me get organized; Pat Ehn kept me going; Homer Milford encouraged me years ago to get busy; Doug Magnus, current owner of the Tiffany Mines, provided me with additional information and pictures; Todd Brown, owner of the Turquoise Mining Museum in Cerrillos, whose infectious enthusiasm permeates this work; Dennis Domrzalski, writer, provided grammatical expertise.

Members of a science fiction writers' group long past: Pati Nagel, Walter Jon Williams, Sage Walker, Sally Gwylan, and Joan Saberhagen.

My original journalism teachers: Tony Hillerman and James Crow.

Most importantly, editor William Baxter, who helped craft Tiffany Blue, as did my husband Arnold Brown, and my mother-in-law Anne Brown.

Heartfelt thanks to all of you.

Patricia McCraw

viii

Santa Fe Region about 1900
Santa Fe to Cerrillos, 20 miles

N

Places shown: Santa Fe, Agua Fria, Cochiti, Rio Grande, Santa Fe River, La Cienega, La Bajada, Bonanza, Turquoise Hill, Santo Domingo, Rio Galisteo, Cerrillos Hills, Turquesa, Waldo, Cerrillos, Madrid, Lamy, Galisteo, A.T.&S.F.

Turquoise Hill Region
Area shown 1.7 miles x 1.3 miles

N

MODERN ROAD • McNULTY'S HOUSE • OLD ROAD

1 - Gem Lode
2 - Muñiz / Tiffany Lode
3 - Morning Star Lode
4 - Blue Bell Lode
5 - Blue Gem Lode
6 - Castilian Lode
7 - Sky Blue Lode

Chapter 1
1892 - 1899

Turquoise Fever

...no material is to be taken from the mines except that to be sent to Tiffany & Company under the joint supervision of yourself and Mr. Sterne.

R.A. Parker, president of American Turquoise Company, to McNulty
June 9th, 1899

THE QUEST FOR PERFECT BLUE

The skies at the Turquoise Hill eighteen miles southeast of Santa Fe, New Mexico, glowed brighter, bluer, and clearer than anywhere else. The sounds quieted and soothed a man's soul. The immense vistas, the adventure, and the thought of riches lured James Patrick McNulty to Cerrillos and its Turquoise Hill in 1892.

A 46 year-old Irish immigrant, McNulty stood five feet six inches tall, weighed in at 175 pounds, and possessed salt and pepper hair that was lately more salt than pepper. His perfectly groomed mustache added just the right amount of decorum to his smile. Twinkling blue eyes contained a hint of mischievousness as well as a warning that people should not take him lightly. And his stare, unblinking and unyielding could hold a man still. Usually, when he had his picture taken, he turned his head a little to the right to hide the notch in his ear made by an Indian arrow. His penchant for action and adventure had taken him by horseback all over the New Mexico territory, and the path from Santa Fe to Denver, Colorado, served as his main route.

2 • Patricia McGraw

Those travels led him to select the Santa Fe surroundings as a good place to raise his son, Eddie, and his two daughters, Agnes and Fannie.

The early 1890s ran rife with rumors of gold, silver, and great mining adventures that teased people, Westerners and Easterners alike, to join the race for riches and land. And with the race on, miners brought their families who demanded laws and sheriffs who enforced those laws. Of course, there were the ruffians and gamblers, and on payday, lots of working men with money in their pockets and trouble in their eyes. It could get rough. But, McNulty, no stranger to a saloon, knew how to steer clear of trouble, and he knew which drinking buddies he could trust.

When McNulty arrived on the Turquoise Hill, he had already enrolled his daughters in Loretto Academy for Girls, where they would be raised in the Catholic tradition of his Irish ancestors. When McNulty's friend, Chauncey G. Story, another miner in Cerrillos, recommended the Irishman to New York investors, that left McNulty and young Eddie free to set about the business of turquoise mining.

Story's backers accepted the recommendation and appointed McNulty manager/supervisor of the American Turquoise Company (ATC) mine holdings just north of Cerrillos. The five claims, the Castilian, the Muñiz, the Morning Star, the Sky-Blue, and the Gem lode mines, produced gem quality turquoise so much in demand back East. And most of the turquoise produced by the ATC was shipped directly to Tiffany & Company in New York City.

In recent years, turquoise had captured the attention of investors, jewelers, gemologists, miners, and politicians, and it all began with a simple declaration from a Tiffany gemologist. Backed by well-heeled investors and his close connection to Tiffany, that gem expert single-handedly pushed up the value of the perfect sky-blue turquoise and raised what had been a nearly worthless stone to gem level. Turquoise quickly became extremely profitable.

Although at the mines the living conditions challenged even the hardiest of men, McNulty took on the project. He hitched his wagon to turquoise, so to speak, and bet on the hope that the gem would bring wealth to everyone. No amount of natural hardship would ever force him off the mines. In spite of the fact that the remote, waterless area was no more than a playground for howling, swirling wind and lightning storms, McNulty rather liked the view.

Cerrillos, the nearest town to the Turquoise Hill, lay only eight miles to the south of the mines. Its train station gave direct access to the East Coast. It boasted water, stores, saloons, dynamite, and equipment, everything needed for a successful mining enterprise. Travelers from the East found hot meals and warm beds. If nature denied water to the gold fields and the Turquoise Hill, it supplied it in abundance in the town. Arroyos or natural cuts through the hills were the paths through which miners could move water, wood, food, equipment, and ores.

Cerrillos provided many of the comforts of a big town: one newspaper, a hotel, a couple of smelters, several boarding houses, and sixteen saloons. Rumors of gold finds made their way into the newspaper, but the more reliable news came out of the saloons. McNulty's daughter described the town as "fairly alive with teams and wagons which lined the roads in every direction," wagons full of ore to be shipped by train to smelters in faraway states. On every corner one could see a saloon. There were sixteen of them. But around those saloons you didn't see loiterers or children playing. Minors, as well as women, were excluded by law from such places; and men who had taken too much were not permitted to remain in town. Cerrillos had pretensions.

At the turquoise mines McNulty found a ten by twenty foot miner's cabin, roomy enough for McNulty and Eddie and close enough for Eddie to attend the school in Cerrillos. The cabin, built out of wood slats chinked with stone and covered with adobe, protected the occupants from the weather. Simple, but warm, the house's wood stove served for heat and for cooking. Kerosine lamps lit the building at night. McNulty's time in tents on other mining sites made him appreciate a house with a real roof. It had served other miners and probably would serve many more.

McNulty's metal trunk banded with wooden straps held his treasures: a picture of his deceased wife, Agnes Dunn, and his three children; a rosary; white shirts; dungarees; literature, including the poetry of Robert Burns; and the glasses he needed for reading at night. A straight razor and sharpening strop; a pitcher and bowl; and a chamber pot. Thus was his small collection of personal items.

McNulty's gold and silver mining experiences translated readily into turquoise mining. It was no wonder that when he received orders the work began immediately. He blasted, hauled out the rocks, and sorted them in search of the highly prized blue color. McNulty faced long hours of hard work, as well as lots of double entry bookkeeping. Just because he was the supervisor didn't exempt him from the rock breaking and hauling.

For mining positions, the physically weak need not apply. Mining days averaged 10 hours, from a little after sunrise to late in the day. The tools of the trade were dynamite, pickaxes, shovels, and lots of rope. Large, empty whiskey barrels stood next to the shafts, ready to be lowered down, filled with rock, and hauled up by the horse-driven whim, which was a pulley and gear system powered by a horse walking in a circle.

Inside the mines McNulty and other miners picked and hacked at the walls of the shaft. The hammers clinked against the hard rock and sounds of stones dropped into buckets echoed in the shafts. They broke down the large rocks into manageable sizes then filled the barrels and buckets. On the surface the miners packed the rock to McNulty's home or nearby tents for sorting. The work required great physical strength since buckets or boxes of turquoise sometimes weighed more than 100 pounds. Other days were taken up by the dangerous work of setting dynamite or black powder charges. That was delicate work. Blasting in the turquoise mines demanded care for personal safety but also to protect the gems.

The turquoise was normally sorted into several piles. Raw stone with turquoise embedded went in one pile and raw stone containing nuggets or slabs went into another. Once he received his instructions he shipped off the stones in boxes, usually cigar boxes, with weights ranging from three pounds to six pounds. McNulty carried the sealed boxes by horseback or by buggy to the Wells Fargo Express office at the train station in Cerrillos on a weekly basis. Other times, when the mine ran with a full crew, the miners worked in sorting tents or sorting areas, but the turquoise nuggets, chips, and pieces McNulty always removed himself.

At the mines the day was punctuated by three meals: breakfast, lunch, and supper. If the hunting were good they had meat; rabbit or the occasional deer. Sometimes mutton was purchased from Cerrillos. At some cost, water had to be hauled all the way from Bonanza Creek, two miles north, or Cerrillos far to the south. Rain barrels stood around the cabin in the event it ever rained.

Meals usually consisted of biscuits, eggs, vegetables, apples in season, and many times a stew. A grocery list written by McNulty noted the important items of the day and their prices: groceries (including flour and coffee, miscellaneous items), $17; wood and water, $2.75; meat, $1.20; Plowman, $2; meat, $1.50; mutton, $1.75. The same leather covered record book showed that water was $1.25 on the 14th, the 20th, the 25th, and the 30th of the month. And those were 1890s dollars. One dollar and twenty five cents represented for a regular laborer a whole day's work.

The American Turquoise Company
Importers of Diamonds and other precious Stones.
Andrews & Doty
Sole Agents,
207 Broadway
New York, Feb 7th 1893

J. P. McNulty
　　Dear Sir —
I enclose the money to pay the enclosed bills also pay me for month of January.

J. P. McNulty	78.00
E. J. McNulty	31.25
Felix Mares	35.60
Bills Cerrillos Suply Co	18.55
Harkness	1.50
	$164.90

and have enclosed receipts to have signed and mailed to me.

ATC letterhead proclaims the high hopes of the newborn mining venture.

People got by with help from each other. Another of McNulty's lists showed he loaned a fellow miner: four drills- two 24" drills; one 18" drill; one 15" drill; two Gads; one pinch; one shovel; one four pound hammer; 25 pounds Giant Powder; one windlass rope. (The miner repaid only four pounds of Giant powder.)

The unending drudgery at the mines was interrupted by Sundays, the day of rest and more. The *Cerrillos Rustler* noted in 1891, "C.G. Story came in from the Turquoise mine to attend church Sunday. Young men are apt to be religiously inclined when there are plump and pretty young ladies to go to church with."

ENTER TIFFANY & CO.

Turquoise in the middle of the 1880s had little value, but in 1892, following Tiffany & Company's gemologist George F. Kunz's declaration of the gem status of turquoise, the value of the stone jumped. Immediately, Charles Lewis Tiffany secured a supply of the blue stone for his jewelry. People screamed for Tiffany jewelry, and Wall Street dug deeper in its pockets to increase turquoise output. What followed was the explosive growth in the price of turquoise, the extreme demand for sky blue colors, and the "blue age" of American turquoise production.

A clipping in the territorial governor L. Bradford Prince papers, dated in pen 12/03/1892, stated that "Mr. George Kunz, the noted expert of Tiffany, New York, and the highest American authority on gems, says to a New York newspaper: 'Look at that. Is not that an exquisite blue? It is the blue of a sky upon a perfect June day. That is a turquoise, far and away the finest in America, and it came from these new mines in New Mexico. It is worth $4,000. ...it is probable that gems to the value of $200,000 a year may be obtained from this mine.'"

Almost overnight a carat of cut and polished turquoise, about the size of a small pea, ranged from $8 to $20. Turquoise of an "off color" had no established price and those stones were used for inlay work on cabinets and table tops. Only the sky blue stone achieved gem status, and Kunz declared that the very best came from the Cerrillos mines.

Kunz, a year older than McNulty, cut a dashing figure with his perfectly groomed mustache and beard. Dark curling hair parted straight down the middle framed his face, and his light colored eyes squinted as he assessed gems. He enjoyed his worldwide jaunts in search of the perfect gems for Tiffany, and he gloried in the difficulty of obtaining those gems. He always said it was the expert who gave a stone its value. That was his job.

"...we might as well state it flatly – no one not an expert can trust his eyes in this matter of selecting gems; for if all else be well, how shall he know whether or not an expert can trust his eyes in this matter of selecting gems; how shall he know whether a certain stone, undoubtedly genuine, is worth ten or a hundred or a thousand dollars a carat? This is a matter of expert judgment of perfection and color and quality. The amateur's eyes may give him its beauty, his jeweler must give him its value," he said.

Gem buyers should obtain their treasures from a thoroughly reputable firm such as Tiffany & Company, Kunz advised.

Turquoise had been fashionable throughout the ages, varying with historic trends, and Kunz had made a study of it, but the relative ease of obtaining Persian stones had kept its value low. When Kunz saw that the turquoise from Turquoise Hill was the signature color of Tiffany blue, he recognized the possibilities. After all, a New Mexico stone had already been part of the same Tiffany collection that had garnered awards at a Paris exhibition in 1889. "The true Persian blue with no tinge of green and without inclusions of matrix [silver, copper, or gold veins] is the ideal; and when this pure color is found the value of the stone is hundreds of times higher than that of the off-color stone." And this is what Kunz saw coming from New Mexico.

With the worth of turquoise established and its status raised to that of gem stone, Kunz's work was done.

Next, Charles Rutt Andrews and Joseph G. Doty arrived in New Mexico, where they intended to begin large scale production of turquoise. Andrews and Doty both had direct connections to Tiffany, Andrews himself recently retiring from that premier jewelry company. McNulty was made superintendent of the mines.

Within four months of taking over the reins of the American Turquoise mining operations at Cerrillos, McNulty's first letter of instructions arrived from his friend, Story. That letter bore the address Turquesa, in care of the Turquoise Mine in Santa Fe County, a new mining town in homage to the turquoise production going on there. It consisted of only three miner's cabins, yet its tiny area intrigued and enticed all types of Eastern investors as well as promoted gossip about great riches below the surface. News of Turquesa spread widely, even in New York where Story's headquarters at 207 Broadway lay only a short 10 minute walk from Tiffany and Company.

C.G. Story to McNulty, July 19, 1892
> *Friend Mac, ...have Mike* [O'Neil] *help you close up opening at shaft as I want that opening kept closed. You need not try to timber it any as I will work in a new place when I come down. Would like to have you write me once a week how things look...*

Story had been working in the Cerrillos Hills for several years, and when a market for turquoise appeared he had incorporated the American Turquoise Company. He set up 16,000 shares of stock at $100 per share on January 29, 1892. And, of course, as was true of so many Easterners, he yearned for adventures in the West.

By June The Farmer's Loan and Trust had provided operating capital of $250,000 in exchange for the deeds of the Castilian, the Muñiz, the Morning Star, the Sky-Blue, and the Gem lodes. The American Turquoise Company now had a hefty loan to repay. Andrews, newly elected president of the company, Doty, and Story set about extracting turquoise, and putting that turquoise on the East coast market, with most of the gems going directly to Tiffany & Company.

The American Turquoise Company will "carry on the business of mining turquoise and manufacturing it into merchantable gems, and selling and dealing in the same in either a crude or manufactured state, and to erect and construct all such works and the equipment ...as may at any time be deemed necessary for such mining and manufacture, and to buy and sell any property as may be lawful ...to acquire, hold and dispose of any turquoise mining property..." the incorporation document stated.

Although the officers of the company frequently visited McNulty and directed operations, the financiers stayed in the background. The sons of Allan Pinkerton, of the Pinkerton Detective Agency, James Stillman, president of the New York City Bank, and Charles Lewis Tiffany of New York jewelry fame poured cash into the venture as they dreamed of the riches that would come from the sky blue stone. But it was Andrews and Doty who directed McNulty throughout that first big year, 1892. These gentlemen from the East arrived by train, looking very "Eastern" in their silk top hats and long tailed coats. They exchanged these for proper mining attire when they arrived, but the people of Cerrillos took note of their movements and activities just the same. The bankers, gem dealers, and jewelry makers from the East enjoyed their jaunts to the West, and when they returned home with quantities of the now-esteemed sky blue stone, they basked in the accolades of their peers and of Charles Lewis Tiffany. They also brought back stories of adventures in the hills.

For his trips west Andrews dressed neatly, with a starched collar shirt, a frock coat, and a top hat, but at the mines he changed all that for the traditional mining garb of hobnail boots, dungarees, and pale shirt. His curling, graying beard and moustache covered his lips while his blue eyes missed little. After a lifetime of assessing the worth of diamonds and other gems, he needed only a glance to establish their value.

That acute business sense made Andrews a perfect agent to present the stone from the ATC mines to two jewelry concerns: Alling & Carter of New York and Chicago, and Tiffany & Company of New York. Story's unerring ability to find veins and pillars of turquoise and McNulty's ability to secure the most reliable workers as well as his skill at extracting the turquoise led to an efficient operation that kept the two eastern concerns well supplied with the gem.

Doty stood as a contrast to the taller Andrews. Around five foot five inches, he possessed dark brown eyes and big black bushy beard sprinkled with grey. His stocky frame looked as if he could carry stones forever and scramble up and down ladders easily. His handwriting indicated an educated man with flowing, bold quill pen strokes. That boldness carried over into his business dealings as he traveled East to supervise the cutting, polishing, and sale of turquoise. Always he demanded more output from the mines. After all, the company had bonds it had to pay off.

As turquoise prices rose, cash flowed to the mines and weekly shipments of turquoise arrived in New York. Sometimes cash arrived in special Wells Fargo envelopes, double red wax seals on both sides. At other times Andrews, Story, or Doty delivered the cash.

ATC optimism matched the turquoise output. For the first 10 months of its mining operations, $290 per month on average arrived at the mines and into McNulty's hands. Jewellers and investors thought the money well spent. And no wonder, because the estimates of the

10 • Patricia McGraw

output of the mine reached $200,000.

Now that Story had the mines up and running he informed McNulty that Andrews and Doty would be his new bosses.

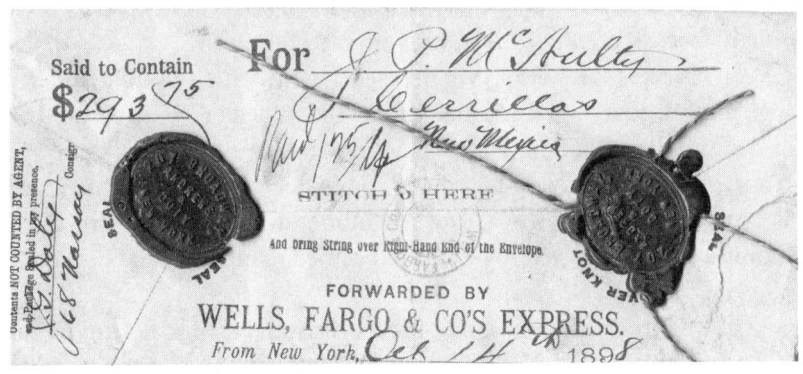

This pouch contained the money for payroll and expenses: $293.75 on October 14, 1898.

This is McNulty's log book for 1898, and his pencil. The notes he took contributed to his very accurate work reports and payroll accounts.

OF DEADLINES AND DEPRESSION

The days in the mines were long and hard. And there were other dangers; lightning strikes, rattlesnakes, and claim jumpers and trespassers. It took a sharp eye and steel nerves to deal with it all. The average pay for a miner hovered between $1.50 to $2 per day in 1893. ATC paid experienced miners $2 per day and McNulty earned $3 per day, high wages for the time. And McNulty insisted on paying equal wages for equal work no matter the miner's ethnicity. In return for higher than average wages the ATC demanded secrecy and loyalty, and this fueled even more speculation among the local population over how much wealth came out of the ground.

One to eight people worked the mines during 1892, with Felipe Mares and 19-year-old Eddie (McNulty's son) being noted on the wage rolls the most often. As supervisor, McNulty averaged 24 days per month. Other miners sometimes worked as little as three days and as much as 25 days per month. Just like clockwork, at least most of the time, Wells Fargo pouches or sealed letters arrived with cash for the payroll and the bills. One of the pouches with $72 in it disappeared and was thought lost. But four months later, the pouch appeared at the American Turquoise Company's New York office with the money still inside.

Speculation about the stones and their resulting value kept gossipers talking for months in 1893 as they schemed to join in the hunt for perfect blue. Politicians and their friends considered every angle to wrest the mines from the hands of ATC. The most common way to take over another person's mine was for noncompliance with the 1872 Mining Law. Mine owners were required each year to prove they had invested $100 or more in mine work, or that they had dug a 10 foot deep shaft, tunnel, or trench. If McNulty failed to produce each year's Proof of Labor, the mines would be up for grabs and could be jumped for new owners. Always, people watched McNulty, hoping that he would miss his yearly assessment deadline. McNulty, strong, crafty, and hard working, kept up with the assessment work, and he did more than the required amount. Claim jumpers remained disappointed; politicians plotted; and the watchful sheriff and his family had to look elsewhere for a way to steal control of the Tiffany mines.

One of McNulty's notes showed that the Castilian mine assessment work extended by 19 feet in one year; the Sky Blue expanded by 13 feet; and the Morning Start increased by 15 feet. "Shaft drift and slope work; sorting and retimbering the mine at a cost of over $2,000," McNulty wrote. This expenditure was 200 times more than that required by law, and the physical work represented 50-75 percent more than required. No slackards allowed on these mines! Everyone stayed busy as the ATC directors moved in and out of New Mexico. They worked alongside McNulty and his miners. They saw firsthand the dangers surrounding the mines. And they went well armed. Some, concerned for McNulty's safety, thought he should always have a body guard. They had heard of the "troubles" McNulty experienced with Pueblo Indians and local thieves coming into the mines to take turquoise as fast as McNulty pulled it out of the ground. And they also saw potential claim jumpers, like turkey vultures, circling nearby and waiting.

Other industrious miners filed claims adjacent to the ATC mining group in hopes of a share of that wealth, or perhaps to practice "slant" mining. This illegal but difficult to detect practice meant digging underground across the boundary lines and into the rich areas of the ATC land. Real or imagined, slant mining caused trouble on many a claim. While miners and New Mexico politicos wrestled for riches, the depression of 1893 hit the east coast and dried up the sources of outside capital. Investment in mining became much less attractive.

The bankruptcy of a major eastern railroad sent shivers through the banks and businesses dependent upon railroads. A depression followed and the stockmarket plummeted downward. By the end of the year, ATC owed $659.50 to shop owners, McNulty, and others in the Cerrillos/Santa Fe area.

Doty explained to McNulty that tough financial times meant outstanding debts and slow payments for all. Patience and trust would have to go a long way. In mid January of 1894 McNulty totalled the bills again as Doty had arrived in Cerrillos to pay them all off. Doty distributed the cash and then turned his attention to the search for the sky stone. He directed McNulty to where the stones should be removed. Teams of eight miners worked through January and February. Doty could sell the stone if he could get the right kind as the demand for quality turquoise showed no signs of slowing.

But it was not only the depression that affected business. Suddenly, on February 6, a telegram arrived indicating trouble at the American Turquoise Company. Ordered to New York at once, Doty faced a fight for control of the company.

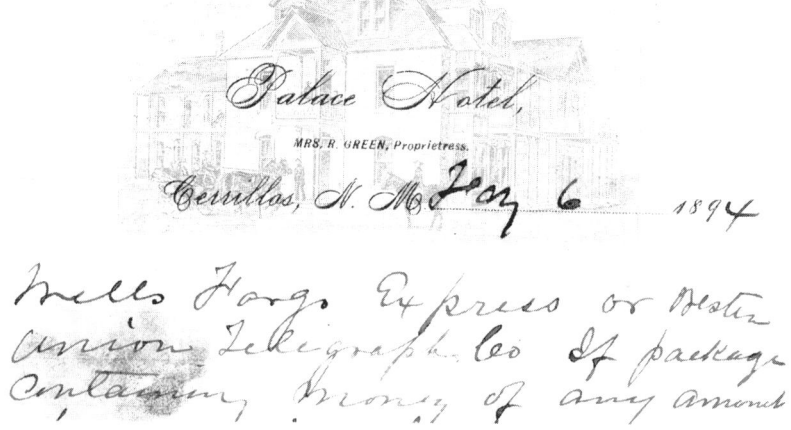

Doty dashed this note off on Palace Hotel stationary before he took the train back to New York.

THE RIGHT STONES

In 1894, before rushing off to New York, Doty sent a rather cryptic letter to McNulty: "You and Alex work together until I get back and I am sure you will be able to make things go all right. My business in New York is of such importance that a day is liable to be very expensive to do." He also wrote that he expected the arrival of an important package that McNulty should save for his return.

The telegram had arrived just six days after Andrews stepped aside as president and turned the American Turquoise Company over to R. G. Rolston, president of the Farmer's Loan and Trust Company, the bank that held the original $250,000 loan for the mine operation. Rolston probably considered foreclosing on the mining enterprise, but apparently decided to let it go a little while longer in hopes that his bank would be paid off. Clearly, Rolston considered selling the mines to others. Finally, the handwriting on the wall stated: "Produce or lose the mine."

Another month passed. No letters came from Story or Doty. McNulty waited. Extremely bad news arrived in the March 14, 1894 *Jewelers Weekly*. John Andrews, the guiding light and major mover of all turquoise from the ATC, had died. This opened up ATC for a takeover by the loan company, a possible ousting of Doty as the sole agent for ATC as well as a loss of his shares in the company, and a possible break with Tiffany and Company.

Doty did not return to the mines within the promised week's time, but two months later he wrote McNulty. Although Andrews' name still graced the letterhead, the headquarters of the ATC had moved to a less prestigious location.

Doty's motto, "Keep business as usual," pushed him to find the blue stone: no perfect blue meant no ATC. Doty insisted on pushing forward with the mine work no matter what the cost as he raced to pay off the bonds and keep his shares in the ATC.

Employees numbered five in 1894: Felipe Mares, Juan Narbiel, E. Marez, Santiago Leiba, and Georio Naranjo. In April and May there were only two employees: Felipe Mares and Georio Naranjo. For June, July, and August McNulty's log book showed no activity. Work resumed in September, October, November, and December with miners F.J. McMahon, Felipe Mares, and Georio Naranjo on the payroll. Naranjo received $1.50 per day while the other two received $2 per day. The directors of ATC promised McNulty continued operations. At the same time, Rolston, ATC president, hinted at bankruptcy proceedings along with the sale of the mine, although he didn't mention it directly. With the death of Andrews and the reorganization of the company, ATC moved to make sure the

McNulty's Winchester was marked with the masonic symbol, and it bears evidence of much hard use over the years.

mine would be saleable should the need arise. Unpaid bills mounted. Then McNulty received a telegram, and he knew that the business of mining had turned desperate. The Irishman was instructed to welcome attorney John McClure in Santa Fe on a Friday evening in 1894. McNulty's task: total all bills and get ready to pay them off. A few days after the telegram had arrived, McClure, money in hand, stood in front of McNulty. After a brief visit with McNulty at the mines, McClure sent a report to the ATC which encouraged the company to expand. That expansion fed the local gossip mill. Now McNulty needed to go about well armed, and he needed more than just a shotgun. He needed something with a little longer range, something for hunting as well as for protection. Authorization for the purchase of a new Winchester repeating rifle quickly came.

McNulty's log book for 1894 noted that in September, October, and November weekly shipments of stone left the mines and headed to New York. Each box contained around five pounds of stone.

By 1895, Doty pressured McNulty for more stone and better results. Heavily in debt, Doty scrambled for more turquoise — his mining shares, at risk. McNulty received an unusual request from Doty — a departure from procedures that McNulty should send the turquoise directly to Doty instead of Tiffany.

Over the next few months disappointment characterized Doty's letters to McNulty. The miner suspected things could not be going well back East. Still, he kept at work.

PLOTS, POLITICIANS, & STRANGERS

It was a clear, brisk day in November of 1895, with a blue sky overhead, when McNulty went out to hunt. Two workmen sorted turquoise on the dumps.

He saddled up his white mare, Nellie, then headed out to look for game. Later in the day he returned to find four strangers standing on the slope above the Muñiz mine. They had come across the top of the hill, and they took a great deal of interest in what was before them.

McNulty stepped off his horse and rushed up the slope. Immediately, he ordered the men off the property, but the men demurred. They introduced themselves as James Purdy, James Vroom, Mr. Jones, and Mariano Sena.

Purdy informed McNulty that the group was out picnicking and had come to look at the mines. Later in the conversation, Vroom and Purdy hinted these mines might fall within the boundaries of the Jose de Leyba land grant. At one point, the men questioned McNulty about the value of the output of the mines, perhaps even suggesting a dollar amount of more than $200,000 per year. As he later testified, McNulty responded, "I will not put in under $200,000."

He then escorted the four off the property and told them not to return. McNulty considered the affair over and done since he couldn't understand how the foursome could possibly have any type of land grant claim. The time period for applying land grant claims had long past, and the mine had been considered abandoned. The incident was forgotten, although McNulty did write a report to ATC.

Letters from Doty in 1896 alerted McNulty that Doty's demand for more stone could not be met. Foreclosure lurked in the background, threatening Doty's position, and McNulty knew that his job could be on the line as well. Doty insisted on a full mining crew in January and February. The crews ran six men in January and 15 men in February, seven of whom worked a full month 24-25 days. The others worked on average 15-20 days. In March the workforce numbered 11.

Doty told McNulty, March 4, 1896, "My men have examined [the box of stones] carefully and can't find a single stone worth cutting. The large chunks are all spotted and not one of them will cut a marketable stone that will bring any price. If there are no stones in the mine worth cutting I will have to close down the work." He had to have good, marketable stones if he was to survive the takeover of the American Turquoise Company. Nothing short of perfection could save his business.

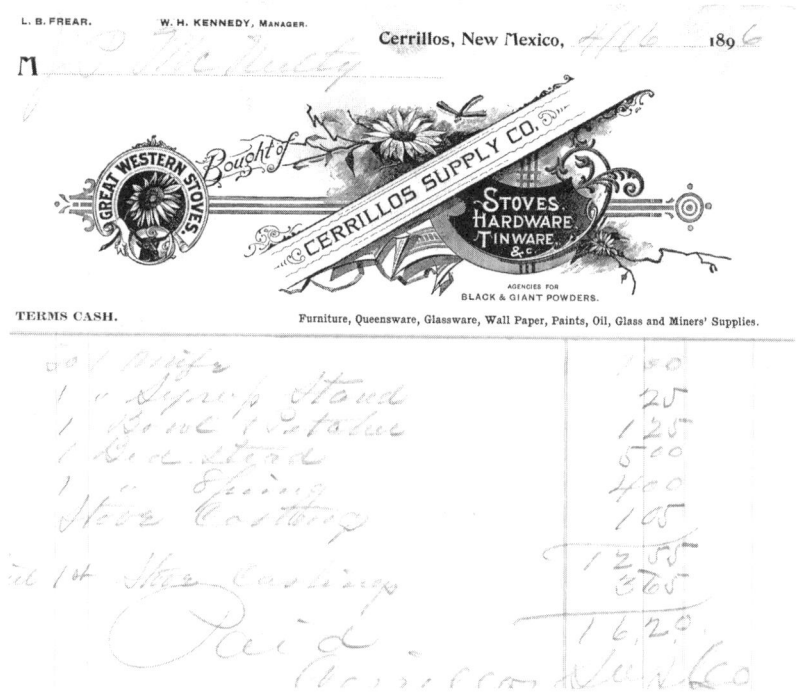

Cerrillos Supply Company Bill.

In April McNulty found time to go into Cerrillos for supplies. The Cerrillos Supply Company, managed by W. H. Kennedy and supplying furniture, Queensware, glassware, wallpaper, paints, oil, glass and miner's supplies, issued a cash invoice for: 1 knife, $1; 1 syrup stand, .24; 1 bowl and pitcher, $1.25; 1 bedstead, $5; 1 bed Spring, $4; stove castings $1.05; another stove casting, $3.65. The bill totaled $16.20. The Cerrillos Supply company touted itself as the agency for both Black & Giant Powders.

Mine work continued until finally Doty received what he wanted, and he ordered McNulty to follow the turquoise lead even if it harmed the mine to the point of making it worthless. Taking all visible blue stone out signaled to potential buyers that the mine no longer contained any turquoise, thus making it impossible to sell in the future.

While McNulty wrestled with finding more stone, the United States economy experienced the effects of "free silver" mania, a movement to establish silver as a second, after gold, monetary standard for the U.S. The government was supposed to buy all silver output from mines across the nation at a rate of one ounce of gold to 16 ounces of silver. However, in 1896 the government declined to continue buying silver at that rate, with a devastating effect on the American Turquoise Company mines. The investors cut back. Doty pointed out that banks wouldn't make loans in the west and that investors were keeping their money close at hand.

Just when they thought things couldn't get much worse, McNulty received two court documents. One was a summons in a case of ejectment requiring ATC to pay Mariano Sena, the mine visitor from the previous year, $50,000 in damages. The other was a lawsuit to prevent removal of turquoise from the ATC holdings and to remove ATC and McNulty from the mines. McNulty, however, consulted with company attorneys and then carried on with his work.

The four strangers who had visited the mines almost a year earlier made their move. They filed suit. Soon known as the Sena Land Grant case, it would define and direct the future of turquoise mining on the Turquoise Hill for more than a decade. Politicians, sheriffs, and court clerks, and even a governor, conspired to take the mines from those alien New Yorkers.

For two months the mine was effectively shut down, with McNulty the only laborer. The company and Frank Clancy, New Mexico attorney to Mariano Sena, sorted out details. The ATC, surprised by the lawsuit, took time to consider the suit's effect on business. Finally, by November, the company re-started mining activities. Clancy had noted that it was of no use to sue McNulty, but rather his client, Sena, should spend his time going after the big investors.

McNulty sorted through stones that had already been dumped. The loan company, Farmer's Loan and Trust, told McNulty that it did not desire to spend much money on the mines, but to send everything he could find so that the holiday demand for turquoise would be met. Lawyers had advised ATC that the mining activities could continue under the cloud of the two pending lawsuits, and that McNulty should be the ATC representative in New Mexico.

The lawyers from the East wrote McNulty on December 30, 1996. "In order to carry out the legal requirements of the Territory of New

THE TERRITORY OF NEW MEXICO

To the Sheriff of **Santa Fe** County, Greeting:

You are hereby commanded to summon **J. P. Mc NULTY** to be and appear before the District Court of the County of **Santa Fe**, in the First Judicial District of the Territory of New Mexico, on the first return day occuring not less than twenty days after service hereof, if the defendant served is a resident of said Judicial District, or on the first return day occuring not less than thirty days after service hereof, if the defendant served is not a resident of said Judicial District, then and there to answer unto **Mariano F. Sena**

in a plea of **ejectment** to the damage of said plaintiff **Fifty Thousand** Dollars, together with interest and costs of suit; the first Monday in each month being a return day, and each defendant being required to enter his appearance in the office of the Clerk of said Court on or before the return day on which this writ is returnable, or judgment by default may be rendered against him. And have you then and there this writ.

WITNESS the HONORABLE *N. B. Laughlin*, Associate Justice of the Supreme Court of the Territory of New Mexico, and Judge of the First Judicial District Court thereof, and the seal of said District Court, this

McNulty received this summons that was to define the future of turquoise mining in New Mexico.

Mexico we have designated you the authorized agent of the American Turquoise Company, residing at Turquesa, upon whom process may be served. We have filed a certificate of this fact and fixing Turquesa as the principal place where the business of the Company is carried on in New Mexico."

For the American Turquoise Company, things went from bad to worse. Eighteen ninety-seven began with legal foreclosure proceedings on the ATC as well as an advertisement for the sale of that company. The Farmer's Loan and Trust Company foreclosed for the amount of $85,481.52. The trust company put the control of the mine into the hands of Howard Carter and William Alling. Letters mentioned Doty less and less. Alling and Carter had the mine deeds filed in their names but they held the mines in trust for the bondholders, James Stillman, the Pinkertons, and Tiffany, until the ATC could be reorganized without Doty. At this point, Doty still issued the mining orders, even though he spent most of his time as gem agent and not in the field. He insisted McNulty work in the same area where they had found turquoise before. McNulty did not search out new sources for the gem and even as payroll fell behind, McNulty continued mining. He trusted Doty.

Payroll for November and December (including McNulty's salary) reached $574, and powder, fuses, and caps cost another $5.

Powder, fuses, caps and explosive work proved to be one of the most dangerous aspects of mining, The *Cerrillos Rustler*, August 5, 1898 related one incident in a neighboring district:

> "Carelessness: O.W. Alexander ascribes the explosion by which he was crippled at Bland last week to carelessness on part of a new assistant. Mr. Alexander had drilled and loaded a battery of fourteen machine holes, five of which were to be "spitted" by one man and nine by himself and 2 assistants. He gave explicit directions to his assistant to "spit" the long fuses first, but the fellow reversed the process by spitting the short ones first and the long ones last. The result was a premature explosion. Mr. Alexander says that his left ankle was crushed to a pulp and a considerable quantity of Albemarel ore was injected into his body. Dr. Grace for several days thereafter employed his time prospecting for ore on Mr. Alexander's person and got pay rock every time he dug a prospect hole."

Another incident showed how much disease affected life during the 1890s. A smallpox outbreak in Albuquerque forced a circus to arrive early in Cerrillos. It had to go around cities with smallpox. Apparently, the mining town of Cerrillos behaved better than its more sophisticated sister in receiving the circus performers, and a news story related the event: "Geo. W. Hall's circus, after successfully running the gauntlet of abuse and smallpox in Albuquerque and other towns, arrived in Cerrillos one day ahead of time. They exhibited here and they were apparently free from contagious diseases. This is a better account than Albuquerque visitors have been able to give of their town."

Cerrillos, grown up in 1898, contained a store for every purpose. The ads in the *Cerrillos Rustler* told of life in a small town: Kendall dealt in lumber, doors, and windows; Tony Trossello, city Livery, promised the best rigs and the finest turnouts in the city; James Williams carried the finest and most complete stock of Imported and Domestic Goods that can be purchased (he owned J.L. Gatzer & Company). Williams also promised to travel to Madrid, Bland and neighboring towns for those who needed tailoring services. J.F. Williams owned the Cerrillos Livery, Feed and Sale Stables where he boarded horses and rented out good teams and careful drivers. The Bullion, owned by Warren Graham, handled the celebrated Jordan Whisky; Lemp's Beer Always on tap. The Fair, owned by S. Golding, carried dry goods, furnishing goods, shoes, hats and grocers. Golding's ad stated, "We guarantee fair treatment and reasonable prices." Julius Muralter, merchant tailor, offered the latest summer styles. H.C. Yontz, watchmaker and jeweler, said that his store specialized in fine turquoise and "gem setting neatly done."

Even in the face of the lawsuit by Sena, 1898 ended pretty well for McNulty. ATC paid all the bills for the year, and McNulty fell in love with an Englishwoman, Emma Hawley, whom he married on December 19, 1898.

Emma, a transplant from England, had joined the myriad of women coming to the west to look for a husband. Her common sense approach to life and smart business sense made her a close match for McNulty. Her arrival in his life marked a noticeable change in the way he conducted his bookkeeping. His log entries became more organized and he made handwritten rough drafts of all the letters he sent back East. She even began writing some of the letters for him at his dictation. The first drafts, made in pencil on Big Chief tablet paper, showed a laborious process that McNulty considered important. McNulty wrote some letters three or more times before he finally sent one off.

His new wife, a little shorter than McNulty, could stand on tiptoe and look him directly in his eyes. When angry, her blue eyes flashed and her checks took on a rosy hue. A strong woman, McNulty could never take Emma for granted. She handled a shotgun almost as well as her husband. She shared many of the duties at the mine. She showed dignitaries around, she fixed meals for McNulty and the workers, and she watched the mine entrances to make sure unauthorized people did not enter. Visitors remarked about her congenial and generous nature, and many enjoyed her guitar and organ playing.

Doty congratulated McNulty on his marriage, and telegraphed him to allow a mining engineer named Sterne to examine the mine since the man had a purchase option on it. The mining claims had been foreclosed in bankruptcy proceedings with Howard Carter, Chicago jeweler, and W. R. Alling, New York jeweler, named as trustees for the bond holders. The bond holders looked to get out of the turquoise mining business – if the price was right.

Alling, the largest jeweler in the East, was renowned as a watchmaker. He once awarded a $1,000 watch, a work of art, to a local police captain for the captain's work in stopping burglaries of jewelry stores. Alling enjoyed fast buggy horses, perhaps a little too fast. Two years earlier the 62 year-old had suffered an accident when he took a turn too fast for the buggy. Maybe now he saw managing ATC as a little less hazardous to his health than driving a horse buggy. One of Alling's first tasks at the reins of the company was to send a Pinkerton man, Frank Murray, to Cerrillos to look over the mines. At Stillman's request one of his associates, Robert Parker, assumed the day to day responsibility of the mine.

The new owners pressured Doty to either produce more quality turquoise or leave. At one point Doty told McNulty that the company owed him $90,000, and the only way to get that money was to follow fashion which required nuggets of a conspicuously large size. But the nuggets McNulty sent were too small.

The turquoise from the area developed a reputation for being difficult to work. The soft and chalky turquoise shattered into pieces as cutters tried to work with it. But the truth was large nuggets were harder find.

Then, one day a letter from Doty arrived bearing a red-ink stamp, "Removed to The Anderson Bldg 12, 14, 16 John Street." These abrupt changes of address in the past had hinted at a major upsets in the American Turquoise Company. Was this another? McNulty surely noticed the forceful quality of Doty's letters and doubtless saw a change in mine ownership in the offing. At this point, however, McNulty remained steadfast. And he improved the quality of his record keeping too. He shared his thoughts with the company owners and his increased concern about the new man who had come to town to look at the mines.

A flurry of letters ensued. McNulty reported in detail on the visiting engineer's actions but McNulty stopped short of accusing him of outright theft. Alling and Doty both told McNulty to give Sterne limited access to the mine — including the opportunity to blast holes, but not the ability to actually do any mining.

McNulty hosted Sterne for the next three weeks, and during that time Parker proceeded to supplant Doty. (Parker, a banking man, headed up the credit department of the National City Bank of New York.) Parker sent letters of introduction for Sterne, and he instructed McNulty to deliver all turquoise directly to Tiffany and Company in New York.

The new address red-stamped across the letterhead that hints of impending turmoil for Doty.

Manhasset House, a well known haunt of the rich.

24 • Patricia McGraw

McNulty & Friends
Dialogs on Mining
1892 - 1899

C.G. Story to McNulty, August 17, 1892
Say, Mac, don't allow anyone on the dumps no matter who they are.

C.G. Story to McNulty, February 22, 1893
Friend Mac.. I told Allan to send Philipe $2.00 per day; Ed $1.50 and yourself $3.00 per day as I agreed when I left. ...Say, Mac, send me all the stone you have. Express it to 17 West 30th Street. I am glad that the bottom of the shaft is looking better.

J.M. Allan [Story's partner] to McNulty Jan 14, 1893
    I enclose to you $87.00 for December pay for yourself and the Mexicans. As Story gives it to me, it is $81.00 for you and $6.00 for the Mexicans. I enclose a receipt for you to sign and return to me. Story tells me you had not got the November money yet when he left. I sent it to you on Dec. 16th but if you have not got it let me know and I will send it to you again and look up the lost package. I only put in this $77.00 as I take out of it $10.00 which Mr. Andrews gave you when down there. Hope you are getting on well with the shaft and finding some stones.

J.M. Allan [Story's partner] to McNulty, May 18, 1893
    After this long delay, I got back the $72.00 sent you December 14, 1892 for your Nov pay. Will write you again in a day or two when I get the time for April.

C. G. Story to McNulty, Jan 25, 1893
Friend Mac: Your letter dated the 16th I received last night. You say that the work goes on nicely and that you are getting some good sized stones.

When you get cigar box full send them to the address I give in letter - don't fail to do assessment work on claims you located by Bottom Dollar. Have the boy and Phillipi [Felipe] *do it. Allan has sent you money up to January 1st. I will see that January money is sent as soon as you send in time for it - say, Mac, you know that claim in Bottom Dollar Gulch just below the road the Vulture. ...the one just this side of where Bennett was working when we were there? They located it the 22nd, the same day that we located ours at noon. Well, you watch it and jump it in your own name if they do not do their work by Feb 22nd at noon. I will write you again in a day or so. Send mail and stone to address below.*

J. M. Allan [Story's partner] to McNulty, Nov. 25, 1893
   Some time next week Mr. Doty and Mr. Story expects to start down to the mine and they will go prepared to pay up all bills due to miners, yourself and the store bills, and will start up work on the mine in good shape. We have gone through some hard times but are now putting things in good business shape. I wrote to my bro Alexander sometime since to go out and assist you and take his Winchester along. You ought to have some one with you all the time.

John R. Andrews telegram to Doty, Feb. 6, 1894
   3:30 p, Feby 6 1894: Dated New York, NY to Joseph G. Doty You must come home at once. Arrange with men to go on with work and you can go back in one week.

Doty to McNulty, Feb. 6, 1894
   You and Alex work together until I get back and I am sure you will be able to make things go all right. My business in New York is of such importance that a day is liable to be very expensive to do.

March 14, 1894 Jewelers Weekly.
   The Death of J. R. Andrews: John Rutt

John Rutt Andrews

Andrews, of Andrews & Doty, of 207 Broadway, New York, died suddenly Tuesday night of last week at the house of Dr. Richard Scholfield on West Fourteenth street, New York. Mr. Andrews, who had been ill, left his office Tuesday evening to call on Dr. Scholfield for an examination. He telephoned his wife in Englewood, N.J., that although he was not seriously ill he would spend the night in the city. At about half past 12, shortly before retiring, he expired. ...When, in 1870, two years after their incorporation, Tiffany & Co. moved to their present location on Union square, they purchased the entire plant of Mr. Andrews who then became a stockholder and general manager of the jewelry manufacturing department. He was also connected with the precious stone department. ...[Andrews sold all his Tiffany stock in 1887 for $400,000.] On the formation of the American Turquoise Company in 1891, Andrews & Doty, who had previously disposed of much of the product of the company's mines, were appointed its sole agents. Mr. Andrews was also elected president of the company, and retained that position until about three months ago. The recent misfortunes of his firm weighed heavily upon Mr. Andrews. ...Funeral services were held last Saturday in the First Episcopal Church, in Englewood, N.J. Among those present were: J.G. Doty, of Andrews & Doty; Mr. Rolston, president of the American Turquoise Company; ...and several representatives of Tiffany & Co. The employees of Tiffany & Co. sent a beautiful floral emblem.

Doty to McNulty, May 4, 1894

The stones are all right for color but they still come out very imperfect when cut. If you push in the direction that you are getting them you must...

find the right kind. These are better than anything we have had yet. When you write me let me know how deep you are running this drift down the top. ...we are leaving in your hands and under your entire control a property that has cost us a great deal of money & one that we look on as being very valuable. ...And we are treating you and look on you as one of us and want you to feel that our interests and your interests are the same. As you know the present holders of this property put out $35,000 just before I came down and they expect me to get enough money out of our sales to pay all other expenses. ...When the collections for the month come in we will send you part of the money due. You must have a little patience and remember that while the company owes you a few hundred dollars, they are owing me ninety thousand dollars. ...But I expect you to do the best you possibly can on your end and help us along during the present depression. It's impossible for me to make the present depressed state of business plain to you, but it can't last much longer. ...you want to give everybody the impression that you know what you are doing and that you are satisfied. Then there will be no trouble.

Doty to McNulty, May 4, 1894

When you write or send any stone send it to J.G. Doty, 68 Nassau St. Now don't get your tail down like a whipped dog and hold up your head & keep up your spunk. You have got a good thing & it won't be long before you will be willing to admit it. P.S. The stones from Arizona are not worth looking after. I don't even think they are turquoise.

R. G. Rolston to McNulty, Sept. 7, 1894

```
     ...we desire to have all the claims listed
at the Sheriff's office paid, and paid
promptly, but we want first to get a de-
tailed statement of these claims.    ...Turner,
McClure & Rolston [law firm] ...are our counsel
and have charge of the legal portion of the
matter.    ...we want to pay them and get them
out of the way and release the mine from all
```

floating indebtedness. We do not desire that you leave the mine, but that you will keep in your present position. You need give yourself no uneasiness as to funds being sent to meet all the indebtedness.

McClure to McNulty, Oct. 4, 1894

I have made a report to the Farmer's Loan and Trust Company of various matters in connection with the mine, much to their satisfaction. ...I will, at this end, do my utmost to have you promptly supplied with such money as you may need in the working of the mine. ...I am sure your work will be appreciated by the people here as they have every confidence in your good judgment and interest in the success of the Company.

McClure to McNulty, October 31, 1894

I am glad to hear that you are beginning to find your work there goes on satisfactorily and hope that you will be able to furnish good material for cutting, and that you can send a box each week as you have been doing. Mr. Doty will be in a position I think, to place the stone upon the market to good advantage.

McClure to McNulty, Dec. 10, 1894

We have arranged to send Mr. Harry Wood to the mines in Grant County, for the purpose of having him do the necessary work to insure the control of the mines by the Turquoise Company. If the Indians trouble you very much, in addition to having the protection from the Governor and the authorities, would it not be well for you to procure a good Winchester Repeating Rifle with the necessary ammunition? If you think it well to do so, we will authorize you to make the necessary expenditure for that purpose.

Doty to McNulty, Oct. 23, 1895

I am coincidentally disappointed from here. But I can't tell what the next week may develop. Ship the two boxes of small stuff to my office in my name and at the same time write Mr. John McClure what you have done and give him the weights of the boxes. And you must also notify my people. Ship them as freight.

Doty to McNulty, April [March] 4, 1896

Your box shipped April 17, 1896, just received. My men have examined it carefully and can't find a single stone worth cutting. The large chunks are all spotted and not one of them will cut a marketable stone that will bring any price. If there are no stones in the mine worth cutting, I will have to close down the work. We have at least a barrel of stone here that are better than what you are shipping us. Your payroll amounts to something over five hundred dollars a month, and I can't possibly get that amount out of the stone shipped. I am waiting anxiously to see what you will get from the Old Castillian.

It's a great deal more importance to me that this should be successful than it possibly can be to you. If you know of any place or any way in which you can find such stone as I want, go about it and get them. I don't care about the expense when I am getting the proper results. But I can't find the money to pay expenses when I don't get any results. P.S. Now don't write any doleful letters but get some stone out. The Bond holders are getting ready to take action here and I want results.

J. G. Doty to McNulty, May 9, 1896

Stone taken out of Old Castilian received. There is very little difference between them and the stone you have been sending us which leads me to believe that there is any quantity of fine stone to be found there if you only go about it in the correct way. You have had charge there for four years and we have paid out quite a lot of money.

But does it strike you at all singular that during the time Story was there he was always able to find stone. When Mr. Andrews was down for one day and a night, they got more good stone in that time than we have had since and while I was there we shipped more value than you sent us in the last four years.

If you can't find good stone for us I will certainly be obliged to recommend some kind of changes and I will have to go about it very quickly. The box previous to this did not cut a single stone and the last box was very little better. All the large pieces are so badly spotted that they are not salable. I don't expect you will be able to send me what you don't find. But I do expect you to work when you can find such stone as we want. I don't like to write you in this way but I must have results. ...What you have got in the ground there is worth nothing until it is sent here and cut and treated and put on the market. I don't like to write you in this way but I must have results. From what I can understand you seem to think you are sending me stones that are worth no end of money. But I know exactly what I am getting.

J. G. Doty to McNulty, June 3, 1896

The box received yesterday is the best you have ever sent and I would rather have a box like that than a hundred pounds of the stone you have been sending. After you take the pillar out follow that color no matter where it may lead you or what effect it may have on the mine...

J.G. Doty to McNulty, July 23, 1896

The silver excitement has made it impossible for me to get money to pay our liens and keep the work going. In fact, business is dead and I can't see any reason for it to improve under existing circumstances. People who have money will not part with it. The Banks won't make any loans and if this thing continues we will have to shut down entirely. Do the best you can with the two or three men you have. ...Don't do any work on the Muniz at present as the product from there is not up to the standard that we want. These are troublesome times and we depend on you to do the best you can for us and we will do all we can on this end of the line.

District Court papers, Subpoena in Chancery, Sept. 25, 1896 & District Court Summons filed by F.W. Clancy to obtain possession of the mines dated Sept. 25, 1896

    The Territory of New Mexico to J.P McNulty and American Turquoise Company... [requires you] to answer unto a bill filed against you by Mariano F. Sena. ...This is a suit in chancery brought to enjoin defendants from mining and removing the valuable deposits of turquoise from the tract of land commonly known as the Jose Leyba Grant.

Turner, McClure & Rolston to McNulty, December 30, 1896

    In order to carry out the legal requirements of the Territory of New Mexico we have designated you the authorized agent of the American Turquoise Company, residing at Turquesa, upon whom process may be served. We have filed a certificate of this fact and fixing Turquesa as the principal place where the business of the Company is carried on in New Mexico.

Doty to McNulty, October 23, 1897

    I sent you $300 last week and at the time thought I would be able to send the balance before this but the money I expected from Europe did not arrive, consequently cannot send yours until it does which in all probability will be next week. ...the assessment work will have to be done before the first of the year. I want you to give this your attention and have it recorded in the names of the following: William R. Alling of New York and Howard Carter of Chicago as trustees. Be sure to attend to this immediately.

Wm. R. Alling to McNulty, March 1, 1899

    Your letters to Mr. Doty and yours to Mr. Rolston are all sent to me to read. The mine is held by myself and Mr. Carter of Chicago as Trustees for the Bondholders. I had Mr. Doty write you, as he is our agent. You do not know me personally although I have been a Director and had much to do with it ever since Andrews and Doty have managed it. He wrote you a letter of introduction to Mr. Frank Murray of Chicago who has spent the winter in Santa Fe for his health. I have known Mr. Murray many years and he is all right. The Pinkertons hold some of our bonds, and as Mr. Murray is their principal man in Chicago I thought it best for you to meet him. I think he will tell you Sterne has nothing to do with them and I would request you not to tell anyone who Mr. Murray is unless you have his permission as he may not care to have it known. Any time you can give me any points you think would be of advantage to the company I would be pleased to hear from you.

J.G. Doty to McNulty, May 25, 1899

You will receive a letter today from Mr. R. A. Parker who represents Mr. James Stillman who is one of the largest bondholders. I don't know who Mr. John Andrews [different from John Rutt Andrews, Tiffany jeweler] *is but they are to examining the mine for some Chicago people who are expecting to make an offer for it. I have already made an offer but can't close until they make their bid. Let them examine the property thoroughly but they are not to do any work. That is they are not to do any mining... P.S. ...I telegraphed you today. If you cannot find any better specimens than last shipment to stop work. The box contained plenty of good color. But there was not a single piece that we could make any use of.*

McNulty to Doty, May 20, 1899

Dear Friend: Many thanks for package of money received and enclosed you will please find receipts for the same. In looking over the bills I find that you have sent $2.50 too much so I paid the $2.50 to the Cerrillos Supply Co towards this month's account for which I send you receipt. I was pleased to receive your last telegram as Mr. Sterne threatened to make it troublesome for me if I did not let him have whom he pleased to take in the mine with him; and I am not that kind of a man to be easily scared by any man until I know that he has authority to do so. Some of the parties whom he wanted to take into the mine with him are the ones that I had suspicions of getting stone from the Mexicans a little over a year ago when I sent a telegram to New York ... asking for a detective to be sent here.

McNulty to Alling, March 11, 1899

Wm. R. Alling Esq., ...I would have written you long ago had I known your address with regards to the property as it is in very bad shape. Mr. Frank Murray was here and all through the mine. ...I have shown him everything and gave him all the details about the past working of the property and the future prospects which he said he would write you all about. ...I have told him all about the man Sterne and he said he would find out who Sterne was. ...there may have been lots of men that has had more experience in turquoise mines than I have but there is not very many of them in New Mexico.

I have told Mr. Doty two years ago that the pocket of stone was about worked out but he would not believe so now it is worked out so now Mr. Alling, I will tell you as a friend, I am now going on the eighth year in charge of this property and I have done honest and faithful work for the company. ...I would advise you to sell this property if you can get a good price for it and not wait until there is another big pocket of stone struck as it has yet to be found. ...I had to go by orders not to do any development work at all but work where I could find stone. So now the bank is robbed of stone none but a few scattering stone left.

McNulty to Parker, May 31, 1899

Not knowing what Mr. Sterne's business was here, and hearing so many rumors that he was here hunting up the affairs at the company, and he talked around to the people in Cerrillos that the parties he was representing received no dividend, and tried to find out how much stone had been shipped this past two years; I did not give him all *the information that I would have done had I known what he was examining the mine for. Very true there is no good stone in the mine at present and there must be a lot of work done before we can find any as the pocket where the stone was is worked out, but nevertheless I can fool any one that I know is coming to buy it; as experts know but very little about Turquoise Mines. I will say to you as a friend that I would advise the company to sell the mine if they can.*

R.A.Parker for NY Bondholders of American TC, May 25, 1899

Mr. Doty has shown me telegram sent you this morning by the request of the bond holders of the American Turquoise Company. I represent the New York bond holders, of which the largest is Mr. James Stillman, President of this Bank [The National City Bank of New York]. ...it is the desire of the bond holders that Mr. Sterne and his men be permitted to examine the mine with a view to reporting to parties who are contemplating making a purchase of same. ...The authority given is only to enable them to view the property as it stands, and not to make any extended operations.

Parker to McNulty, June 6, 1899

You have my thanks for the candid reply you have made, and you can serve the interests of the Bond Holders further by enabling Mr. Sterne's representatives to properly examine the mine. ...In a letter received from that gentlemen today, he states that he wishes to be permitted to direct some of the work in both the Castilian and Story Muiz mines, and to send specimens of turquoise, etc., as may be obtained, I desire both yourself and Mr. Sterne's representatives to pack, seal and address the same to Tiffany & Company, Union Square, New York. This is to be done in each other's presence, and both to see that the shipment is made accordingly. The Railroad receipts for the goods are to be sent to me for Messrs, James Stillman and Tiffany & Company..such other operations as these people make, you will watch, and nothing is to be taken away except that to be sent to Tiffany and Company under the joint supervision of yourself and Mr Sterne.

This is McNulty and his family prior to 1892. To the left is Fannie McNulty who saved her father's letters; next is Agnes Dunn, McNulty's first wife; Eddie McNulty stands between his mother and father; to the right is Agnes, the baby of the family.

JAMES STILLMAN, President.
SAMUEL SLOAN, Vice President
A.G. LOOMIS, Vice President
G.S. WHITSON, Cashier
Wᴹ A.SIMONSON, Asst.Cashier

No. 1461.

WALTER H.TAPPAN, Asst.Cashier
ARTHUR KAVANAGH, Asst.Cashier
HORACE M. KILBORN, Asst.Cashier
JAMES A STILLMAN, Asst.Cashier
C. JANSSEN, Manager
        Foreign Exchange.

THE NATIONAL CITY BANK
OF NEW YORK.

DEPOSITORY OF THE
UNITED STATES, THE
STATE AND CITY OF NEW YORK.

CAPITAL & SURPLUS
$5,500,000.
CABLE ADDRESS "CITIBANK"

New York, June 6th, 1899.

Mr. J. P. McNulty,
    Cerrilos, N. M.

Dear Sir:-

    I am in receipt of your esteemed favor of the 31st. ult., contents of which have been duly noted. You have my thanks for the candid reply you have made, and you can serve the interests of the Bond Holders further by enabling Mr. Sterne's representatives to properly examine the mines.

    In a letter received from that gentleman to-day, he states that he wishes to be permitted to direct some of the work in both the Castillon and Story mines, and to send specimens obtained, East. I wish, therefore, that you would allow this work to be done, in your presence, however. Such specimens of turquoise, etc., as may be obtained, I desire both yourself and Mr. Sterne's representatives to pack, seal and address the same to Tiffany & Company, Union Square, New York. <u>This to be done in each other's presence</u>, and both to see that shipment is made accordingly. The Railroad receipts for the goods are to be sent to me for Messrs. James Stillman and Tiffany & Company. I know,

---

The National City Bank of New York served as the depository of the United States and New York City. Robert Parker underlined his instructions to make sure that McNulty and a visiting mining engineer sealed the turquoise shipments and sent them to Tiffany and Company.

Chapter 2
1899 - 1900 Part I

Plots and Rattlesnakes

I leave New York on the 23rd of June for Paris, and I have been in hopes that I could take with me some good clear stone to have put on exhibition by Tiffany & Co. at the World's Fair there.

R.A. Parker to McNulty, May 24, 1900

SON OF A SEA COOK!

McNulty's cabin and three other dilapidated small miner's cabins sat on the Turquoise Hill down from the Muñiz mine. A sorting tent covered the northern portion of the Muñiz rock pile. Early morning sunlight glinted off the hills, turning them brownish golden, and scrub juniper trees dotted the golden expanse.

Halfway up the tallest of those hills lay the Muñiz claim with its 100 foot shaft partially covered over by a wooden platform. To the west was the Castilian Mine, a gash in a low hill that measured about 32 feet wide by 75 feet deep. Outside both mines were huge piles of rock, carried there by hand or in small tram cars. As McNulty's workers removed the rock they searched it for flecks of color or anything that might be valuable. Those stones they set aside for McNulty to remove the excess stone surrounding the turquoise. The company was adamant. It wanted only clean turquoise and did not want to spend money to ship any turquoise containing imperfections such as matrix or rock. Gold, copper, silver, or stone threads appearing as spider veins in a turquoise nugget were not highly valued by Tiffany, who wanted only the perfect, pure blue that matched his signature color.

Some of the perfect blue occasionally found its way into the dump piles outside the mines, and on slow mining days McNulty would pick through those rocks. The turquoise-flecked mini-hill there functioned as a reserve should the price of turquoise rise and should matrix turquoise ever become sought-after. The dump at the Castilian lay scattered around that shaft, and McNulty started a few larger piles to the south of the mine opening. Rock was hoisted up the shaft and piled into one of the tram cars that ran from the mine entrance to the dump pile about 40 feet away, where the car was upended.

On dynamite blasting days the hills reverberated. Even the birds cleared the area as the miners set the blasts off. To begin opening a shaft, a miner hammered a one-inch round metal drill into the ground. Each carefully counted hammer stroke moved the drill through solid rock to a certain depth, as each count equated to a measurement. First, the miners had to set up the drills. Then came the hammer strikes, and finally the dynamite. Double jacking, the most common method for drilling, required one man to hold the drill and the other to wield the hammer. Once the drill reached a depth of two or three feet it was withdrawn. Dynamite was packed in the hole, set off, and then the miners removed the rubble. They averaged six feet of timber-supported shaft construction each day. Day after day the process continued in the quest for the sky blue stone.

It was an unusual day when McNulty allowed anyone other than himself to blast in the tunnels and shafts. That day came on June 15, 1899, when the bond holders sent a Chicago mining engineer to the mines to check them for profitability. ATC ordered McNulty to help out the engineer in any and all endeavors, but at the same time, ship any stone recovered straight to Tiffany. The boxes were to be sealed in the presence of both McNulty and the engineer. And the engineer, known only as Sterne in McNulty's letters, blasted in several places in the tunnels.

Sterne evaluated the claims for possible purchase or lease. He had spent the previous day nosing around in Cerrillos, talking with residents about the output of the mines, and when McNulty learned of Sterne's activities he grew more protective. McNulty knew the people in Cerrillos loved gossip, and none loved it more than the train station agent, Charles E. Harney, who handled the turquoise shipments. There is no doubt that agent let Sterne know all about the turquoise he shipped, and more. There was no telling what he said.

This is one of the few pictures existing of the Castilian Mine taken in 1900 by mining engineer H.D.C. Richards. Jack, the dog who saved McNulty's life, stands next to his friend.

While McNulty clearly felt threatened by Sterne's presence, the mine supervisor tried to keep a professional demeanor. All the same, McNulty watched the engineer closely. Sterne's hunting jacket contained too many pockets which could be filled with valuable pieces of turquoise. Sterne was not subject to search when he left the property. (Other employees were searched each day.) Besides, Sterne insisted on bringing in outside workers, workers who may have been involved in stone theft the previous year. For McNulty, that was about the worst thing Sterne could do.

Sterne pawed through the dumps as he looked for the sky stone in veins and pillars, but by the time Sterne left McNulty knew this man would not be back. Sterne did not find easily accessible turquoise, or perhaps the bond holders wanted too much for their share of the mine. McNulty expected more visitors, more trouble, more work, and more explanations so long as the mines were on the market.

No matter what Sterne thought, McNulty knew that lots of turquoise lay below the ground and mining was still good business. Mining created many a town and provided a livelihood for hundreds of

40 • Patricia McGraw

miners and shopkeepers. While those towns thrived on miners spending their money, miners thrived on getting information from their friends and neighbors as they visited in a more "civilized" setting.

The miners found provision and entertainment at the camps where they could pass a few hours, get a few drinks, and if they stayed over night, good food and a warm bed. McNulty and his wife, Emma, enjoyed trips to the largest of the mine towns in the area, Cerrillos. Visiting friends or strolling the streets or delivering cigar boxes of turquoise to the train station agent provided a break from the drudgery at the claims. With each cigar box shipment came speculation and rumor about the mine's output.

A news story clipped by McNulty described the excitement that surrounded a typical mining camp, in this case nearby Carbonateville. "Each night we could hear the hobnail shoes shuffling down the hillside headed toward the blacksmith shop with picks and dull steel. George Loya was the blacksmith and a noble man, too. The miners, with the pockets full of very valuable specimens, their enthusiasm could not find words to express the value; smiles told their thoughts; companionship was waiting everywhere to tell the great future just beyond... It was the headquarters in good weather, for the miners to put on the big boast, specimens enough to fill a wash tub they had

McNulty left nothing to memory. He listed names of witnesses in the Sena case along with the cost to get the witnesses to court. Mike O'Neil stayed in Santa Fe for six days. McNulty hired a wagon to transport the witnesses to court and he paid for their hotel rooms.

brought to show their comrades. It was a peaceful meeting. Only each one had the best mine in the district."

The land grant case loomed like a malevolent spectre, casting a pall over all the work and activities of the mining venture. Four years ago the case had been thrown out of court because Sena had failed to prove ownership. This year, 1899, the Sena group decided to prove the Jose de Leyba Land Grant actually existed, and then they could prove ownership, maybe.

This second case interfered with mining, compelling McNulty to gather information and reestablish contact with the old residents who would be witnesses. None had changed their stories about the land grant although some had been approached by the Sena group and asked to avoid telling the truth. McNulty decided that during the court hearing the witnesses would have to be separated and kept away from the Sena people. As he contacted them, he made sure they were willing to stay in Santa Fe as the guests of ATC. At the same time, he listened to their stories and took those reports back to company's lawyer.

All the same witnesses from four years ago agreed to testify again. There was always the risk one or more might fall victim to misfortune — planned or otherwise — so they all had to be deposed before the court session. This time the company's lawyer, Edward Bartlett, took the depositions in front of a judge in District Court.

With his witnesses standing by and ready to go, McNulty waited for a court date. Apparently the influence of Mariano Sena, whose brother was the clerk for the New Mexico Territorial Supreme Court, reached to the lower Court of Land Claims. The case was delayed. And delayed. A court date would be set, then McNulty would contact the witnesses, and the court date would suddenly be changed and pushed back several weeks. For the new court date, McNulty had to make the rounds again and inform the witnesses of the new time.

While he waited on the court, McNulty spent June and July of 1899 working the dumps alone. The summers were just too hot for many workers. Recent blasting had left enough rock at the bottoms of the shafts and tunnels to keep McNulty sorting for a good long while. At night he and his wife chipped out the turquoise nuggets by kerosine lamp light. They packed cigar boxes for shipment. They wrote detailed letters to the company. When time permitted, they repaired the cabin. Since ATC assured them that the McNulty's superintendent position was safe, they felt fairly secure in their future.

During the summer, McNulty's daughters, Fannie and Agnes, now in their twenties, visited. One morning Fannie heard a characteristic rattling under the house. She called her father who came at once. He could see a coiled rattlesnake, and he reached down for a rock. As he did so the snake jumped its full length and struck him on his hand.

"He got me!" McNulty cried, as his dog Jack rushed in to take on

Late into the night, McNulty and Emma chipped rock away from the turquoise nuggets by the light of this kerosine lamp. The spice can to the left and the snuff box to the right were shipping containers for the turquoise chips. A rock from the Tiffany mine sits at the lower right.

the rattler. Jack killed the snake, but he, too suffered what might have been a fatal bite in his paw. Agnes grabbed the dog and sucked on the wound. Jack survived.

McNulty's more serious wound required a doctor's care. Fannie hitched the horse to her father's buggy while Emma dressed the wound and placed McNulty's arm in a sling. By this time McNulty, in great pain, could barely climb into the buggy even with help. The family wrapped him in a blanket. Fannie urged the horse faster down the rough road leading to Cerrillos, and they didn't stop until they were at Dr. Friend Palmer's office at the Palace Hotel. The doctor grimly examined McNulty's arm, now black, blue, yellow-spotted and swollen. The arm, the size of a well-muscled thigh, looked about ready to burst open. The pain was excruciating, and whenever touched, McNulty shouted his favorite epithet, "Son of a sea cook!"

Dr. Palmer took out a knife and cut two gashes just above the snakebite, and he warmed a poultice, wrapping it over the wound. Within a few days McNulty was back directing the mining operations.

TOO MANY LAWYERS

As the winter of 1899 appeared, Emma and McNulty hoped the harsh weather would miss them. The cabin was not in the best of condition, and they expected a November addition to their family. Drafts came through the chinks, and when the wind blew, the temperature dropped. Blankets and a small pot bellied stove were what they had for heat.

The days passed quickly, as miners hauled up rocks iron bucket by iron bucket and whiskey barrel by whiskey barrel. All the while McNulty actively sought potential buyers for the mine, but only rumors and land speculators appeared. There were no real offers.

The *Silver City Enterprise* of Friday, September 29, 1899, helped keep turquoise fever high... "There are valuable beds of turquoise in New Mexico, which surpass the turquoise of Persia, which have been pronounced by experts to be the finest, purest and best in the world and surpass any other turquoise in lustre and permanent sky blue color."

Turquoise fever ran rampant in Cerrillos, and papers had taken up the new name for the old Muñiz mine. It was now the Tiffany mine. People took notice of the happenings at the Turquoise Hill.

Everyone knew that the cigar boxes shipped by Wells Fargo arrived at the premier jewelry company of the nation. The mines had to be extremely valuable since Charles Lewis Tiffany helped finance them, and he created great jewelry masterpieces. Gossip had it that there were untold riches below the surface. And the Sena group determined that those mines were worth a lot.

The Sena case involved a great number of lawyers, all in it for the money. Too many lawyers, as Edward L. Bartlett, a New Mexico attorney who represented McNulty, wrote. Teams of lawyers from New York and Colorado represented the ATC. And Frank Clancy, a New Mexico attorney, represented Mariano Sena. These would battle in district court to decide who owned the mines.

As September rolled around McNulty tallied his witnesses for the Sena Land Grant case. He had the oldest residents of the area including: Nasario Gonzales, 83 years old; Jesus Narvais, 80 years old; Francisco Romero, age 83; Jose Benevides, age 72; and Susano Leybo, 66 years old. They testified that they had never heard of the Jose de Leyba Land Grant and that the land in question had been "used by the community from time out of mind and without objection from anyone as public pasture land."

At the end of September 1899 the District Court dismissed Sena's case on a technicality. It had been filed in the wrong court. Land grant cases were supposed to be filed in the Court of Private Land Claims. That meant that the Sena group — Mariano Sena and his lawyer, F.W. Clancy — had to re-file the case in the proper court, which meant that now the United States would also be named as a defendant. The case was based on Sena proving that his land grant was valid and that the title was for 16,000 acres, not 16 acres.

Alling, trustee for the ATC bond holders, expressed his satisfaction over the apparent victory in his letter of October 19, 1899: "...as we understand the laws here it is impossible to begin any more suits on old Spanish claims as the time limit has long passed, and if this man continues to annoy us it is quite possible I will take some action by which the Government can take charge of him." He brushed off the lawsuit, not even considering the possibility that Sena would return to haunt the Easterners.

McNulty pointed out that the lawsuit had to be brought against the United States Government, not just the ATC, and he believed Sena intended to do just that.

One of the participants in the Sena scheme broke away from the others after the court judgment and tried to shake down the Farmer's Loan and Trust Company. But the shakedown failed since his information was so old. Farmer's Loan and Trust had ceased to hold an interest in ATC now that the Alling group had taken over the company.

McNulty expected another lawsuit because he knew Sena received his money from a well-heeled New Mexico politician and others who had been amassing land fortunes by dealing in old Spanish land grants, and intimidation through the courts was one of their tactics.

The tram tracks led to the Castillian mine. To the right of the horse driven whim stands an unidentified man, McNulty, and his mare, Nellie.

As the Sena case consumed the finances of the ATC, McNulty saw that Doty no longer issued any of the mining instructions. This ominous development heralded the removal of Doty and the installation of new managers. The three bondholders, however, remained the same: the Pinkertons, Stillman, and Tiffany.

McNulty's new source of instructions, the banker Parker, had decided that he could administer the mines from a distance, relying on McNulty's reports and a map on his desk in New York. McNulty noted this and suspected things had heated up for Doty. The bond holders had changed their minds about selling the company and instead looked to oust Doty and gain control of his shares. Alling, too, took a back seat in the running of the mine and let Parker call the shots.

When another mining engineer, H.D.C. Richards, sent by the bond holders, arrived on the Turquoise Hill, McNulty read the signs — a change was in the offing. The bond holders refused to let go of the mines. Richards' report, once delivered, would determine the future of both the mines and of McNulty.

McNulty and Richards examined very carefully every inch of the

Castilian and Muñiz mines. Richards pointed out areas most likely to contain turquoise, and together they determined future work places. Richards thought that aggressive mining combined with scientific knowledge would result in profit. In the past McNulty had simply found veins, pillars, or slabs of turquoise by luck. Sometimes turquoise appeared in hanging shelves or in the rock walls. But under the old company's instructions, McNulty could mine only what could be seen — a technique used in gold and silver mines where veins could be followed until they played out or disappeared. Turquoise followed no such rules, and by those restrictions the company limited McNulty's ability to search for new turquoise pockets. Since McNulty knew this approach would cause problems later, he used the need for regular assessment work to dig and blast in likely places where turquoise might be. Those prospect holes could be turned into tunnels or shafts that could eventually lead to more turquoise.

Richards and McNulty recognized the poor management practices of the bankers in the East, and they hoped that with more direction and science from their side the mines would produce more turquoise, more profit, and the Easterners would expand operations. Richards also promised McNulty to talk with the bankers and see if some improvements could be made for his living conditions. Clearly, poor housing reflected adversely on the company and did not impress potential investors. Besides, that winter the cold drafts might prove very unhealthy for Emma and her expected child.

Just as anticipated, a cold winter blew in and along with the wind came the flu that kept miners home sick. At the beginning of the winter both McNulty and his wife avoided the sickness, though many times McNulty did not have a full crew at work.

After Richards departed and just before Thanksgiving, 2:45 p.m. on November 17th, 1899, Ethelred Patrick McNulty was born. The baby required lots of attention from Emma and McNulty, and heavy blankets to guard against the winter chill. When Ethelred wanted attention, he threw his little arm over his head and uttered an appealing cry. His parents wrapped him up more closely in Emma's crocheted brown blanket to ward off the cold that permeated the cabin. If visitors arrived on the claims, they always asked after the new baby.

But mining took no holidays, and while McNulty worked in the cold, Emma stayed inside to tend to Ethelred and prepare the meals. As the winter drew on, so did the mine work and letter writing.

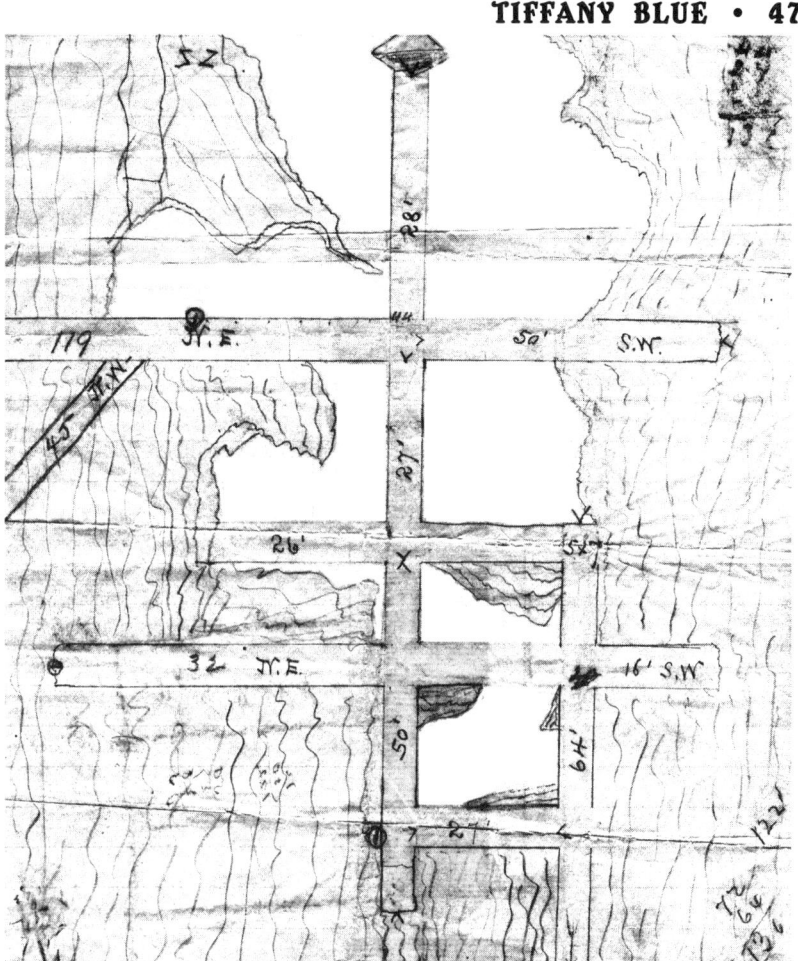

The map shows the shafts, tunnels, and drifts in an unidentified mine. This most likely is the type of drawing McNulty sent back East so that the bankers could follow his progress.

Letters passed regularly to and from the banker, and if McNulty was surprised when one day a letter from Parker said, "Doty is now out of our service," he did not show it. Doty had always tried to pay McNulty all that was owed — even if it did arrive late. Apparently, Doty's bid to gain controlling shares of the company had failed. The current management threw him out, along with the former trustees. The bond holders took hold of the operational reins and they decided R.A. Parker was the right man to take over the day to day control. Parker looked after Stillman's mining interests, and as representative for the largest financier in the cooperative, his position carried great responsibility. The New Yorker had no previous experience in the mine fields, but that did not deter him from his task to bring perfect blue to Tiffany. Parker negotiated an exclusive contract with Tiffany for the mine's gems, and no other shipments of turquoise went to any other jeweler in the world.

Outsiders would stop to offer McNulty money for a single specimen of turquoise, but he never took up the offer, and he refused to engage in gossip or rumor mongering so prevalent in the press at the time.

McNulty gave Parker a crash course in mining. The most important thing was the assessment work which was required each year in order to retain the claim. Assessment meant that miners had to prove a minimum of $100 was spent in maintaining or improving the mine, which might be done with 10 feet of work in a tunnel, shaft, drift, or cross cut. Any claim on which the assessment work had not been performed was open to anyone who wanted to claim it on January 1st of the following year. In order for the company to obtain a patent — ownership of the surface and mineral rights on the property as validated by the United States Government — there could be no pending assessment work nor any pending legal matter over the mining claim. For the past seven years McNulty's assessment work on all four mines, the Blue Gem, the Morning Star, the Muñiz, and the Castilian exceeded the legal requirements, but the Sena case precluded the issuance of any patents. It was McNulty's own stubbornness and sheer determination to do what was right that kept him working on the assessments. Never once was he late with his paperwork, and that fact must have mystified the Sena plotters.

Nothing surprised McNulty, and when he heard Richards' services were no longer needed, McNulty just shrugged his shoulders and moved on. Richards told McNulty that it was because the company didn't want to pay him, and he asked McNulty to note the turquoise coming from a certain nearby claim. Since demand for turquoise ran high, Richards was eager to act as an agent for that claim's owner, Mike O'Neil. (For its own mines the ATC was the exclusive agent.)

By the end of 1899, Parker instructed McNulty let him know when Doty ever appeared in New Mexico since Doty still owed the first American Turquoise Company $10,000, and the successor company

Edward L. Bartlett,
SOLICITOR GENERAL
OF
THE TERRITORY OF NEW MEXICO.
SANTA FÉ.

May 10th, 1900.

Mr. J.P. McNulty,
    Cerrillos, N.M.

My Dear Sir:-

    The Court this morning handed down a unanimous opinion in the Sena case against the United States and the Company, rejecting the grant on the ground that it was imperfect and was not presented in time in this Court, and was therefore barred by the statute of limitations. The opinion affirmed all the positions I took in my brief. I have notified Mr. Parker today.

    Mr. Clancy gave notice of an appeal, which they may perfect, although I doubt it, as the expense of going to the Supreme Court, outside of attorneys, fees, for the necessary printing, etc., will be considerable, and the hope of reversing this decision can't be very great.

    I hope the baby is better, and with regards to Mrs. McNulty,
I am,
        Very truly yours, *Edward L. Bartlett*

The Solicitor General of the territory of New Mexico tried to derail Sena's efforts to gain ownership of the mines. He said that too many lawyers made it impossible to conduct an effective case.

wanted to collect that money. McNulty told Parker that O'Neil had sold some stones to an agent who then took the turquoise to New York, but that was as much as he knew. No further information was available. Interestingly, McNulty added that there was only one person who knew the colors and the real worth of turquoise — Fred Kunz, the Tiffany gem expert.

January of 1900 turned very cold, and McNulty purchased more fuel for a stove so that the men sorting the stones had a place to warm their hands. They had spent the previous days filling buckets, then hoisting them out of the mine and wheeling the rocks to the dumps. Now they turned to the work of breaking the rocks and were sorting them into piles for McNulty, who worked on the stone at night.

Timbering shafts and building ladders filled many days. For January, though, the only stone McNulty found was dispersed throughout the rock formations in the mine and very difficult to get out. McNulty continued reporting the number of feet he had worked and describing the direction of such work, as Parker kept track of this on his maps. While mining work continued, Edward Bartlett, now Solicitor General of the Territory of New Mexico, carried on the legal battle in court on behalf of the United States Government and the American Turquoise Company.

For the case, McNulty's responsibilities still entailed rounding up the witnesses when the Court of Private Land Claims finally put the Sena land grant case on the docket.

The officials of the Land Court planned a picnic at the mines with the company's lawyer, Bartlett, and they looked around the Turquoise Hill trying to identify landmarks. The picnic was termed a success. A few weeks after that visit McNulty gathered up the witnesses and drove them into Santa Fe for their depositions. While the legal battles raged, interest in exactly what was going on at the mines themselves increased.

A FINE SIGHT

Curiosity led tourists to the area, and an article appeared in the *Indianapolis News*, dateline April 22, 1900. F.M. Sloan wrote the story about his visit to the mines, and it was stories like these that kept many across the nation focused on turquoise and the Southwest.

> A party of eight, we left Santa Fe early on the morning of March 20, in a large picnic wagon for a trip to the famous 'Tiffany turquoise mine,' which is located south of Santa Fe eighteen miles. We drove at a brisk pace over a fine road surrounded by beautiful scenery. Mountains in front of us; mountains to right of us; mountains to the left of us; all around us, in fact, rising range above range or standing grand and solemn in solitary peaks. Some with their snow-capped summits, others far away, enveloped in that purple haze peculiar to a mountainous country.

A New Mexican Turquois Mine

F. M. Sloan provides a glimpse into the process of turquoise mining in New Mexico.

[Special to The Indianapolis News.]
SANTA FE, New Mexico, April 22.— A party of eight, we left Santa Fe early on the morning of March 20, in a large picnic wagon for a trip to the famous "Tiffany turquois mine," which is located south of Santa Fe eighteen miles. We drove at a brisk pace over a fine road surrounded by beautiful scenery. Mountains in front of us; mountains to the right of us; mountains to the left of us; all around us, in fact, rising range above range or standing grand and solemn over all, there was a blue sky flecked here and there with ragged, fleecy clouds that drifted lazily. We rode for many miles without seeing a house, but finally passed two small American settlements in a little green valley. Near by was a clump of cottonwood trees, the only trees on the road, if we may except the stunted cedars and pines, which are plentiful. Grazing in this valley, we saw a flock of several thousand sheep, guarded by herders and dogs — a fine sight. After several more mines were passed, we came to a small stream of water where we found a town consisting of a very few houses, which boasts the name 'Bonanza.' It sprung up during a mining excitement, like a mushroom — got its growth, you may say, in a night. The hillsides around are covered with 'prospect holes,' where, alas, many well laid plans and hopes are buried. A little way beyond is the Mexican settlement, with the queer little adobe church.

Two miles farther on we reach 'Turquesa', where the turquoise mine is situated, as bleak, barren a spot as can be imagined. The nearest water is the little stream I have just mentioned two long miles away; the nearest people too, are there. Here in a small adobe hut, for it can scarcely be dignified by the name of house, lives the superintendent of the mine, with his wife, a sweet-faced woman, and their baby of four months old. She gave our party a hearty welcome. It is so seldom she has visitors that she was very glad to see us. We went into the house, where she made us a cup of tea, and we ate our lunch, which we brought with us. Then, regretting the absence of her husband, who had gone to Cerrillos ten miles away, she said she would show us the mine. Visitors are not very welcome, and are not allowed to go to the mine alone.

The superintendent, or his wife, in his absence, must go with them. We climbed up the mountain path and came to the mine, a great, well-like shaft, 200 feet deep, with rough boards covering all except the mouth, down which there is a perpendicular ladder, over it a pulley with a strong wire rope and two huge iron buckets. This is worked by one horse. The rock is blasted and brought to the top in these buckets. It is then assorted, all that contains turquoise is saved, and the refuse is taken to the dump in a small tram-car. A rude blacksmith shop for sharpening and repairing the tools, four Mexicans, the superintendent and his son — this is all there is to this great mine.

The turquoise is picked out of the rock by the superintendent himself with a small hammer. It must be of a certain color, or it is rejected. A peculiar shade of blue is what gives value to the stone. It is shipped from the town of Cerrillos in cigar boxes, a box being worth, as we were told, as much as $10,000. We were of told a pair of turquoise cuff buttons that were recently sold for $800. I think they must have been set around with diamonds. All around are beautiful specimens which you are told are worthless, because they are 'off color,' but you are not allowed to pick up the smallest piece. Every one is closely watched, and it is almost impossible, even if one were tempted, to secure the smallest specimen. And it would almost certainly cost the superintendent his position, which is a responsible one, were it known that he allowed any one to carry away any of the precious stuff. Even the workmen are searched before leaving the place.

The mine was first discovered and worked in a rude way by the Indians, long centuries ago. They went down thirty or forty feet. A pole or trunk of a tree was their means of going down or coming up. They used the beautiful blue stones for ornaments, making necklaces, bracelets, armlets, eyes for their fetishes or gods, and other things of it. They did not cut and polish it as we do now, but made holes in the pieces and string them on the dried sinews of deer. Afterward the mine was worked by the Mexicans [Spanish] in a small way. It is the finest turquoise mine in the world.

Five miles from this is another mine, but not valuable, as the stone is not as good a color, being slightly tinged with green. It is being worked, however, with profit. These mountains are rich in undeveloped treasures, and the great industry of New Mexico must be mining. Rich deposits of gold, silver, iron, copper, coal, sulphur and many kinds of precious stones have been found. — F.M. Sloan, April 22, 1900.

Demand for turquoise ran high during the early months of 1900.

Sometimes McNulty found good color, but most of it was in small stones which he dutifully sent on to Tiffany in New York. This was not enough. Parker needed many more gems. Demand far exceeded supply, and more workers and new sources were called for. Parker asked McNulty to recommend someone as superintendent for the ATC mines in Grant County.

Although Parker drummed into McNulty that finding turquoise and shipping it was his only priority, he also pushed McNulty to find more workers, cheap workers. He couldn't attract enough miners, especially since he couldn't guarantee them adequate and consistent hours. There was no housing because the few cabins at the mines were unlivable.

By 1900, Parker relented and allowed McNulty to obtain bids to build an inexpensive house. After all, the company had an image to uphold.

DEATH STRIKES

The first week of May 1900 brought the Sena hearing to court where Sena himself attempted to bribe witnesses, while a little latter he gave false information to the Santa Fe newspaper, the *New Mexican*. McNulty subsequently corrected that story.

The Land Claims Court determined that the ATC owned the mines and that no land grant existed for that area. McNulty and Parker both hoped that this decision would finally be the end of all their legal troubles. Once they got the patents for the mines the need for assessment work would disappear, and they could concentrate on turquoise. When Sena's lawyer, Clancy, announced that they intended to appeal, both Bartlett and McNulty figured there was no chance of reversal, in spite of the fact that Sena was backed and funded by the powerful and well-known politician, Soloman Luna. With the decision rendered, McNulty returned to the mines only to find his infant son deathly ill.

On May 24, late in the morning, McNulty's family gathered, waiting for the child's death. An hysterical Emma screamed and struck at

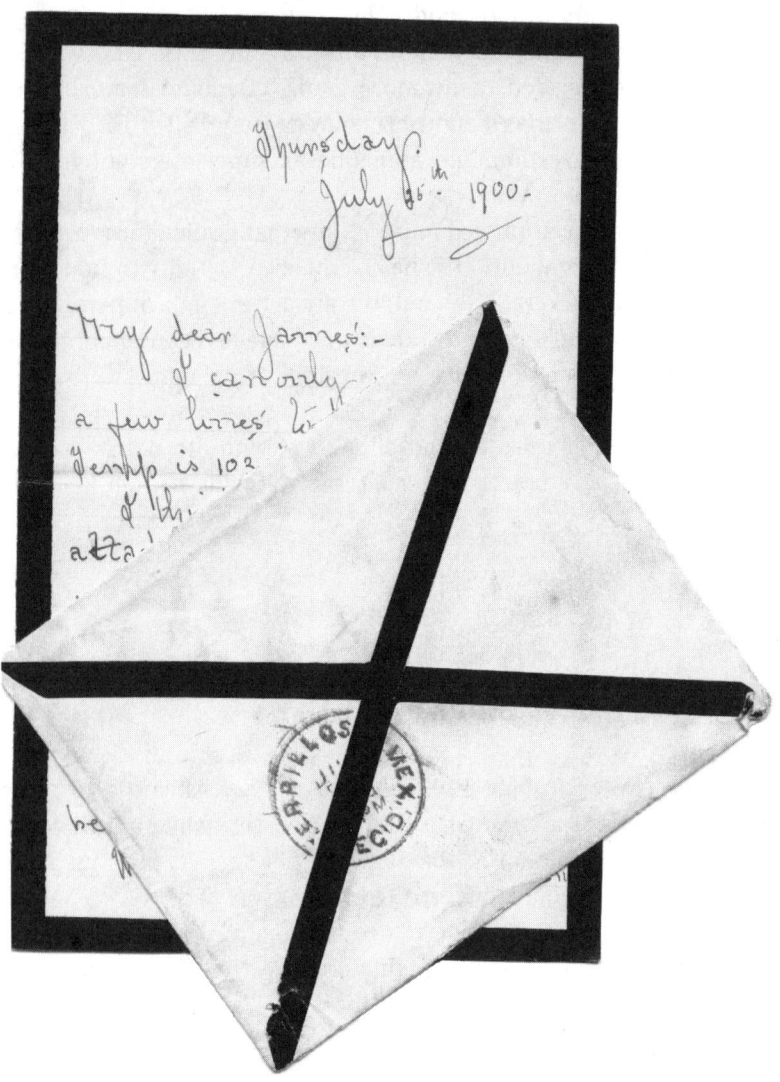

Black bordered mourning stationary let the world know of Emma's pain two months after her son's death. She seemed unable to deal with the reality of that death.

family members as Ethelred gasped, then died. Fannie had to restrain her stepmother from throwing herself on the body. Emma did everything in her power to keep them from taking the child for burial. Finally, Ethelred was taken away and buried. Emma returned to an empty house and McNulty stayed in Cerrillos.

The mining world knows no time of mourning, and two days after the funeral, McNulty, nursing his sorrow and a hangover, returned to mining operations. A simple entry in the family bible marked Ethelred's passing: "Ethelred Patrick died at 1:15 p.m., May 24, 1900, Thursday at Turquesa."

In a letter that arrived a few days later, Parker stated that he required a perfect blue stone, as he planned to attend the World's Fair in Paris and a perfect gem might garner for Tiffany & Company the award for best of show.

McNulty & Friends Dialogs on the Sena Lawsuit 1899-1900, Part I

McNulty to Wm. R. Alling, August 1, 1899

I went to Santa Fe yesterday to get instructions from Ed. L. Bartlett who is my attorney in the damage suit brought against the ATC in 1896. ...It will be tried in Court next month and Mr. Ed L. Bartlett's opinion is that the other party will get no longer stay. It must come to hearing this time. ...We have already procured several witnesses who have lived here all their lifetime and have never heard of any tract of land commonly known as the Jose Leyba Grant until this suit started.

I must go amongst these witnesses this coming week and take an interpreter with me and remind them of the statements they have already made two years ago and also try to find some more of the old Mexicans that have lived here all their life time that we could not find two years ago; but I have heard since that they have returned. It is our opinion that the grant is a fraud; nevertheless, it will cost the Company time and money and I have to hire teams to take the witnesses to Santa Fe. They live so far apart that it will keep me rustling to get them there. Of course, I will notify them to be in readiness from the 4th to the 12 of Sept.

McNulty to Alling, October 24, 1899

I will tell you what I know about it. The grantees claim to have a perfect grant and if so they can get it in to the land court at any time but they must prove that they have such a grant. We will know all about it when the Court meets in December. Of course, we have no more to do with it when it is in the land court; the government must do the fighting now. They have got a grant of 12 or 16 acres but they claim 16,000 acres.

Bartlett to McNulty, February 16, 1900

I have arranged with the United States to take the testimony of our old witnesses in the turquoise case here in the Court of Private Land Claims next Friday. ...and the U.S. Marshall will be down early in the week to subpoena them. I wish you would let them know that it is in our interest, and make it comfortable for them turning up. It might be well for you to come also to encourage them. ...but we think it best to secure their testimony at this time for fear of accidents, and a possible delay in hearing the case. ...The U.S. Attorney, Surveyor, special agent, and myself are coming down Monday to look over the ground. There also will be a picnic party with us who 'want to see mines.' I will see you on that day, and regards to Mrs. McNulty and the baby I am sincerely yours...

McNulty to Parker, March 1, 1900

I went in with them [the witnesses] to Santa Fe on the 24th and kept them from being mixed up with the Grant people. One of my witnesses swore in court that the grantees tried to bribe him to turn over with them for there was a lot of money in it, but they all gave a good straight testimony to the judge in court. I think we will have a clear case when the court opens in April.

McNulty to Parker, May 9, 1900

...*in regards to our case in court, I think we will come out all ok which I expect General Bartlett has written to you about it. Sena was so angry with me that he or some of his party had published in the Santa Fe paper a false statement of my testimony in the case which I had contradicted in the next day's paper on the 5th.*

Bartlett to McNulty, May 10, 1900

The court this morning handed down a unanimous opinion in the Sena case against the United States and the Company, rejecting the grant on the ground that it was imperfect and was not presented in time in this Court, and was therefore barred by the statute of limitations. The opinion affirmed all the positions I took in my brief. ...Mr. Clancy gave notice of an appeal, which they may perfect, although I doubt it, as the expense of going to the Supreme Court, outside of attorneys, fees, for the necessary printing, etc., will be considerable, and the hope of reversing this decision can't be very great. I hope the baby is better, and with regards to Mrs. McNulty, I am, very truly yours, Edward L. Bartlett.

McNulty & Friends Dialogs on Mining 1899-1900, Part I

McNulty to Wm. R. Alling, August 1, 1899

...*now with regards to the selling of this property, I think there is a good opportunity of doing so to the Syndicate. While I was in Santa Fe yesterday, I had quite a talk with Judge Victor, their agent, whom I am well acquainted with. He read a letter to me from the Eastern party stating that* they were well satisfied with the properties that he had already obtained and in their opinion, they thought he had everything outside of the ATC property that was worth taking. Then came my opportunity to put in a word, so I told him that the property was for sale, then he wanted to know your price and that I told him I could not tell him for at least two weeks.

McNulty to R.A. Parker, June, 1899

Mr. Stern and his men are through exploring the mines today. I have shown him every place where stone is to be found and I let him work wherever he wished to. The specimens that he and his men have taken out will be shipped to Tiffany and Company tonight by Wells Fargo Company Express. I cannot say whether he smuggled any stone in his pockets or not, as he wore a huntsman coat with many pockets in it. I had not the authority to search him...

Parker to McNulty, October 31, 1899

It has been decided by the bondholders to reorganize The American Turquoise Company, and with that purpose in view we have sent to New Mexico Mr. H.C. Richards, a Mining Engineer, to make a thorough examination of all properties owned by the ATC, and to superintend such operations as he may deem advisable. You will therefore be kind enough to assist Mr. Richards in this work, as we know you will, having always shown the proper spirit in this connection. There is no disposition to dispense with your services, but on the contrary, as it is the intention of the new Company to work the properties vigorously, there will be more need than ever to have the work properly done by parties on whom we can rely. Mr. Richards will in all probability remain with you for about a month, and we hope that your combined efforts will result to the advantage of The American Turquoise Company and, as a consequence, of yourselves. For present, no more shipments are to be made from our property to Mr. Doty.

I am about to negotiate with a firm here to handle the product of our property, and instructions will be sent when arrangements are completed.

McNulty to Alling, November 14, 1899

Mr. Richards was with me all last week and I gave him all the minute details about the property. On Saturday afternoon, I drove Mr. Richards into Santa Fe, and we had quite a consultation with Mr. Bartlett concerning the Patent, in which Mr. Bartlett advised Mr. Richards to notify Mr. Parker not to make a transfer of the property from your name until the Patent is obtained, as the property has been in your name since the foreclosure of the sale and the papers for the patent at that time was made out to you and Mr. Howard Carter. Should a transfer be made before you obtain the patent, new papers will have to be made out for the new company. The important matter about this is that the grant people had filed their former suit against the A.T.C. and the property belongs to you and Mr. Carter and the grant people do not know anything to the contrary.

H.D.C. Richards to McNulty, December 6, 1899

Mr. Parker requests me to tell you to ship the stones you have on hand by express to him at once at the above address. It seems to me it will do well to put in every possible stone that you can. I have told Mr. Parker that I directed you to proceed with two men in the east drift of the Castilian, and that you have been requested to save an assay sample from clear across the lead each day, which is to be numbered and dated, so that the record for each day and its showing will be perfectly clear, and to proceed on that work until further directions; also that I directed you to continue the cross cut west in Muniz until lead pinches or shows promising development, upon which you will advise here for further directions as to work in the cross cut. In case of pinch in the cross cut, you are to put your men on that tunnel running south and work out to the hill below the present dump. I have suggested to Mr. Parker the advisability of having you put two men in the tunnel at the same time that you are working two more in the cross cut. ...I have talked with Mr. Parker and he gives permission to put two men at once in that tunnel. I am mightily pleased at this concession on Mr. Parker's part for I believe it will help you out in future operations, and possibly may show some Turq. as you go out to the face of hill. This will give you six men, and with $50 worth of tools and powder you should be able to make a fine showing by January first. I felt like congratulating you on the showing you will be able to make now that I have induced Mr. Parker to let you have six men, which I felt you had need for.

Parker to McNulty, December 15, 1899

...am pleased to learn that the work you are doing in the mine is looking better than when Mr. Richards was with you. That gentleman wrote you on the 6th inst. authorizing you to put on two more men in the tunnel. I agreed to this on statements he made, and while I want you to have all the men, within reason, at your command to prosecute this work, I wish as much as possible to guard against any superfluous or immediately unnecessary work. My desire is to get out Turquoise, and in endeavoring to get it, to develop the mine, but I do not wish any scientific work done with a view to getting Turquoise out at some distant date. Therefore, in the matter of this tunnel, on which I am not thoroughly clear, I should like you to advise me what results you expect to gain from it, and whether in forming it you expect to obtain some stone. Mr. Richards informs me that the property has been goffered to a great extent in the past. While I do not wish to have anything done which could be construed as an injury to the property, I am particularly desirous, during the next two or three months, to get some good Turquoise, and don't want to have work done for the sake of work and thus wish to put before you what our intentions are. In short, THEY ARE TO GET OUT TURQUOISE. ...I shall always appreciate your giving advice, as being on the ground many points will come to your mind which will be of service to us. Suggest you will please make up an account for labor, etc. ...send same to me as near the first of each month as possible, and on the 15th check will be forwarded to you. All stone fit for shipment I wish forwarded to me... So far as you have seen from your present work in the Castilian, what indications are there of gold?

O'Neil and McNulty pose at O'Neil's Blue Bell turquoise mine, three miles south of Turquoise Hill. Although fierce competitors, they remained friends throughout the years.

McNulty to Parker, around December 20, 1899

Now in regards to this matter about doing any superfluous or immediately unnecessary work, I wish to say that there never has been any unnecessary work done by my orders heretofore, nor shall there be any done hereafter. The work I am doing now is the assessment work on four claims and it is being done in the best place for the benefit of the property. At that same time it is prospecting the Muniz. The work which is being done on the southwest drift, which Mr. Richards called a tunnel, I am having it done for the assessment work on the Gem claim. It will take all of this month to finish the assessment work on it. Should you wish the work to be continued next month it could be counted for the assessment work for next year and when it is driven to the surface it can be used as a tunnel and will be of great benefit to the property in prospecting the hill from that level which is 45 feet under surface at the shaft.

As the drift goes through the hill it gains in depth. The formation in the drift looks favorable for turquoise as far as I have gone, but whether I will be able to get stone I cannot tell at present. The drift has been driven 6 ft. at present for this year's work. The cross cut I am driving northwest is 94 ft. from the main shaft where I am having the assessment work done for the Morning Star claim; the cross cut is 52 ft in length, 9 ft. of it has been done this month.

I am not quite through the quartz dyke yet but it is looking better every day as it shows more small colors which indicates to me that there must be more turquoise ahead in the hill. Please let me know if you wish me to continue the cross cut next month. In regards to the Castilian property I have struck no lead ledge or spur that looks favorable for gold in my opinion, but I have taken samples each day according to Mr. Richards' orders. The drift is in 7 ft. at present for this month. The cross cut I am running west is 6 ft. in length. The formation looks favorable for turquoise as there are small pieces of stone all the way through. I will take all of this month to finish the assessment work.

You will please let me know if you want me to continue the work there or not. I have got but 5 men to work as it being difficult to get American miners to come here there being no houses for them to live in. I have chosen the best I could find from the cheaper miners. Now Mr. Parker, I have found no turquoise so far where I have been working that *is worth saving as I have been doing assessment work and prospecting the property at the same time. As the mine has been goffered out of stone there are only two places in the mine where I may be able to find some. One is in a pillar near the bottom of the shaft and the other at the bottom of the winze. Should you wish me to work there, I shall need the force I have now to do this work to advantage and will also require about 1,000 ft. of lumber for repairs in the shaft.*

Richards to McNulty, December 18, 1899

I had a lot of specifications made up regarding the work on both the Muniz and the Castilian as well for machinery, supplies, work, your house, shaft house, etc, but all of this was of no interest to Mr. Parker who is a bank man and not a mining man, and therefore does not see either the point or the value of my suggestions.

Parker to McNulty, December 27, 1899

Do you know if O'Neil is shipping any stones to Doty? If he is, please find out on what terms, as I am particularly anxious to know if Mr. Doty has any money, as he owes the late Bond Holders in the vicinity of $10,000. Any information that you can obtain on these points, or in fact on what is being done by O'Neil or any one else handling turquoise in your neighborhood shall thank you to advise me.

McNulty to Parker, January 2, 1900

I have never met any expert yet that knew anything about turquoise except Mr. Kunz who is Mr. Tiffany's expert when he was here about 8 years ago. Mr. O'Neil has got better stone in his property than I have shipped to New York for the last three years.

Parker to McNulty, March 31, 1900

Do you not think you could send this stone broken up in larger pieces? Our lapidaries often state that if the pieces were larger

64 • Patricia McGraw

they could do a better work. In a box received a week ago, there was a very large piece, and I hope you will endeavor to continue to send more of that size. From April first we shall have our own lapidary shop when I hope to achieve better results from the material you send.

McNulty to Parker April 7, 1900

In regards to sending larger pieces of stone, I shall always try to do so but the majority of the stone is hidden in the rock and I have to break the rock to find the stone. The men do the sorting in the rough and I do the last sorting and trimming. Since I shipped you that large piece of stone I have not been able to find any more of that kind; but I am driving now, trying to find some more of the same kind as I think it has gone in further through the wall.

...In reply to your request asking me if I know of any one trustworthy and competent to go to Grant County... There is a great temptation to a man in charge of Turquoise Mines as I have been offered a great many times from $10 to $50 for specimens. It therefore is a hard thing for me to recommend a stranger; there are scarcely any miners who know anything about turquoise mining as it is entirely different from gold and silver mines as they work on the lead matter all the time. But in turquoise mining you have got to know the formation that carries stone as there is no lead to work on but deposits in pockets here and there through the rock.

...Should you wish to send me to Grant County to start the work as you say, I can safely do so as my son has worked for me for 7 years and he knows all about the property [the Muñiz and Castilian] and I can trust him while I am gone.

Parker to McNulty, April 12, 1900

I wish to keep our lapidaries well employed, and know that I can depend upon your co-operation by prompt and repeated shipments of stone.

TIFFANY BLUE • 65

Parker to McNulty, May 24, 1900

I leave New York on the 23rd of June for Paris, and I have been in hopes that I could take with me some good clear stone to have put on exhibition by Tiffany & Co. at the World's Fair there. I hope, however, even yet that in the course of a couple of weeks you will send some large pieces which will turn out about the right color that I want for this purpose. I am very glad to learn the success Gen. Bartlett has achieved so far in regard to the Sena case, and hope that we shall not be further molested by the parties. Please push the work along as fast as you can.

Pinkerton's National Detective Agency.

FOUNDED BY ALLAN PINKERTON 1850.

ROB'T A. PINKERTON, New York.
WM. A. PINKERTON, Chicago.
PRINCIPALS.

GEO. D. BANGS, GENERAL SUPERINTENDENT.
New York.

ALLAN PINKERTON, ASST TO PRINCIPALS & GEN'L SUP'T.
New York.

OFFICES.

EASTERN DIVISION.
JOHN CORNISH, ASST GEN'L SUP'T
New York.
NEW YORK, 57 BROADWAY.
BOSTON, 30 COURT STREET.
MONTREAL, MERCHANTS BANK BUILDING
PHILADELPHIA, 441 CHESTNUT STREET

MIDDLE DIVISION.
E. S. GAYLOR, ASS'T GEN'L SUP'T
Chicago.
CHICAGO, 201 FIFTH AVENUE.
ST. PAUL, GERMANIA BANK BUILDING.
KANSAS CITY, 622 MAIN STREET.
ST. LOUIS, WAINWRIGHT BUILDING.

WESTERN DIVISION.
JAS. McPARLAND, ASST GEN'L SUPT
Denver.
DENVER, OPERA HOUSE BLOCK.
PORTLAND, ORE. MARQUAM BLOCK.
SEATTLE, BAILEY BLOCK.
SAN FRANCISCO, CROCKER BUILDING.

ATTORNEYS,
SEWARD, GUTHRIE & STEELE,
New York.

TELEPHONE CONNECTION.

DENVER
OPERA HOUSE BLOCK
J. C. FRASER, SUPT.

Denver, _____ 190_

The Pinkerton Agency, the world famous detective agency, had offices in many cities. Founder Allan Pinkerton's sons were major investors in the Tiffany Mines, and throughout the years made their officers available to investigate the goings on around the mines.

Fred Harvey, of Harvey hotel fame, produced many books in response to America's fascination with the Great Southwest. This volume was McNulty's own.

Chapter 3
1900 Part II - 1901

Perfect Blue

> ...he wants you to use every effort possible to get stone. ...we are very much in need of it. ...send such stone as you have on hand from the Castilian by freight, but that from the Muniz [Tiffany mine] to come by express...
> James Matthews, secretary of American Turquoise Company, to McNulty,
> November 26, 1900

SEND MORE TURQUOISE

By mid-summer life at Turquoise Hill had assumed a rhythm, with miners looking for work, McNulty searching for turquoise, and the banker from New York, Parker, guiding the mining operations he had never seen and quite possibly never understood. McNulty regularly sent mine descriptions back East so that the banker could map exactly where he dug, blasted, and cleared tunnels, winzes, stopes*, and shafts. Matching descriptions against a map at long distance led to misunderstandings, notwithstanding the expertise of the mining engineers who assisted Parker with those maps. Although the demand for turquoise was so great now that almost any type of stone was marketable, Parker continually criticised McNulty's turquoise. It was of poor quality with too much matrix and not the right shade of blue. Cerrillos turquoise was often somewhat soft, and that quality earned it the reputation for being difficult to cut and polish, yet, once

---

* winze: a shaft inside a tunnel - stope: an underground room

the jewelers worked their magic the gems took on a luster that commanded a high price. Despite Parker's complaints about quality, someone clearly made money on the turquoise McNulty sent. Estimates and rumors put the output at around $200,000 a year in 1892.

At the same time the company's insatiable appetite demanded all grades of turquoise, mining activity slowed due to the financial strain of the Sena case. No matter, the work was driven by dreams of finding the perfect Tiffany blue stones, and sometimes those dreams were fueled as much by gossip as by what was in the rocks.

A number of people watched the Tiffany mines for the chance to make their fortunes: miners located new claims adjacent to the ATC, Cerrillos merchants inferred mine discoveries from the supplies that were purchased, and Santa Fe, Denver, and New York lawyers waited for their turn at the legal spoils.

McNulty regularly received letters telling him the turquoise he sent wasn't worth much. But then the next letter would plead, "Send more, send it quickly." An ordinary person might have walked off such a job, but McNulty's Army experience had made him more tough and astute than an ordinary person, and not so easily discouraged.

Although McNulty's paychecks, payrolls, and expenses received prompt and detailed attention, his living quarters escaped the notice of Parker until numerous visitors came back with tales of McNulty's living conditions. Eventually, Parker realized the dilapidated house reflected on the company, and he took action. He requested that McNulty figure out a way to build a new, inexpensive house.

The heat of July days forced miners to shelter. The Turquoise Hill sat in such a remote, dry area that travelers were few, and many would-be miners considered it unliveable. A traveler from Cerrillos to the mines could make the fastest time on horseback along the path that followed the bottom of a draw, barely a road. Buggies and wagons could also travel that same rough road, but it was hard on rigs and harder on the passengers. The drive or ride to the mines from Santa Fe, to the north, was a much smoother, more comfortable trip. Easterners and lawyers preferred the Santa Fe route.

At times on either road McNulty was known to let his horse choose the direction. Even the Cerrillos road, as rough as it was, was so often travelled that it was passable by both man and horse, night or day. The road could be rough in other ways too. Carrying cigar boxes to the train station, McNulty was customarily armed with his Winches-

Emma, McNulty, and the dogs, including the one who saved his life, stand outside their old house. Note the timber prop on the wall to the right that held the house up.

ter or his shotgun. His other constant companions along the trail, hawks and robins, flitted, graceful visions in the far distance. These lonely treks were as much a part of the mining operation as breaking apart and sorting the rocks.

To distract himself from the loss of his son McNulty had his work. But Emma, tied to an empty house full of memories of her first child, endured times of deep depression and times of sicknesses. The laudanum provided by Dr. Friend Palmer of Cerrillos didn't help her dark moods nor provide relief for her bilious attacks. Trips to Santa Fe and visits to friends cheered her some, while in July of 1900 she spent whole days in bed.

A good job and hope kept the Irishman at the mines. More than that, he knew his circumstances were better than those of his friends. He had a roof over his head, albeit a leaky one and about 18 inches out of line. He had a job that paid well and regularly, usually. And his family surrounded him. The measure of a man was by his family and his work, and all things considered, McNulty had done well.

During one of her stays in Santa Fe, Emma wrote to her husband

and closed the letter with love and kisses. Love. Without Emma the evenings at the mine could be long and lonely.

McNulty's most memorable days came when his daughters, Fannie and Agnes, and his son Eddie were there. Fannie, the great cook of the family, prepared the meals, and his son helped with the mining work. And in those light moments of family life his now grown children raced buggies around the hill and wove their tales of turquoise and New Mexico.

Against this domestic backdrop, mining beckoned, and the few experienced miners willing to work at Turquoise Hill usually lived within five miles of the mine. If they owned a horse, they could make it to work in a timely fashion, but otherwise it was an hour or more of walking each way. At the turn of the century sheep raising was a major activity in New Mexico, and during lambing season most of the workers tended to business back at their homes. Of course, during the rainy season no one wanted to live in hot, sweltering tents.

Most days of the summer McNulty worked alone, filling buckets with rock and hoisting the turquoise laden stones to the surface by the whim. His work was mapped by tunnels and shafts, but the true measure of his work lay in the soreness of his muscles.

A BOGUS STRIKE AND A BAD STRIKE

In 1900 there appeared in several newspapers a series of articles that immediately excited potential new investors and bond holders alike. It didn't matter that the stories came from dubious, unnamed sources and the "facts" stretched far into the sunset. Turquoise news was big everywhere, even in Europe. This news took the bond holders by surprise. What they read and what they thought they knew did not at all agree.

> One of the richest strikes of turquoise ever known in the history of the world was made in the American Turquoise company's mine near Cerrillos last week. For size, purity of texture and delicacy of color, they have never been surpassed, so it is said by experts who have

examined the gems. Their value is, of course, fabulous, and they will probably be bought by the crowned heads of Europe. The largest turquoise in existence belongs to the crown jewels of Spain, and was taken by the Spaniards from these same mines over two hundred years ago. A large trust has attempted to secure all the turquoise around in the district for the last year, but so far their efforts have been unsuccessful. New Mexico now produces more turquoise than the mines of the world combined. Persia formerly held that record until the mines of this territory were discovered. — *New Mexico Mining Record*, July, 1900.

Two unidentified newspapers in New York re-printed stories on the turquoise finds in New Mexico, and both contained datelines of East Las Vegas. McNulty suspected his friend and competitor, Mike O'Neil, may have been the source of the stories. O'Neil's motives for spreading the stories were that this story might make his own mining claims suddenly more valuable and easier to sell.

When Parker, company president, returned from Paris, he demanded McNulty explain the stories' origins, since the bond holders were besieging him for news about the great turquoise finds reported in the papers. McNulty had kept track of O'Neil's movements and determined that O'Neil had been in Las Vegas about the time the story was put out. The mystery was solved: O'Neil had employed that most valuable tool of the miner's trade, the bogus strike, to up the value of his own claims.

Possibly spurred by the news stories and possibly spurred by optimism, Parker insisted McNulty speed up the turquoise shipments. The recent meager production of the sky stone hindered the company's ability to pay its bills, and all the while demand for the stones ran high. Parker thought that McNulty, or perhaps Doty in the past, had hidden away some turquoise that could now be sent to Tiffany. McNulty set the banker straight. He said that the mine had little visible turquoise and that the dumps had been thoroughly worked over. As to a hidden stash of turquoise, the utterly ridiculous suggestion deserved little response.

Ultimately the ATC desired to patent its claims so that assessment work would no longer be necessary and the company would have a government-recognized document by which it could fend off future troublemakers. Getting that patent work fell to McNulty, and he spent many hours arranging for surveyors to plat the boundaries of the claims. The process should have been easy, but of course nothing connected with the mines was ever easy.

McNulty had arranged for a surveyor to come to the mines, and he hosted the man and his son for the week. One August afternoon near the end of the surveyor's visit a fast moving thunderstorm enveloped the Turquoise Hill, taking the surveyor and his son by surprise. Later, McNulty counted himself lucky that he had not been on that hill.

> The Surveyor has been here all week and I am very sorry to tell you of the sad accident that happened to him and his son. As we were about to finish up on the Castilian claim, a storm came up at 2 o'clock yesterday afternoon. While the surveyor was standing with his instrument, a bolt of lightning struck him on the top of his head and ran all the way down to the sole of his foot and burned his garments and body and cut two gashes on his head. His little boy was struck lightly on his head and limbs, and his eyesight is very much affected. I sent to Cerrillos for the Doctor immediately and had a message telephoned to his relatives in Santa Fe and his brother and another doctor with him came out and took him to Santa Fe last night and when he left my house he was in a very critical condition... I have had a very hard time in locating the corners for the surveyor on the Castilian claim, as it is fifteen years ago since it was located. — McNulty to Parker, August 18, 1900.

McNulty followed up with a trip to Santa Fe to check on the surveyor, but the man, still in critical condition, could not muster the strength to sign an affidavit as to the relocation of the mines. The delay might prove costly — it kept the hopes of the land grant litigants alive, and the Sena people appeared to have unlimited funds.

With patent plans temporarily shelved, McNulty turned his attention to his house. He hoped to have a warm, new cabin before the cold and snow set in. Of course, he also had to continue with the necessary assessment work at the mines.

McNulty's work report for 1900 said the Blue Bell and the Blue Gem claims reached the 44 foot level. On the Muñiz property he had prospected for turquoise leads. He worked on the Castilian claim at a depth of 55 feet where he found stains of turquoise but knew that the rock formation was not the right one for large finds. At the same time McNulty panned for free gold but found none. Then, in September, the clear blue skies turned dark and cloudy. Rains poured into the shafts and caused mud slides. McNulty reported that running water loosened the walls and threatened cave-ins, which meant even more expense for the company. He described the opening over the Castilian as being around 60 feet in length and 20 feet in width. Ladders between platforms every 20 feet or so provided stopping places for miners or visitors descending into the mine.

LONG DAYS, LONGER NIGHTS

Turquoise mining differed from gold, silver, lead or coal mining. Turquoise formed in pockets or pillars, and sometimes veins, but the vein could quickly disappear. Just as easily and without warning just a few feet away a new pillar might be found. As productive areas appeared McNulty would open up a small room or stope which would then be worked out. Tunnels pursued veins deep into the hill, but tunnels were not a way to find individual pockets. As rock was cut, blasted, and moved out from the side of the hill, other workers would cut across the hill in the quest for veins. This cross cutting exposed possible veins, pockets, and flecks of turquoise that could be scooped up, chipped out, and the best of it sent back East. Yet Parker prevented the exploratory operation from going full force — McNulty's orders from the banker were to follow only veins and look for visible turquoise. McNulty insisted that development work could pinpoint more turquoise. Parker didn't listen, and he just insisted on more production from the visible turquoise.

Parker, at the same time he derided the quality of the stones he was getting, suggested McNulty put on more men immediately. Parker eventually relented, backtracked, and then said McNulty's work was fine and the stones needed to keep coming. In fact Parker even suggested that he was "content" with the quality of the stones.

Parker encouraged the new house by permitting McNulty to order 3,000 adobes or mud bricks at a cost of $25. Workers completed about 350 adobes a day, hauled water for $2 a day, and averaged 20 barrels of water daily. As Emma had now rejoined him at the mines McNulty was particularly anxious to have his house done.

Some workers made adobes while McNulty directed others at the mining, but Parker's demands for turquoise simply could not be met with what he was finding. The long days began and ended with moving, blasting, and chipping stones. Things never changed.

Mining engineers noted that Parker's approach to mining didn't agree with good turquoise mining principals. In fact, he "gophered" the mine, thereby decreasing its value by taking out visible turquoise. H.D.C. Richards, a mining engineer who had earlier visited McNulty, commented, "Mr. Parker had views regarding the operation of the American Co's. properties which differed from mine, for the time being; next year may be different if certain steps he contemplates are taken and the patent difficulties are removed."

By October Parker's nervousness and uncertainty about the ownership of the company's claims appeared in his letter to Edward Bartlett, attorney for the company in New Mexico. He needed some positive news for the stockholders, the Pinkertons, Tiffany, and Stillman, and he needed a good prediction of their chances in the land grant case.

Bartlett refrained from expressing an informal opinion. It had always amazed him the number of attorneys with whom he had to deal — there were New York lawyers who directed Colorado attorneys who in turn directed Bartlett regarding the actions that needed to be taken in New Mexico. And the time involved in such convoluted maneuvering made it difficult to get information, and even more difficult to get prompt payment.

The Colorado lawyers, too, wanted to deal with McNulty, who provided the witnesses. This most confusing situation could be handled only one way — with common sense. All evidence pointed to the fact that the land grant did not have the Tiffany mines within its purported boundaries. It would just take time for all the attorneys to sort it out. The testimony of old residents in the area supported the contention that no land grant existed, so McNulty felt secure in his job and his ability to keep the mine going. The question was, did the company have enough money to keep paying out big legal fees to redundant lawyers?

As usual, McNulty expected that the Christmas season would push the company to demand more stones, and just like clockwork the expected letter arrived authorizing him to employ more workers and have them work in three different places. McNulty commented that the walls and rock showed the blue color but not in a substantial amount. He pushed the work and he sent what he could.

Toward the end of 1900 McNulty's house neared completion, and he looked forward to a neat little cottage. The three room house, built in an L shape, would keep the cold winds away. Unfortunately, some snow and rain destroyed some of the adobes and forced a delay. While the adobes dried, McNulty hired his own men to make more to replace the damaged ones.

For the next 60 days McNulty kept the shipments of turquoise going to Tiffany. After a day of heavy work, he retired to his house, put on his glasses, and along with Emma they chipped out the blue colors by the yellow light of a kerosine lamp. They averaged a cigar box of turquoise per week.

At the end of each evening, before he went to bed, McNulty took a horseback ride around the claims to make sure they were secure and that no one hid in the darkness. Sometimes it was dangerous, as he occasionally met Pueblo Indians waiting under the cover of darkness to take that day's left-behind turquoise. Most times the only signal McNulty had to give was a wave to send the trespassing Pueblos on their way. He hoped that if they knew a guard watched the area, that would suffice.

Cigar boxes were filled with turquoise chips and nuggets before being shipped off to Tiffany. McNulty used snuff boxes for the smaller chips. Each cigar box weighed close to five pounds.

On visits to Cerrillos McNulty customarily made the rounds of the saloons — in a mining camp, the best places to hear the latest and most up to date information. Whatever he heard that might interest the company he promptly reported.

He heard that Doty had reappeared in the area, possibly working with O'Neil. One day in November McNulty and O'Neil sat chatting, and O'Neil offered that Easterners as a rule declined to pay top dollar for his, O'Neil's, turquoise and, tried to cheat him out of some promised money. Also, promises made didn't count for much until actual dollars lay on the table, and both O'Neil and McNulty agreed this was the first rule of the mining business. Some days the stories had the sound of truth, and other times a tale would reach McNulty's ears that made no sense. McNulty and O'Neil, lifelong friends, were two of a kind — highly competitive miners who knew there was a great get-rich-strike around the corner, or at least a means of making a living.

As the winter progressed, so did McNulty's house. He and Emma could visualize moving into a snug home — one that would remain warm in the winter. The delay the rain had caused didn't seem to matter any more. Here stood a home that anyone could enjoy, built of adobe in a draw that shielded it from the wind. If only the weather warmed up for a few days the house could be completed, and McNulty and Emma would be comfortable for a change.

In 1900 McNulty experienced much difficulty keeping workers. The hard work discouraged the slaggards, and many of the other workers were sick. Although McNulty had completed the assessment work and filed the Proof of Labor, there was still cleaning to be done so that next year's work would go more smoothly. Never one to wait, McNulty toiled to secure the company's claims for the coming year. The cost of labor and supplies for 1900 amounted to almost $4500.

The company log book detailed the work done in 1900: removed a pillar, 15 feet; winze seven feet, cross cut, 4 feet for a total of 26 feet driven through solid rock in the Muñiz mine. And this was just January and February of 1900. The next entry listed 41 feet of tunneling, shaft, and winze work being completed April through May. And so it was throughout the log book — more than 400 feet of blasting through solid rock in four different mines.

DISAPPOINTMENT & JEALOUSY

For unknown reasons McNulty carefully preserved this news article, which he had cut from a local paper. The story illustrates life in a small town, along with the dark side, the tragedy of a respectable family.

Murder and Suicide
A rejected lover shoots his sweetheart then kills himself
Special to the New Mexican
Cerrillos, January 5 — About 12 o'clock last night, while this town was in seeming repose and peaceful slumber, a horrible tragedy occurred, prompted by disappointed love and raging jealousy. Duncan McIntire, a young man of good enticements and character, employed in the Madrid coal mines, fatally shot Miss Etta Anderson, an estimable and attractive young woman, at her residence here, because, upon being urged to marry him, she declined to do so. He then turned the murderous pistol on himself and fired, dying instantly from the effects of the shot. Miss Anderson died in about thirty minutes. Both are well connected, they had the respect and goodwill of the community.

McIntire was only twenty years of age, and his innocent victim but 18. The murdered girl was the oldest daughter of Mr. and Mrs. William Anderson, and had many friends. McIntire was a stately young man, but was evidently crazed by love and jealously. The entire community is very much shocked and grieved over the double tragedy.

McIntire had to have worked in the mines the past six years, and had saved about three thousand dollars. The young woman had been attending school in Kansas, and was home to spend her vacation. Both young people had been playing cards when he called her into another room, and after an earnest conversation the shots rang out, one of the shots in the eye of the girl and the other her side. She died in her mother's arms, to whom she said "Goody-by" before the last breath had fled.

Miss Anderson leaves a father and mother, one brother and three sisters. McIntire leaves a widowed mother, one brother and four sisters. Both young people were active church workers.

The year 1901 began inauspiciously, an omen of the difficulties to come for the company and for McNulty. The land grant case headed to court, and that meant more witnesses and more trips to Santa Fe. Company business kept McNulty running between Santa Fe to Turquesa. At the same time he moved forward with mine development and turquoise production.

HURRY UP AND FIND MORE

The new year greeted McNulty with his new house only two weeks away from being occupied. While he worked the mines Emma painted inside and then whitewashed the outside of the house. McNulty suggested Parker come for a visit since the house would be done by his arrival. Parker considered coming to New Mexico, but he didn't know when. A visit to the mines would now be easier on the banker, since the timbers and ladders had been repaired and the housing accommodations were much improved. McNulty anticipated that the visit would educate the New Yorker on the workings of a turquoise mine. Parker could bring his maps and they would see how well they matched the descriptions McNulty had been sending him.

McNulty tried to inject some optimism in his letters at the beginning of 1901: "the cross cut in the Castilian is looking favorable... I have been getting a few stones out and also from some waste rock stored away in the mine [Muñiz]..."

This, however, did not coincide with Parker's view of the situation. The banker's letters were a litany of complaints. High expenses, inferior stone quality, the financial drain of the legal battles: all these had put the company in dire straits. Parker ordered the workers discharged and the mine shut down, and he told McNulty to give no reason. Why? Perhaps it was to reduce supply and thereby inflate the price of the turquoise, but Parker didn't share that information with McNulty.

It took no reading between the lines to see a direct connection between the shutdown and the Sena case. Stock holders met and decided their dollars should be directed to legal fees instead of mining, an indication of their concern, and of the uncertainty over the

McNulty received many of these types of telegrams over the years. One day he was ordered to layoff workers, then a short time later, he would receive a telegram ordering up more workers.

outcome. The hearing was set for early in the year.

Several members of the Private Land Claims Court had asked McNulty for samples of the turquoise as remembrances. McNulty passed along the request to Parker, who immediately suspected a plot, thinking the members of the court wanted to find out the value of the turquoise. Parker hesitated to grant the request. McNulty requested permission to give samples and tried to explain to Parker why this was wise. "They merely asked if I would give them a piece of turquoise in the rough in remembrance, as it was one of the hardest cases they had to fight in Court." Parker relented. The court members could have some Tiffany turquoise — but nothing too valuable!

The exchange had not helped McNulty's relations with Parker. His requests were inspected twice; every receipt analyzed, questioned again, and then grudgingly orders or money issued. The stockholders appeared to be expecting bad news all around — bad news from the court and bad news from the market. An unfavorable decision would put all the company holdings and finances in jeopardy.

McNulty guarded carefully the information he sent to New York as he struggled to make sure every detail was completely accurate. Should a mistake in paperwork occur he immediately corrected it in writing, and in duplicate. He strove to answer every possible question. And

80 • Patricia McGraw

he kept a most detailed accounting of his expenses.

Less than two weeks after McNulty received orders to discharge the workers, he received another letter to find stone and ship it immediately. Those orders also included instructions to re-hire the recently discharged workers. "Hurry up and send more," were the orders from Parker. "Look for whatever may have been hidden away in the mines in previous years." To add insult to injury, Parker said that Doty found more turquoise regularly than McNulty had found in three years. "Business is done for profit or not at all," Parker concluded.

McNulty immediately shipped a small box of turquoise all of which came out of the dumps. He noted that he blasted here and there in the mine walls where he thought there might be any chance of finding turquoise. "A mine is a prospect hole in the ground, and when the mine is robbed of stone," McNulty said, "no turquoise can be found."

Still, Parker pushed the miner to look in every nook and cranny for perfect blue turquoise gems. McNulty searched and re-searched played out areas along with any place where the blue might be hiding. At the same time Parker expected McNulty to host potential buyers the company sent his way.

> April 7th
> Hotel Dewey
> Welton St
> Denver
>
> To J. P. McNulty Esq
>   Dear Sir
>   I enclose letter of introduction from Mr Murray, which will be sufficient guarrantee of my stability & bona fides. &

Before any one could visit the mines, the company required McNulty to be presented with a letter of introduction. Louis Marks, sent by the Pinkertons, oversaw their interest in the mines.

ANOTHER RICHMOND IN THE FIELD?

McNulty wrote to Parker about the progression of work and said that he expected to find more turquoise. The miners dug out little rooms or stopes by chipping out the ceiling, since no turquoise could be seen in the walls or on the floors. The slow work created rubble that had to be removed before anything else could be done, and that meant transfers from bucket to bucket and transport to the dump. Then came preliminary sorting, and the last step was a trip to McNulty's house where he assessed the value and chipped away excess rock. And for this he had only four workers. It was Parker who held back permission for a full work force.

Finally, a shipment arrived that delighted the New York bond holders. The next order was to work in the drift and ship all stone as soon as possible. McNulty had found the quality of stone they wanted.

As May 1901 rolled around so did lambing season, and the pool of desirable workers dwindled. American miners demanded steady work before they signed on, and McNulty could never guarantee that. But because Parker was expecting to come to New Mexico he allowed McNulty to take on whatever workers could be found. The banker intended to visit the mines in comfort. In fact, he wanted the mines safe for an "Eastern gentlemen" such as he. McNulty looked forward to the visit.

When the end of May arrived, McNulty received a letter from the former U.S. Surveyor General, Chas. Easley, who now entered the melee as an attorney for ATC. And another lawyer, of course, meant an additional financial burden for the company. The Sena group headed to court again, this time in the Court of Private Land Claims.

Then the payroll for May did not arrive. That it was late was not unusual, but this time because workers were in short supply it was disastrous. McNulty delegated one miner each day to go to Cerrillos in case the payroll arrived, which left the mines even more short handed.

Halfway through 1901 Parker sent word to pick up the pace and at the same time keep expenses down. McNulty's orders were to work only where turquoise could be seen. He searched urgently for veins, slabs, and pillars, but encountered only flecks and small bits. The

THE AMERICAN TURQUOISE COMPANY.
52 WALL STREET.
NEW YORK

August 27th, 1901.

Mr. J. P. McNulty, Supt.,
    Cerrillos, N. M.

Dear Sir:-

    I am in receipt of your favor of the 23rd inst., and note your remarks relative to the necessity of timbering Nos. one and two shafts and the Castillian.

    Please advise me by return mail what it will cost to put in the necessary timber to make all safe, according to your understanding. Perhaps it would be as well to obtain bids for this work, if you and your men are not in a position to do it yourselves.

    As General Bartlett advised you, I have been expecting to visit the property, and if the work should be done before I arrive I desire to know exactly what is necessary and the cost of same, otherwise it can remain until my arrival, which will be probably in a month.

    I am not accustomed to going down mines, and as I desire to see all that belongs to The American Turquoise Company I would like the means of descending and ascending to be such that a man, not accustomed to the work like yourself and your men, would not come to grief, so you had better have this part of the business attended to at once.

    Yours very truly,
    R. A. Parker
    President.

In other words, I do not want to run the risk of "taking a header" down a shaft and breaking my neck.

Parker, company president, asked McNulty to make sure the mines were safe. The banker wrote, "In other words, I do not want to take the risk of 'taking a header' down a shaft and breaking my neck." This single letter shows Parker's cautious, careful nature.

turquoise had been worked for almost nine years, and the days of easy pickings were gone. Now only luck led to anything profitable.

    McNulty customarily followed the local and regional newspapers with an eye for the mining news, and in July he learned that Doty was back in New Mexico and was mining turquoise a bit to the south of the American Turquoise holdings. McNulty hadn't actually seen Doty, but he learned that the former ATC mine manager was selling whatever he had on hand quickly. And those sales were out of state.

The registrar for land claims refused to accept the patent application of ATC until the Sena land grant case was resolved. It appeared that New Mexican officials were purposely thwarting the aims of the ATC and bleeding its finances. Parker lamented the fact that the former company hadn't taken care of the patents much earlier, and that a lot of trouble could have been avoided if they had. And he questioned whether some unsavory or corrupt politicians were working against them. He wondered if someone with deep pockets was financing Sena, since he most likely didn't have large resources of his own.

Parker wryly commented, "...there is some prejudice being exercised against our interests and rights to lead the Register to throw out our applications on the rest of our mines. Who is at the back of Sena? Has he money enough to prosecute all these suits, or is there another Richmond in the field, who is merely using Sena's name and claim?"

Then, uncharacteristically, Parker voiced his disappointment, "...I recognize the difficulties which have beset you in our affairs, and it is a source of much regret, undoubtedly to you as to us, that it has not been possible to overcome them.."

All this meant that McNulty had to work all of those claims in order not to lose them.

More disappointment came when some unexpectedly heavy rains damaged the mines. That damage needed to be repaired before Parker's visit, so funds were committed to purchase the necessary timber for the repairs.

McNulty worked and awaited Parker's arrival, but the banker sent no word about a date. September and October passed, and Cerrillos was alive with gossip, and some of it traveled. Doty apparently had passed through Cerrillos again. Parker asked McNulty to pass along any information about Doty, and an explanation of how people might have gotten secret ATC information.

Regarding the secrets, McNulty responded that people in Cerrillos loved talking about him. In addition, Doty inquired at length about the Tiffany mine. Doty's inquiry alone may have been enough to fuel more rumors.

"...I do know that there are some people in Cerrillos who are envious of me because I will not tell them anything about the property...," McNulty told Parker.

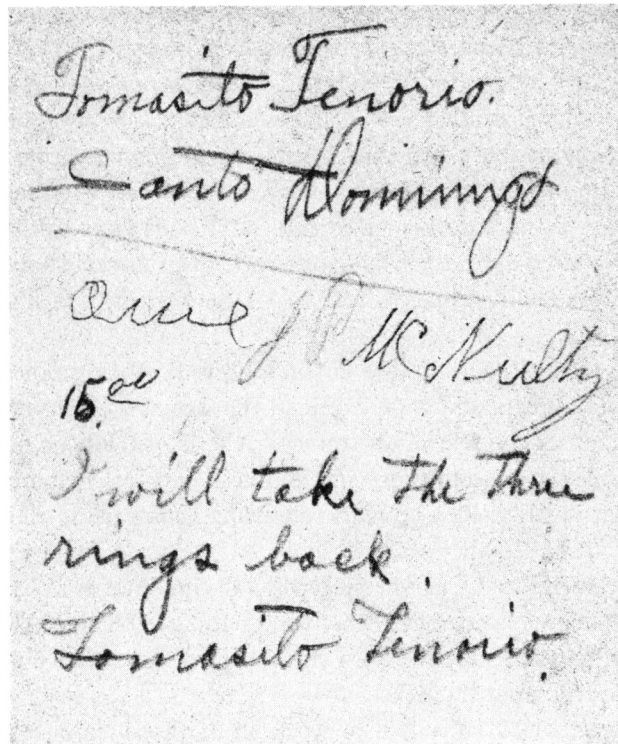

At a time when banks were few and not available to most people, McNulty served as "the banker." In this case for Tomasito Tenorio from Santo Domingo Pueblo.

TWENTY-THREE CIGAR BOXES

The numerous trips up and down the Cerrillos road took its toll on McNulty's buggy and harness. Since it needed replacement, McNulty requested the company purchase a buggy, harness and a strong road wagon. The company agreed. Ever frugal, McNulty saved the company money by purchasing a second-hand buggy and harness, and he also bought a new black mare, which promptly bucked him off. The mare was fresh and young.

In November of 1901 big changes came to the ATC mines — Eddie, who had been his father's right hand man, decided to go to work in

Arizona for his father-in-law. That meant that the second most experienced miner the ATC had was hired away at a salary of $125.

When the news of his son's departure came to the ears of the ATC, the company requested more details which McNulty quickly supplied. Eddie's new job included setting up machinery and frame timbers near Prescott, Arizona.

To fill Eddie's position McNulty needed someone steady, hard working, and experienced. And in spite of the fact that McNulty enjoyed his whisky — in moderation — he found fault with those workers who spent too much time in saloons. He demanded reliable, honest workers in return for good pay, and those who didn't drink alcohol to excess. Finally, he found a good worker whom he promptly hired.

Adjacent to the ATC claims McNulty had staked a couple of claims for himself — the Blue Bell and the Blue Gem — at the top of the Turquoise Hill above the Muñiz mine. Since the demand for perfect blue turquoise was strong, McNulty considered selling his claims. He talked to A.C. Ireland, a pharmacist and land broker in Santa Fe, who said he had found a buyer. The asking price: $15,000. Ireland cautioned McNulty that in the past outside interests had caused deals to fail. Sometimes when people heard that a buyer was in town they would spread rumors specifically to scare him away.

Fledgling landlord and occasional pawnbroker of sorts were added to McNulty's resumé. He acquired rental properties that would provide income in his old age; his pawn brokerage helped out friends such as Tomasito Tenorio, who borrowed $15 in return for McNulty holding onto some Santo Domingo jewelry.

The end of 1901 totaled up to 277 feet of tunneling, winzes, crosscuts, raises, and shafts in four mines. The amount expended on the mines alone, not including legal fees, $4202.02. Shipments totaled 23 cigar boxes, each around five pounds and containing chipped-out turquoise; and seven large boxes containing 2 cigar boxes each as well as larger rocks and stones.

When McNulty paid the employees they signed receipts for their work that detailed the hours they had worked for that month. Signatures and even spellings were variable, and McNulty commented to ATC that because some workers were unable to spell their names their signatures were written differently on many of the receipts.

McNulty & Friends
Dialogs On Mining & Patents
1900 Part II - 1901

Parker to McNulty, October 17, 1900

So far as the specimens in one of the tobacco sacks is concerned, we do not find it of much value. However, any stone that you do get out, please ship it, and we will see what we can make out of it, no matter what the quality.

McNulty to Parker, October 22, 1900

The few stones in the sack is all I have been able to find in the open cut on the surface. ...which I intend to quit in a day or two and start to work on the Castilian. Where I have been sinking in the bottom level, in the Muniz mine, I have found no stone as yet. ...There is no one interested in the property that can feel more disheartened in not being able to ship you stone regularly than I am. ...The Mexican who had the contract for making the adobes for the house had finished making them *on the 18th inst and I paid him $20 as was agreed to when made and on the 15th inst there came a heavy rain and on the 20th inst it rained also, which have spoiled most of the adobe as they were laying flat on the ground being too wet to pile up. Very true the Mexicans will be the losers as they have to replace the spoiled ones according to the contract. It is a rare thing to have rain in New Mexico at this time of the year and should we not have two or three weeks of dry weather from now on, I fear we shall not be able to get the house up this fall.*

James Matthews, company treasurer, to McNulty, October 27, 1900

```
    Mr. Parker has requested me to write you
to push the work as vigorously as possible
and ship whatever stone you obtain as soon
as you have enough to make a shipment by
express.  It has occurred to Mr. Parker that
possibly you may be able to find some stone
on the dump, or wherever you have been ac-
customed to placing the refuse from the mine.
While we do not expect you can find first-
class stone in this way  it is possible that
we can make use of it  in second or third
grade goods.   ...we are most anxious to re-
ceive all the stone we can within the next
few weeks.
```

McNulty to Parker, November 1, 1900

I have now six men to work since the first of the week. I have put two of the old hands to work again. I have started three days ago to work on the Castilian, and have men working in three different places in the mine. In one of the places I expect to get out stone in a few days, such as specimens which will be green, the color may be better as I go deeper. I shall send you a sample of them as soon as I get enough sorted. I am also sinking the winze in the bottom level in the Muniz which is down now 12 ft from the bottom level, and have found no stone as yet, but the rock is stained with colors, and I intend to sink it at least 10 feet deeper and should I not find stone at that depth, I intend to drift and crosscut from there.

McNulty to Parker, November 5, 1900

The sack marked Castilian 1898 is what I took out and laid aside as Mr. Doty would not handle them. There is also some specimens in the paper sack that I am taking out of the Castilian now, and should you be able to handle this kind of stone, I will be able to send you several boxes of them. The small stone in the sack and the loose specimens is the best in what I have got out of the dumps and the refuse...

Matthews to McNulty, November 26, 1900

[Parker] he wants you to use every effort possible to get stone either from the mine or the dump and ship without delay as we are very much in need of it, but to exercise care in shipping it. You may send such stone as you have on hand from the Castilian by freight, but that from the Muniz to come by express.

McNulty to Parker, November 26, 1900

I heard a little news the other day about Mr. O'Neil and his property which I no doubt you would like to know as you told me to be on the lookout. He has been working his force of men on his turquoise property these last few weeks and I have been talking to him several times, trying to get what information I could and yesterday when he was intoxicated he told me that he had sold 5 pounds of stone to Mr. Burns & Lawson of New York and the next lot of stone he had on hand they only wanted to pay him $100 per pound and that they were trying hard to get a bond and lease from him and he told me that he would not let them have on bond and lease unless they paid him half the purchase price in cash right down.

Mr. Burns is the man who bought the stone for Mr. Doty last year, but I cannot say now who he is buying it for and Mr. Lawson is the son of Mr. Lawson of New York who is president of the Ortiz Mining Grant which is seven miles from Cerrillos. I do not know Mr. Lawson's initials but you may know him by his being president of the Ortiz Grant. I must tell you that Mr. O'Neil is a man that you cannot rely upon for always telling the truth but I will be on the lookout and find out all I can and let you know.

McNulty to Parker, December 15, 1900

I have quite a difficulty in keeping the Mexicans at work regularly as some of them are sick and others quitting, that I intend to make a general change as soon as I can find men that will suit me.

Parker to McNulty, January 14, 1901

We have your payroll for the month of December amounting to $440, and in as much as we have received but one small box of stone during the past month, and that of very inferior quality, we wish you to discontinue work for the present. You, of course, are still on the payroll; and we would like you to retain a cheap helper who can assist you in sorting. Of course, where you see an opportunity of getting and shipping us some stone from what you have in sight you can do so, but we are tired of paying out so much money with so little financial result. The fact of the matter is, Mr. McNulty, your developing and other work does not pay, and I want no more expense incurred until after the Sena trial. You will be kind enough to discharge your men, except as above, and it will not be necessary for you to give any reason why you are shutting down. Please keep this letter strictly confidential.

McNulty to Matthews, treasurer for American Turquoise Company, January 24, 1900

No doubt the signatures on the receipts may puzzle you, but there are very few of the Mexicans who can write, and the one who does the writing does not know how to spell their names correctly.

Matthews to McNulty, January 24, 1901

...ship by first express all the Castilian stone you have on hand in the shape of slabs. ...You need not ship any Castilian stone other than that which you find in this shape. If you are able to obtain any more of this kind in the mine, please express it as soon as possible, and whenever you have enough stone from the Muniz also send that immediately.

McNulty to Parker, Jan 26, 1901

...there is no change in the drift that I am mining in the Muniz mine since I last wrote you and the crosscut in the Castilian still looks favorable, but there is no stone in sight yet.

McNulty to Parker, February 4, 1901

I am still working the crosscut in the Castilian and will continue as I have great faith in it as the rock looks better every day. The drift in the Muniz is not looking very good, and I will not drive it much further. I am still working the dump.

James Matthews to McNulty, February 16, 1901

We notice the payroll is large for this month, and as we have been receiving such a small quantity of stone from you, would ask what is the matter. What we want is turquoise stone, and I will frankly say that we are not getting it. It is not paying us to continue in this way; do you think so?

Parker to McNulty, February 21, 1901

We have every opportunity at this time of disposing of all large pieces, both clear stone and what is termed matrix, and I hope that you will push everything forward as rapidly as you can. I have, I must confess, not been satisfied the way things are going inasmuch as we are spending more money at the mines now than ever Doty did, and yet we are not getting one-fifth the results that he did, and, moreover, there is more demand for the stone now than at any time during the past ten years. ...we know there must be the stuff hidden away in the mines. ...as you know, business is done for profit, or not at all.

McNulty to Matthews, February 22, 1900

Very true the payroll for January was large but I had to have the men in order to be able to make the shipments that I have made, as some of them have been doing development work to see where to find stone, some breaking round here and there, where I could see any stone to take out, and others sorting the dump. ...the mine is merely a prospect hole as there is no development work done on the property yet to amount to anything. I am now in the tenth year in charge of this property and have never had permission to open up the mine through development work, except a little last year as the call is continually for stone and the mine has been robbed till all the stone has been taken out of it.

There is no mine in existence that can hold out and pay its way without doing development work and this property is not like a gold or silver mine where they have a lead or ledge to follow. All I have to follow here is merely certain formation of rock that carries stone. There is a true fissure vein at least 3 feet wide, but it carries no turquoise. It would be more satisfactory to me and the Company if either you or Mr. Parker would come here and look over the property as you would better understand all about the property and the working of it, than you would by sending an outsider.

McNulty to Parker, March 2, 1901

You say there must be the stuff hidden away in the mine, and that it is very provoking to see good opportunities passing by for lack of material. It is very true the stone is all hidden in the rock, and it is an old saying, — that one man can see as far through a rock as another & as the Irishman said a great deal further, and 18 months ago I could see further through the rock where I could find stone than I can today.

Very true, the stone is not confined to this one place, as there must be some more pockets somewhere in the hill and the hill will have to be cut through to find them sooner or later. I cannot do much of this development work, with the force that I have, when there is a continual call for stone as I keep the men sorting and blasting for stone wherever I see there is any stone to be got. ...I have still got a man breaking ground in the Castilian, and I am now under the place where it shows some fine blue colors near the surface, but they are too small to save.

Louis Marks, engineer seeking to lease mine shares owned by Pinkertons, to McNulty, April 7, 1901

I want you to give me option and report on turquoise claims as I feel confident of doing something with it and you can mention in your report that they are the same as the Tiffany mines.

Matthews to McNulty, April 15, 1901

...send by express all the brown matrix stone taken out of the drift from the bottom of the winze, together with any other stone that you have ready to ship.

Parker to McNulty, April 27, 1901

I note what you say in regard to the progress you are making, and would suggest that you put forth every effort to secure as much stone as possible from the drift, - such as you sent us - and as soon as you have enough to make a shipment that you will forward same by express immediately. Any other stone that you have ready at the time, also send by express.

McNulty to Parker, May 11, 1901

It is very hard for me to keep the Mexicans to work now as most of them have ranches to attend to during the summer months; so I will have to try and get some Americans to work, and it is hard for me to get them unless I can promise them steady *work for a few months and that I cannot do unless I get word from you to that effect.*

Parker to McNulty, May 15, 1901

I would suggest that you engage some Americans, and you are at liberty to promise them steady work, if their services are satisfactory, for the summer. Please write me by an early mail as to the weather during the summer season. Which of the following months are the hottest and most uncomfortable in your section, June, July or August?

.McNulty to Parker, May 20, 1901

As the weather here during the summer season, July and August are the hottest months, and then it is sultry from 9 a.m. to 12, and in the afternoon, we have plenty of winds and the evenings and nights are so cool that you can sleep comfortably with a blanket on. The rainy season generally commences about July or August. The most comfortable months are May and June.

Parker to McNulty, June 24, 1901

I wish you would put all the men you can work to advantage there at the [Muñiz] and see if you cannot get out more stone for us than you have been doing. The fall trade is rapidly approaching and I am desirous of having some material to cut up to meet any orders which come to us, and unless we get larger and more frequent shipments than we have been doing we shall be seriously handicapped.

McNulty to Parker, August 23, 1901

I do wish that you would come here soon as the property is in bad shape owing to the heavy rains. The No. 2 shaft [Muñiz] *which is the air shaft has not been retimbered for 12 years, and it is only timbered with 2 inch planks, and is filled in all around with loose ground for over 20 feet in depth and more of the planks are rotten; it is liable to cave in at anytime. The No 1 shaft timbers are nearly all rotten and the heavy rains of late have* made them worse. The Castilian is also in the same condition as the No 2 shaft.

Parker to McNulty, August 27, 1901

Please advise me by return mail what it will cost to put in the necessary timber to make all safe. ...I have been expecting to visit the property, and, if the work should be done before I arrive, I desire to know exactly what is necessary and the cost of same. ...I am not accustomed to going down mines, and as I desire to see all that belongs to The American Turquoise Company, I would like the means of descending and ascending to be such that a man, not accustomed to the work like yourself and your men, would not come to grief, so you had better have this part of the business attended to at once. In other words, I do not want to run the risk of taking a header down a shaft and breaking my neck.

McNulty to Parker, September 2, 1901

...was glad to hear from you to know that you will probably visit the property within a month. ...You need not dread the going down or coming up out of the mines as you will only have to climb the ladders and there are stations on levels from 20 to 40 feet apart where you can rest and walk around and see the places that are worked which you will see on the map.

McNulty to Parker, September 23, 1901

I cannot give the estimates of the prices or the amount of lumber that will be needed at this writing although heavy timbers are $20 per thousand. As you are not coming down here soon, I would suggest that I would only timber the most dangerous places where the timbers are all rotten. The timbers I need right now are not in Cerrillos at present but they may have them in Santa Fe. It will take a few weeks before I can get started to do the timbering as the Mexicans are not suitable men for timbering and I will have to wait until I can get some Americans or do the best I can with the men I have got.

Now, in regards to the work that I would like to have done. I want to run a drift 75 or 100 feet to the east of the bottom of the main shaft to prospect and as the formation looks favorable for copper; should we not find anything favorable in the drift it will not pay to sink the main shaft to the depth that I am working now. ...there will have to be a new shaft sunk midway between the number one and number two shaft, or have the number two shaft sunk to the depth that is required then crosscut to the formation that carries turquoise. The tunnel that I have written to you before about will eventually have to be driven for at least 200 feet or more through the best formation in the hill that carries turquoise. It is merely to prospect to find out where the strata from the number 2 shaft has gone to. Where I am working now in the winze is looking very favorable as there are still fair colors at the bottom and should I strike a pocket deeper down I would be in favor of sinking a new shaft or continue sinking the No 2 shaft to the depth and then crosscut as the main shaft is so far away now.

...it is slow work, but should you give me permission to drive the drift 75 or 100 ft East of the main shaft and I should strike something favorable I would suggest to sink the main shaft deeper. ...Should we sink any of the shafts deeper there will have to be a gasoline hoist as the whim is very slow work. Of course a steam hoist would be better, but as there is no water, it would not pay so well. ...I will ship you today by express all the stone I have on hand and inside the box you will find a small tin box containing some specimens which I would like you to have assayed for gold, silver, and copper, which comes from the east side of the main shaft.

McNulty to Parker, November 12, 1901

I have been able to get an American miner to come to work today and I am on the lookout for another. There are plenty of men in Cerrillos, but they hang around the saloons too much and would not work steady. ...I feel somewhat downhearted and would be much better satisfied if you would come.

McNulty to Parker, November 25, 1901

I got some more timbers hauled from Cerrillos and then I will start to do some timbering. The whim got out of order last week and I had to take it all apart and put new framing under it for the timbers were so rotten that they all crumbled to dust and had to be shovelled out. I have now got it all right for working. ...Now in regards to the Sena case I had quite a talk a month ago with Mr. Reynolds, United States Attorney, of the Court of Private Land Claims, and he told me that he would have to be in Washington when the case was called, and that he thought the case would be dismissed as he could prove it to be a fraud. Mr. Easley expects to get the final papers for the patent before the first of the year.

McNulty & Friends
Dialogs On Newspapers & Gossip
1900 Part II - 1901

.Unknown newspaper, July 27, 1900

Turquoises of enormous size

Rich Find of the Blue Gem in Mines of New Mexico

Largest Stones in the World

Many of the Famous Crown Jewels of Spain Came from Cerrillos 200 Years ago

Special to the Press, July 27, 1900.

News of the richest turquoise find in the history of the world comes from Cerrillos, N.M. The strike was made in the mines at a depth of 300 feet. Experts pronounce the gems just discovered the largest ever found, as well as possessing the greatest purity with the most beautiful tints. A large portion of the gems found will easily polish to the size of small hens' eggs, which ranks them as the largest in the world. Their value is incalculable. Many of the famous crown jewels of Spain were taken from these same mines over 200 years ago by the Spanish invaders of that period. ...The turquoise is a blue or bluish-green mineral valued, when cut and polished, as an ornamental stone.

New York Times, July 27, 1900

During the past year a jewelry trust has made an attempt to secure a monopoly of the New Mexican turquoise ground, but unsuccessfully.

Parker to McNulty, August 6, 1900

On the 27th of July a notice appeared in the newspapers here to the effect that a great find had been made on our property of stones larger than had ever been known before. This has been published and broadcast all over the country, and I have had several inquiries made of me by stockholders and others regarding same. I should like you to write me by return mail what is the meaning of this. No stone received from you thus far would warrant such an extraordinary report, and I should like to know who it was that caused this to be circulated, and what basis there is for it. The reports seem to come from Las Vegas, N.M. Who has interviewed you with regard to the matter? I enclose clippings in question from N.Y Press and N.Y. Times dated July 27th.

McNulty to Parker, August 12, 1900

...in regards to the advertisements in the newspapers about the new strike in this property. I know not from whence it started as I have not been interviewed by any reporter outside of the Santa Fe people and whenever I go there they always want to quiz me about the output of the mine. All I tell them is that she is holding her own and they asked me about this new strike when I was there last week

98 • Patricia McGraw

and I told them if I had made one I knew nothing about it. I was told about the piece that was in the Las Vegas paper and I only laughed as I did not think it hurt the property and my name was not mentioned in it.

I have met many strangers who have asked me how many tons of turquoise do I ship a week and how big is the largest piece that I get out. I tell some of them as large as my fist and when they ask how deep down do I get the stone, I tell them that experts say there is no stone found deeper than 60 feet. No one outside of the Company, myself, & son, knows anything about the depth of the workings, not even the men who work for me know it. I think the advertisement in the papers must have come from parties who own properties adjoining the Castilian claim as there is one stock company got a claim adjoining it & has been selling stock two years ago & some Las Vegas parties, also interested in Turquoise claims around here & further more Mr. O'Neil that owns turquoise claims here makes frequent trips to Las Vegas but otherwise I do not know where such reports originated from.

Parker to McNulty, August 15, 1900

How about that report that was circulated from Las Vegas? I am pestered by correspondence from all parts of the country and Europe about that report, and I feel particularly annoyed that it should have gotten out, but more so as there is no basis for it, and it places the Company, in denying it, in a peculiar light.

Matthews to McNulty, October 16, 1901

Information has come to Mr. Parker's ears which indicates there is considerable gossiping going on about the affairs of our company around Cerrillos and your name is coupled with it. Some people appear to know all about what you are doing and not doing, and Mr. Parker would like to know how this discussion arises.

McNulty to Parker, October 25, 1901

...now in regards to this matter I am still in the dark, as I have never [had] any conversation with any one about the affairs of the company around Cerrillos, and I would like to have an explanation about this gossiping that my name is coupled with, as I do know that there are a few men in Cerrillos who would do me an injustice if they could, and one of them is a man who cashes the check for me in Cerrillos. I understand that Mr. Doty passed through Cerrillos about a month ago, and this man I have reference to had quite a talk with him in the Depot and this man told me afterwards that Mr. Doty asked him a good deal about this property. I do know that there are some people in Cerrillos who are envious of me because I will not tell them anything about the property, and I would very much like to know what all this gossiping is about so that I can give you an explanation if I have said anything.

McNulty & Friends
Dialogs On the Sena Case
1900 Part II - 1901

Parker to Bartlett, October 17, 1900

I expect to hold the first annual meeting of the stockholders of this company on the 5th of November, and while, of course, the progress made during the past year has not been all that I should have wished, under the circumstances, and with the limited amount of capital at our command, and the various obstacles we have had to encounter from mismanagement in the past, I feel fairly well satisfied with the condition. ...I should, therefore, like you to write me a line in the course of the next day or two what you believe to be the final outcome in this patenting and the Sena litigation, and of anything that may prompt itself to your good judgement that would be of service to me in laying before the stockholders in my report.

Chas F. Easley, attorney, to McNulty, May 28, 1901

I suppose you know that Mr. M.F. Sena has filed a protest against the patenting of these claims, alleging that the land sought to be entered is within his grant, etc., etc., which will be the cause of some delay, but cuts no figure in the end.

Bartlett to Parker, June 7, 1901

This is a part of the very unsatisfactory and the unbusinesslike manner in which the former company transacted its affairs in regard to these mines. This firm of Turner, McClure and Rolston I know were greatly interested personally in the mines and they did most of the correspondence and in fact were the persons who directed McNulty in all his operations here. ...the indifference and negligence of the old Company ...caused a great deal of uneasiness and resulted in great loss and expense to the company. ...the affairs of the old company seem to be in a mysterious and muddled condition, and when you first wrote me in regard to taking charge of your affairs here, I wanted it understood that I should have exclusive control, as acting through attorneys in New York, then through Denver and at last myself who did all the work was extremely unsatisfactory.

Parker to Bartlett, August 13, 1901

...we are in no better condition than we were three years ago, notwithstanding all our expense and legal efforts. I realize, of course, that the long delay from '92 to when the present company took hold of affairs may be reasonable ground for the Department to pass unfavorably on our applications for the patents on the Muniz, but it does seem from your letter of the 24th of June that there is some prejudice being exercised against our interests and rights to lead the Register to throw out our applications on the rest of our mines. Who is at the back of Sena? Has he money enough to prosecute all these suits, or is there another Richmond in the field, who is merely using Sena's name and claim? In the present condition of affairs, I do not feel justified to either make a loan to the company or to call an assessment to work the property on a large scale, as I had contemplated had we been successful in obtaining these patents. ...I recognize the difficulties which have beset you in our affairs, and it is a source of much regret, undoubtedly to you as to us, that it has not been possible to overcome them.

Bartlett to Parker, December 2, 1901

[I] now write to enclose the adverse opinion from the Commissioner of the General Land Office in regard to your appeal from the decision of the Register and Receiver holding up your application for patents. The decision and reasoning are a great surprise to me and I consider it all wrong and not sustained by fact, law or reason. ...this action on their part takes me entirely by surprise, because as I wrote you, I did not believe they would raise the money to print the transcript, but it seems they not only have done this, but are making this motion and are seriously going to fight the case in the Supreme Court which I did not believe they could on account of their very flimsy character of their claim, but they have evidently buncoed somebody into advancing them money on the strength of their claim. ...This is the first time such a motion has ever been made in the Supreme Court. ...We knew that the grant claim was so flimsy, that we did not dream they would make a serious fight in the Supreme Court, and supposed the appeal was taken simply for delay and annoyance in the hope of being bought off perhaps.

McNulty & Friends
Dialogs On Home Life
1900 Part II - 1901

Emma to McNulty, July 25, 1900

My dear James: I can only write you a few lines today as my temp is 103 degrees. ...I think I have a bilious attack like I had when I was in bed for four days. I hope I will feel better by tomorrow, and if not will see Dr. Sloan. I hope you are well and will be able to come out here. With much love and a thousand kisses, from your loving wife...

McNulty to Parker, August 24, 1900

Now in regards to the house, it would not be advisable to try and repair it as I will describe to you what kind of a house it is I am living in. It is built of small poles and the ends that are in the ground are now rotten having been in for fifteen years, then there are poles on the top four feet apart and covered with willows and several tons of dirt thrown on the top of that to prevent the cold and rain from coming through. The poles that are standing for the walls are filled in between with pieces of wood and adobe mud and then plastered outside and inside to make it look like an adobe house.

The dimensions of the house are 23 feet long, 11 feet wide and 6 1/2 feet high inside. I have a small room adjoining it built out of logs 9 feet wide and 11 feet long. The most to be feared about the house is of its falling down as both the walls are leaning over 18 inches and I have it braced up with two large timbers, but still it is liable to break between the timbers. In regards to building a new house for about $300 or thereabouts I will inquire from some contractors what size and kind of a house I can get put up for that amount. I think it would be cheaper to have the house built by contract than by day's pay. If it was mining, I could tell how much work a man is supposed to do for a day's work,

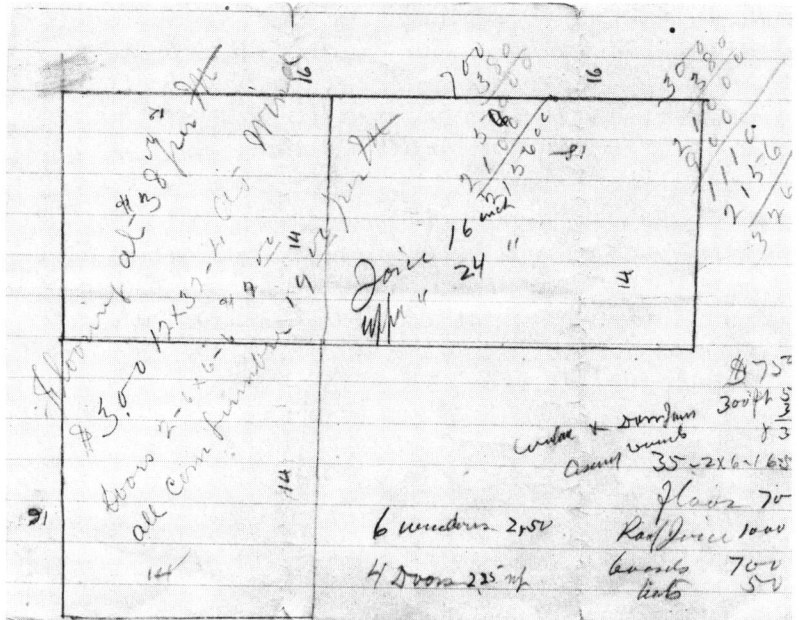

This floor plan shows the calculations McNulty made in order to build his neat little cottage.

but in building a house I could not tell how much work should be done in a day.

McNulty to Parker, December ?, 1900
   I have the house very nearly completed except the ceiling. The rooms have been plastered once with mud and sand mixed and there has to be another coat of thinner mud plaster put on it to fill up the cracks and thoroughly dried before it can be whitewashed on account of the front the outside cannot be plastered until the warm weather sets in as adobes have to be thoroughly dried.

Murray, Pinkerton Detective Supervisior, to McNulty, May 17, 1901
```
     I  am  sorry  to  learn  that  Mrs.  McNulty  has
been  sick,  but  I  presume  by  this  time  she  is
up  and  all  right  again.
```

104 • Patricia McGraw

McNulty to Parker, November 2, 1901

I am short of men who understand timbering as my son has quit work yesterday to accept a position in Arizona with $125 per month and it will be hard to me to find a man to fill his place.

McNulty to Ireland, land broker, December 15, 1901

Of course I will keep our business a secret and know by the tone of your letter that you will also. I would advise you not to call by Cerrillos with your man as the people there blackmail every body that tries to make a sale.

E. J. "Eddie" McNulty, every inch his father's son, cut a dashing figure.

Chapter 4
1902 - 1903

The New Mexican's Peculiar Temperament

The men and creditors are complaining about not getting their money so I wish you would please see to the money being sent...

McNulty to Parker, November 3, 1902

LAYOFFS & RAIDS

The paperwork for the American Turquoise required McNulty to send payroll sheets and receipts to New York every month. The company supplied all forms, which he slavishly followed. Each month he or Emma itemized the payroll, the work done by the miners, and the location of that work. One entry from 1902 showed that prospecting and assessment work completed in the cross cuts totaled a length of drifting of 17 feet.

The 1899 payroll also shows the McNulty's son functioning as the blacksmith for the company. The same payroll sheet shows similar entries for 1901, 1902, and 1900. The ledger page was completely covered from margin to margin with penned entries, some upside down, some scrawled along the edge. Every available bit of paper was covered with notations. McNulty's daughter, Fannie McNulty, with a quill pen and in a flowing hand penned the major headings.

> **Memoranda**
> of Turquesa N. Mex.
>
> Nov 17th 1902
>
> Received of J S McNulty thirty dollars $36.00 as payment in full for work done in the month of October on the Blue Bell and the Blue Gem Claims
>
> A Narbais

McNulty carried little memo books with him wherever he went. When he ran out of company-supplied receipts, he made do with his memo books.

By this time he and Emma may have been the only residents of Turquesa, New Mexico. The post office there had closed in 1899, and their mail was now handled by the post office at Cerrillos.

As 1902 began McNulty devoted himself to carrying out his most recent instructions: sorting the stones from the dump, waiting for Parker to arrive in New Mexico, and bit by bit replacing rotten timbers in the mines. Then, halfway through January, McNulty received a telegram instructing him to stop all work. Legal bills took precedence over mine work, and all the company's assets went to support lawyers and Easterners who were in a territory where lies and deception were the norm, and where politicians' actions depended on their familial relationships or personal friends.

The bankers ordered the layoffs and asked McNulty to continue on his own. McNulty's response was that the mines had urgent need of timber work or the walls might cave in. In his hurried, sprawling handwriting he outlined his concerns, urging the actions that he thought would most benefit the company.

One troubling thing was that the payrolls and bill payments arrived consistently late. Money was so chronically short that, customarily, McNulty paid the mine's bills and the workers before he paid himself. In a rough draft of a letter dated March 1, 1902, he wrote, "I do wish you would please send the men's pay for January as they are uneasy and claim that they should have been paid when they were laid off." Almost as soon as he mailed the letter, the money for January's payroll arrived, a month late.

Several more weeks passed without any word from Parker. Then, in April, McNulty sent a letter advising that the Pueblo Indians had paid him unfriendly visits. They possibly meant to scare McNulty and Emma off the claims. Was this related to the Sena Land Grant case? The two of them watching over 120 acres and a half-dozen or more Pueblo Indians waiting for an opportunity to do mischief was a serious problem just waiting to happen. At one point the Pueblos fired several rifle shots at McNulty, some bullets kicking the dirt only two feet away. McNulty returned fire with his shot gun, and the Indians scattered. Although both McNulty and the Indians were excellent shots, throughout the year not one person was ever hit. All of them, apparently, were aware of the consequences should blood flow.

McNulty promptly requested governmental assistance to put an end to the raids. But all he got was a letter written by the Indian's attorney to the Santo Domingo Pueblo governor, and it had no discernible effect on the unfriendly visits.

When he received no answer from the New York banker about the raids or about payroll, McNulty sent another letter to Parker. On this one his pencil strokes were heavy, making deep impressions on the paper, probably out of anger and frustration. He again commented on the trouble with the Indians and again detailed the dangers he faced living on the claims.

It was bad enough that McNulty hinted about getting out of those mining operations. In what appears to be an effort to raise money so he could leave, McNulty contacted Louis Marks, a miner who had come to the claims the previous year to examine them for the Pinkertons. This time, though, McNulty offered Marks a lease of the claims he owned. The offer was declined, and McNulty stayed on the job.

Finally, on April 18, 1902 Parker contacted McNulty to say he awaited the return to the United States of James Stillman, the largest stockholder in the company. Once Stillman returned from Europe, Parker promised, more money would become available.

108 • Patricia McGraw

THE MAN IN THE IRON MASK

James Stillman, president of the National City Bank of New York and one of the richest men in the United States, had led his bank to become the largest in the United States. A quiet, soft spoken banking genius, Stillman lived in a world of financiers, railroad tycoons, politicians, and high-end jewelers. Because of his unemotional patience Stillman was known as the Man in the Iron Mask. He also served

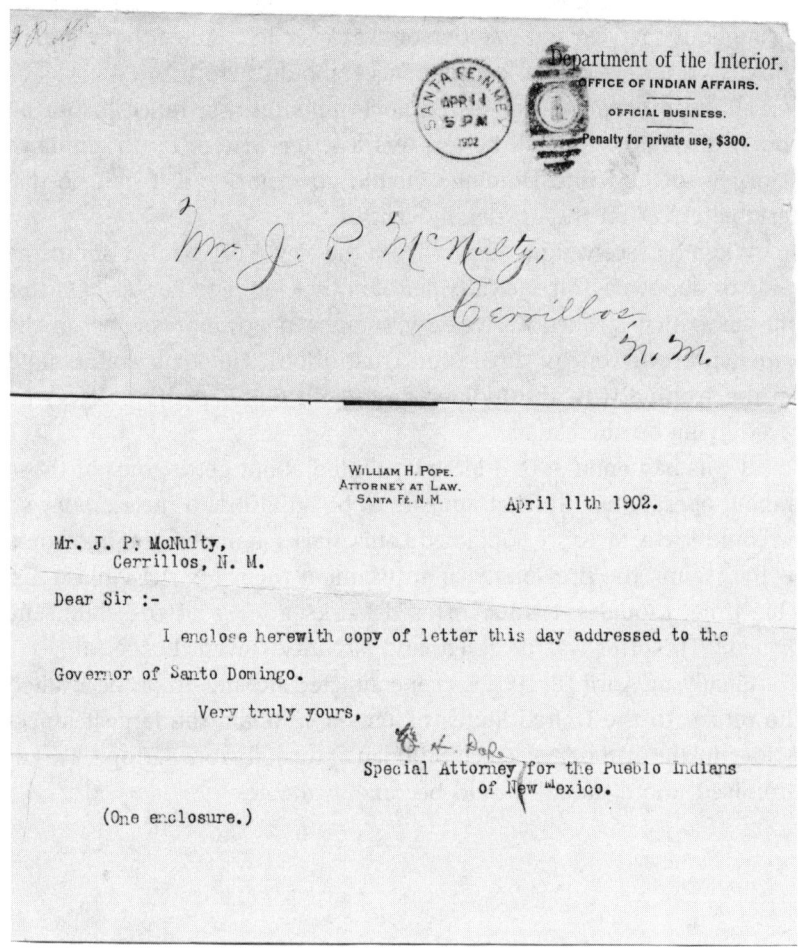

The actual letter written to the pueblo no longer exists, but this note shows a letter was sent. McNulty received no response.

as a financial advisor to United States President Grover Cleveland.

His hair, greying and balding, framed a round face with sharp features. Stillman's wide and varied business interests ranged from insurance to traveler's checks (which he first introduced) to mining, and he had managed to amass a fortune of $70 million. Always impeccably and tastefully dressed — not the image of a man drawn to mining ventures — Stillman was clearly partial to the mining business. Along with his ATC partners, the Pinkertons and Tiffany, Stillman refused to surrender the Cerrillos mines to provincial shyster land grabbers. The bond holders were determined to fight the Sena case to the bitter end.

By mid May the necessary funds from Stillman still hadn't arrived, and McNulty's frustration increased. "Now, Mr. Parker, you said in your last letter that my pay would come in a few days." He added that he had had to borrow money to "get along with."

Over the past few months McNulty had turned down other job offers that would have paid almost as much as the ATC. Though he had been tempted, McNulty's loyalty to the company, along with what was probably his deep sense of proprietorship for the turquoise mines, made it an easy choice. McNulty's blood ran Tiffany blue. Besides, he had absolute faith in Parker's word.

As soon as Stillman returned to Wall Street, Parker obtained the necessary funds and rushed the money to McNulty. And the miner received new orders; hire men and start working the mine. "We are especially desirous that the stone should come from the Muniz [Tiffany] Mine," Matthews, company secretary wrote on July 12, 1902.

Almost simultaneously with the new instructions, Doty reappeared in Cerrillos looking for experienced turquoise miners. McNulty's son, Eddie, fit that bill, but Eddie, McNulty explained, wasn't home. He had moved to Arizona to work for his father-in-law. Doty wanted to start up turquoise production in Kingman, Arizona, and Eddie was part of his plan. McNulty managed to get a letter to his son about Doty's offer, and Eddie accepted. With his son embarking on a new high-paying enterprise, and everyone riding the turquoise boom, McNulty wished them success.

Eddie's mining skills, especially at shoring and timbering, so valuable to Doty, were the same skills McNulty needed back on the Turquoise Hill. ATC never wanted to pay full salaries to timber workers, so McNulty had to make do with the workers he could find that he could entice to work for irregular periods. As the mines resumed operations, a pattern of uncertainty emerged.

The stress of on-again-off-again payrolls, send more turquoise, stop work, and wait for pay impacted the McNultys' marriage. Emma had come under a doctor's care. More and more there were temper tantrums and shouting matches that included slamming doors and

> Cerrillos,
> New Mexico.
> March 2nd 1901.
>
> J. A. Parker Esq
> New York City.
> Dear Sir:—
>
> I am in receipt of your letter dated Feb 21st and was glad to hear from you, at the same time am sorry to learn from the tone of your letter that you do not have confidence in what I report to you about the mine. You say that you all know there must be the stuff hidden away in the mine, & that it is very provoking to see good opportunities passing by for lack of material. It is very true the stone is all hidden in the rock, & it is an old saying, "That one man can see as far through a rock as another", & as the Irishman said a great deal further, & 18 months ago I could see further through the rock where I could find stone than I can to-day. Very true the stone is not confined to this one place, as there must be some more pockets somewhere in the hill, & the hill will have to be cut through

Emma took dictation from McNulty even when they were at odds with each other. Particularly galling to the two was the fact that the Eastern banker accused McNulty of holding back turquoise. The only way to resolve this misconception was for Parker to come search the mines himself.

locking family members out of the house. When McNulty's daughters visited, the fights grew even more pronounced.

NO PERFECT BLUE

Although Emma and McNulty's had their difficulties, they determined that they would stay together. Emma provided housekeeping duties and helped with some of the mining chores, and she frequently wrote out McNulty's letters for him, his own spelling and penmanship reflecting his limited formal schooling. Clearly, she chose to stay because she had no where else to go, and equally clearly she loved McNulty. But the isolation of the mines and McNulty's strong willed daughter, Fannie, made life challenging. Many times they discussed how some rest and recuperation in a more gentle place would be good for Emma. After consultation with the doctor it was decided that once McNulty's back salary arrived Emma should make a trip to her old home in England.

Once again McNulty asked the company to send the payroll more promptly. The workers were dissatisfied with the slow pay and might leave, and now he himself needed the money.

McNulty, completing the all important assessment work, warned the bankers back East that the one pillar of turquoise they had been mining was gone. Mined out. No perfect blue, he told them, was visible anywhere in the mines.

The company's remittances lagged months behind and made it almost impossible to hire good workers. McNulty's skills of persuasion kept most of the creditors at bay, and everyone waited, trusting him. They knew when McNulty had money in his pocket he paid the bills. Once a particularly "bothersome" miner demanded immediate payment, and McNulty took what he had in his pocket, borrowed some more, and made sure the man received his due.

"The men and creditors are complaining about not getting their money," McNulty wrote on November 3, 1902. With payments more than three months behind, workers were laid off and mine work ground to a standstill.

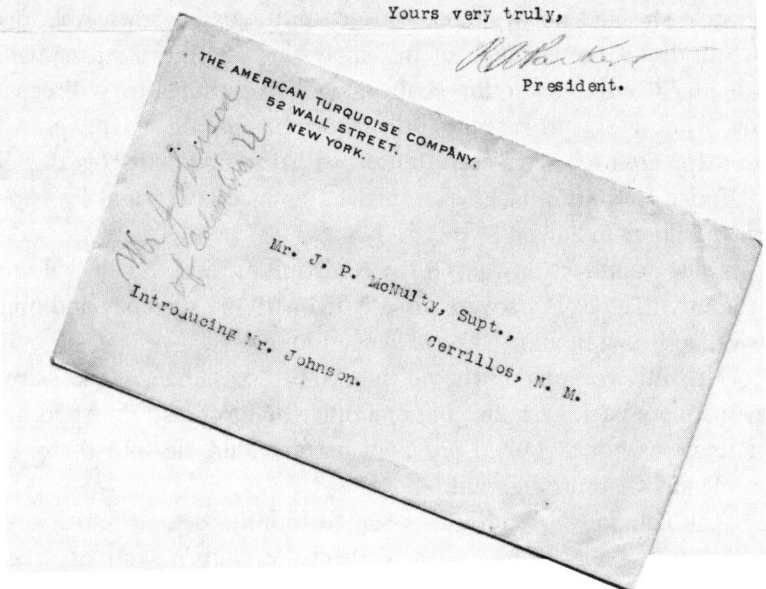

Letters such as these were required before anyone could gain admittance to the ATC properties. This one introduces a professor from Columbia University.

In fact the only turquoise they had recovered, matrix turquoise, was not welcomed by Tiffany's jewelers. And, with the death in 1902 of Charles Lewis Tiffany, control of the Tiffany company had passed to his son, Louis Comfort Tiffany, whose creative interests leaned toward elegant glass. Turquoise had lost a champion. Louis Comfort

Tiffany continued his father's jewelry tradition, but no longer with the emphasis on the blue stone. Besides, the growing supply of inferior turquoise entering the market drove turquoise prices down. The previous year more than 23 cigar boxes were sent, totalling more than 115 pounds of turquoise.

Production at the mines decreased, and investment capital went elsewhere. For the year it appears that no more than nine cigar boxes of turquoise totalling 45 pounds arrived at Tiffany.

NOTHING BUT BLUFF

The year 1903 began with salaries over four months in arrears. McNulty wrote that he wished the Sena case would quickly be heard, and that the work of the mine would start up again. There was no word from the company during all of January, nothing in answer to McNulty's impatient letters to Parker requesting payment. For one letter, dictated to Emma, he went through two rough drafts before it

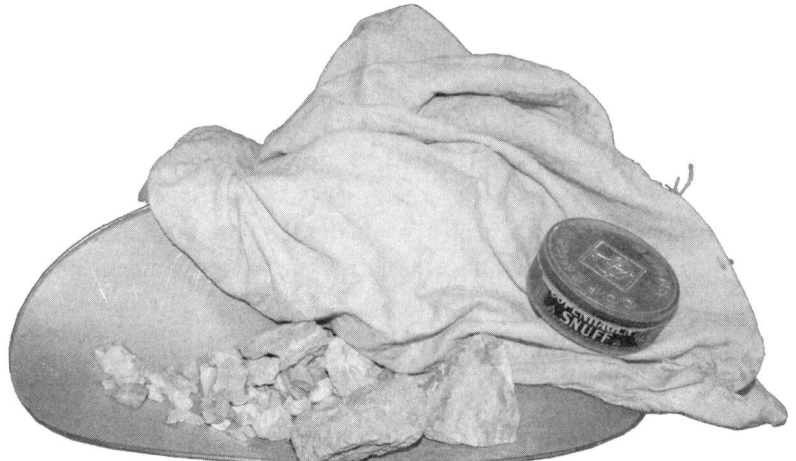

Whether a rock might contain turquoise was not always evident. This scale cup holds the stones, some with visible blue and some, perhaps, with a surprise inside. McNulty's old pillow case holds even more stones. Small turquoise chips, once freed from the matrix, went to fill the snuff can.

was good enough to send. In it he reminded the banker that his letters to the company were being ignored, and that was not acceptable behavior. In fact, he said, this "oversight and neglect" was a very serious matter for working men.

McNulty needed money, the money he was due, to pay Emma's way to England. Her need for a change of scene and a chance to recover her health was daily becoming more evident. It reached the point where neither McNulty nor Emma any longer made an effort to get along. Instead, many days went by when neither talked to the other, Emma making the meals and McNulty eating them in silence. They resolved to separate for a few months to see if things could possibly get better. Perhaps Emma's health would improve and that alone might keep them together.

When the overdue payroll finally arrived it was for only one month. McNulty was forced to turn to his friends for the money to send his wife on her way.

Emma was gone all that summer, and McNulty began and ended those lonely days by sorting through the dump and poking through the mines. When he accumulated enough turquoise to fill a cigar box he would send it off.

On one of his visits to Cerrillos, McNulty, always on the lookout for stolen turquoise, found someone selling stones that he was certain came from the Tiffany. McNulty accused the seller of such, summarily took the stones, and forwarded them to Parker.

By April 1 McNulty had received his salary up to January, and he missed his wife — a little bit. He forwarded some money to Emma, who was then in New York waiting for her ship to arrive from England.

Somehow, while boarding the steamship, Emma's trunk disappeared. Emma lost everything. McNulty sent her more money. Never one to pass up a little bit of humor, McNulty said, "I received your letter and postal card and you can bet your bottom dollar if you have one that I was [glad] to hear that you arrived there all ok. ....Let me know the nearest telegraph office that takes money orders or post office that will take money orders." He concluded that it was good Emma wasn't in the trunk, otherwise, she would be lost, too.

Now that McNulty was alone at the claims, protecting the mines was an even greater challenge. One day as he checked the area he discovered he had had a visitor: Mariano Sena. Sena had put up a No Trespassing notice at the mines. Did Sena think that would be enough

> *as this is a lonesome place to live miles away from any settlement but I am no coward never the less there is danger. M. Send put a Notice up ten feet from the Castillian Claim. Had he put it on the claim*

This is a lonesome, dangerous place, and Sena put a notice only ten feet from the claim.

to move one stubborn miner off the claim? It didn't work. "It was nothing but bluff," McNulty said in his report to Parker of the incident.

The land ownership case was coming up in the territorial Supreme Court, and Sena clearly wanted McNulty and his bosses to abandon the claim. With the help of some of his Pueblo friends Sena hoped McNulty could be encouraged to leave. If the claim should fall to Sena, the ATC would disappear, and Sena expected that he and his backers would all become rich.

Within a few days of receiving McNulty's letter about the sign incident, Parker shot back a letter requesting the miner to meet him on Monday morning at 11:50 at the train station. Parker's long-awaited trip had finally materialized!

The visit went well. For the next few days the two toured the turquoise mines. Everything seems to have met Parker's expectations since he ordered more mine work as well as the sinking of a shaft on a new mine, the Agnes P.

Parker apparently believed what he had heard about the dangers in the wild west, and that had partly been the reason for delaying his visit. It is ironic, then, that Parker's only brush with a bad guy should have happened as he neared home. The banker was robbed on the train just a few miles outside New York City.

McNulty commiserated with Parker over the robbery, commenting, "...it must have happened when you were either asleep or with the point of a gun for anyone to get the best of you."

When Parker settled back into his normal routine in New York, McNulty's pay started to catch up. In August his salary was only three months in arrears, an improvement over the beginning of the year.

A SNOWBALL IN YUMA

Parker contacted Bartlett, the Santa Fe-based ATC attorney, and in a candid letter discussed some of the strategies for winning the Sena case as well as proving company ownership once and for all. Parker, who placed no faith in the honesty of New Mexico courts, directed the legal matters in Santa Fe from his office in New York just as he directed Cerrillos mining operations from that office.

By this time, September 7, 1903, Matthew G. Reynolds, Special Assistant to the Attorney-General of the United States, had joined the lawsuit representing the United States Government, and he had specific ideas as to how the case should be run. Reynolds reminded Parker's attorney that certain areas of the state remained unfriendly to the interests of the ATC, and in those counties facts and truth didn't account for much. "We stand about as much show on any question of fact which the Court may submit to the jury as a snowball would have for existence in Yuma today," he commented. Then he proceeded to discuss the qualifications of the various judges along with their honesty. He added that the jurisdiction of Judge Sluss should be avoided since he had crossed Sluss' path. "...knowing the peculiar temperament of the New Mexican, I thought well to avoid this particular jurisdiction."

Against this backdrop McNulty pursued his hunt for information. He approached the former governor of the territory, L. Bradford Prince, on the topic of the Sena case. Prince agreed to be a witness if necessary, but Parker was not pleased and ordered McNulty to steer clear of politicians.

Parker, in a letter to attorney Bartlett, said that the property was not as valuable as people thought, and the only reason he continued the legal battle was "to defend our own, irrespective of the actual value." In the same letter he assured Bartlett that all legal fees would be met.

The year concluded with the company having spent $2046.47 at the mines and on supplies, and most of that for the required assessment work.

Finally, in November, Emma returned to the mines, much happier and more at ease. For McNulty, some things improved.

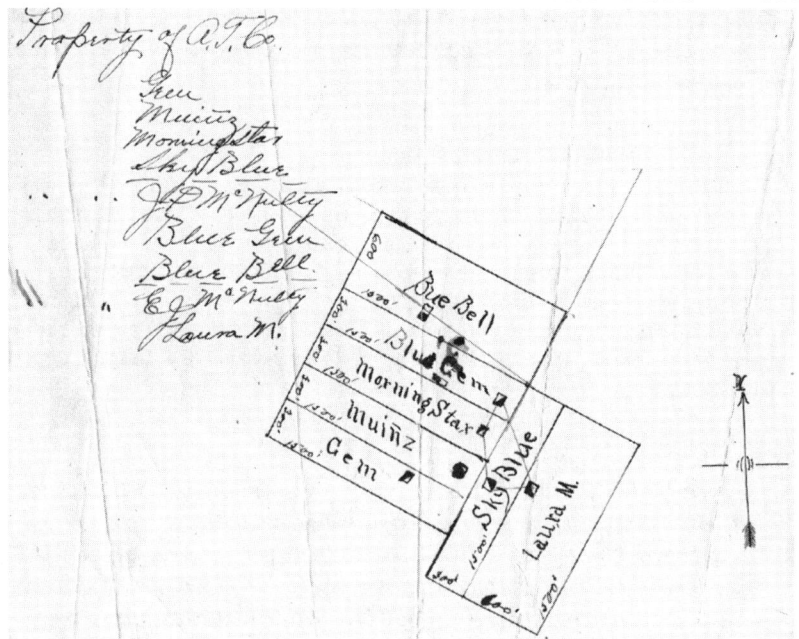

This hand-drawn diagram of the mines was most probably done by Fannie McNulty. The older claims are 1500 feet by 300 feet in size. The two more recent claims are 1500 feet by 600 feet.

McNulty & Friends
Dialogs On Mining & Patents
1902 - 1903

McNulty to Parker, January 20, 1902

...*will comply with your wishes as stated in your letter. I would not have received your telegram in time if it were not that the Mexican was hauling a load of timbers for the mine and the postmaster saw him and gave him the notice to give to me. Then I sent down for the telegram and just got it in time when the men quit to lay them off. I am very sorry that I could not have the timbering finished in the Muniz mine as I have all the lumber here that is* needed. ...I do hope that the Sena case will soon be settled. ...P.S. Please wire me if you will have timbering done.

Matthews to McNulty, February 24, 1902.

Mr. Parker wishes to have you dispense with the services of all the men at the mines with the exception of yourself until further notice, and would have you send him whatever stone you may be able to get by express when you have enough to make a shipment. We will notify you when it is necessary to employ anyone.

McNulty to Parker, March 11, 1902

Now, Mr. Parker, I ask you, as a friend, to please let me know if my position here will last for any length of time, as I have had two positions offered me, and unless you can give me a satisfactory answer, I cannot afford to let the opportunity pass by. My reason for asking you this favor is because as things appear to me, I feel as if I may be laid off any time and would like to hear from you. Of course, I do not intend to leave here at any time without first giving you a month's notice, and would like you to do like manner. I do hope the Sena case will soon be settled.

McNulty to Matthews, April 17, 1902

Your letter of April 10th inst was received and also check for fifty dollars as part payment for the month of February's salary and many thanks for it and enclosed you will please find receipt for same. I wish you would please send me more money as soon as you can as I really need help to pay my bills.

Parker to McNulty, April 18, 1902

I beg to state the reason I have delayed replying to that letter is because I am anticipating putting more money in the business, and necessarily have been waiting the return to town of our largest stockholder. As you know, business has given us no profit.

...and the Sena legal complications have prevented my introducing new capital. ...We have been a little short of money the last week or two, but there is no danger to you on this score, as what we owe you will be paid in a few days now, and hereafter your monthly salary will be promptly sent you as heretofore. ...I do not think that you could do better elsewhere, so we require your services to look after the property until such time as we can operate on a larger scale, when we shall still need you. ...I regret to learn the trouble you have had with the Indians, but trust that is only temporary, and that matters have now resumed their harmonious sway.

McNulty to Parker, June 4, 1902

Mr. Parker, please send me some money if you have not already done so as my creditors have shut down on me. I have borrowed money and I told the parties I would pay them in a week or two. Now it is months since I got it and have to pay big interest on it.

Matthews to McNulty, June 26, 1902

Mr. Parker directs me to write you that he wants you to proceed at once to put on three or four men, and secure all the stone you can with as little delay as possible from wherever it is in sight, and also if you can, without ruining the pillars, get us some stone from them, you are to do so and forward by first express. The trade demands large stones, and we must have them if they are to be obtained.

McNulty to Parker, July 2, 1902

I will say that there is little or no stone in sight, only one pillar at the bottom winze where there are a few small stones and that I cannot get to work at until I finish timbering the shaft. ...It is very hard to get men around here now as there are no idle, but as soon as I can get suitable men to finish the timbering, I will start to do so and try and get *down to the pillar. ...I have written you many times that there is no stone and that there must be prospecting done to find stone. ...No doubt you have heard the Mr. Doty is manager of the Aztec Turquoise Company in Arizona. My son was in El Paso Texas two months ago and the company sent him $100 by telegram to defray his expenses to the mines as superintendant and they bought him a horse and a $125 buggy to go to town with and he has written to his sister since he has been there that there is an abundance of Turquoise in sight but a little off color.*

Parker to McNulty, October 9, 1902

I am greatly disappointed at the poor results you have shown since starting up again. ...I felt certain from your correspondence that there was stone to be found in the pillar which could be cut out for clear turquoise, and unless you can immediately find material of this kind I must ask that you stop work at once, as we cannot afford to pay out money for labor, which bears no result. ...Are there not some stones to be found in the shape of nuggets such as we received two or three years ago? These stones cut better into clear turquoise than any other, and if you can find them in sufficient quantities we might be able to do some business with them.

Matthews to McNulty, November 10, 1902

What is this we read in the newspapers about Mr. Doty and Mr. McNulty shipping a wagon load of stuff out west?

McNulty to Parker, November 15, 1902

In answer to your inquiry about Mr. Doty and Mr. McNulty shipping a wagon load of stuff out West, I will say of this I know nothing about, as I have not heard from my son for several months, but I have heard from other parties that he has been making some large shipments of turquoise from Kingman, Arizona. I do hope the Sena case will be settled for good when it is tried in the Supreme

Court in January and that it will be more encouraging for the company to do more work on the property.

McNulty to Parker, December 2, 1902

I am doing the assessment work by prospecting outside in sinking shafts as the old mine is dangerous to work in until it is retimbered. The first two places I am working on the hill show lots of colors, but they are of a greenish tint.

McNulty to Parker, February 1, 1903

As you are aware my salary has been due and unpaid since the 31 of September and the men for November and December and Cerrillos Supply Co. bill also. And I have been unable to hear from you or Mr. Matthews in reference to the same. It is absolutely necessary that these amounts should be paid to the 1st of January. We are all laboring men depending upon what we earn for our support, and this oversight and neglect has been a very serious matter to us and cannot be longer endured. In order to bring this matter to your official attention, I write these few lines, trusting that the unpaid payrolls will be promptly paid, and that there may not be such delays in the future as you have told me in your letter of April 18, 1902 that there would be no more trouble about the pay coming promptly.

McNulty to Parker, August 3, 1903

I have had a hard [time] to find an American to move his family here as there is no accommodations. But I have got a man now who has worked for me six or seven years ago but I had to promise him steady work and he is moving here today. I have started to sink a shaft at the open cut a hundred yards from the cabin.

McNulty to Parker, September 1, 1903

It has been very hot here this last month so I had the assessment work done on the Sky Blue lode inside in the crosscut in the Muniz mine. I had a long talk with ex-governor L.B. Prince about him siding in with the grant people and he said it was all false and that he would fight against it. So I told him I would have him as a witness and he said I could do so. I must go to Santa Fe this week to find out when the case will be called and give Mr. Bartlett a list of witnesses.

McNulty to Parker, September 27, 1903

Mr. Reynolds told me to get an American right away as there was danger of the grant parties bribing the Mexicans and I really don't know how it suits the attorney and the company. I was in Santa Fe on the 8th inst., and General Bartlett informed me that Mr. Clancy was to take a change of venue to Sandoval County. I protested against it being tried there as there are no Americans living in the County and we would get no fair show in the trial with a Mexican jury. General Bartlett then said that it would make no difference that we got beaten in that County that he would take an appeal but I am glad now as Mr. Reynolds is of the same opinion as myself and has also protested against it being tried in Sandoval County.

McNulty to Matthews, October 9, 1903

The work I have been doing is assessment work and prospecting for stone at the same time but have not found any as yet, so if you need stone, I must have more men to work, and then it will take some time before I could make a shipment. I explained all of this to Mr. Parker when he was here and he thoroughly agreed with me. ...If you are in a rush for stone the quickest way for me to find any is to put some men to work the dump.

Parker to Bartlett, October 14, 1903

It is unnecessary for me to state General that we have every confidence in your integrity, honor and ability, if there was any delay in following this matter up from this end, it was either because promptness was beyond our control, or so far as the check was concerned for $125 its sending was probably due more to proscrastination than anything else, as so far as your terms were concerned, you had issued your fiat, and we had to accept. We have never haggled about your fees but have paid you everything you asked, and while I do not think the property is as valuable as McNulty and some of his local friends consider, we are in this thing to defend our own, irrespective of the actual value. Go on with the case, and you will find that you will not have to sue us for any lawyer's fees as you did other Eastern parties.

McNulty to Matthews, November 26, 1903
I am really surprised about this as Mr. Parker told me himself to get a man with a family that I could depend upon and that I could promise him steady work. I had quite a difficulty in getting a good man and he had to move his things here forty miles in wagons.

McNulty & Friends
Dialogs On Mariano Sena
1902 - 1903

McNulty to Parker, June 2, 1903
I wish things was settled so as work would start up as this is a lonesome place to live miles away from any settlement. I am no coward, never the less there is danger. M. Sena put a notice up ten feet from the Castilian claim and had he put it on the claim I would have taken it down. I have run him from here 7 years ago with a shotgun. This is a copy of the notice.

"All persons are herby warned not to trespass in any manner shape or form upon the property and real estate herein below described being the owner of such real estate and all trespassers will be pros-

ecuted according to the law said property is known as the grant made by King of Spain to Josepha de Leyba on May 25, 1728 and its boundaries are" & *etc. It is nothing but bluff.*

Reynolds to Bartlett, September 7, 1903

This is for your guidance and to enable you to fully interpret and understand my letter of today, in relation to taking the Sena case in Sandoval County. If Fred Otero is the Sheriff of this county and Clancy is the District Attorney, we will stand about as much show on any question of fact which the Court may submit to the jury as a snowball would have for existence in Yuma today. I have no particular objection to the Judge, except as suggested in your letter of the 30th inst., in which you state: "I shall try to have it go to Judge Mills at Las Vegas instead of Albuquerque, as I know the Judge of the latter place is friendly with all the enemies of the Administration." Personally, I assume that Judge Baker would try the case as judge and lawyer. He could not well afford to do otherwise, knowing the case will be reviewed by the Supreme Court of the Territory and Supreme Court of the United States.

Reynolds to Bartlett, September 15, 1903

I thought it would be possible for me to avoid stating the real objection that I have to the case going to Sandoval County. Fred Otero and his father became very much offended at me, if you will remember three or four years ago, when I compelled a re-survey of one of their land grants, growing out of what we supposed and believed to be Fred Otero's interference with witnesses summoned on behalf of the Government. You will remember, Judge Sluss, Mr. Pope and quite a party made the trip to the western part of the Territory and made a personal examination of the same. ...they are very sore over it, and knowing the peculiar temperament of the New Mexican, I thought well to avoid this particular jurisdiction.

Parker to McNulty, September 17, 1903

Permit me to request that you say as little as possible to Prince or anyone else who are antagonistic to our interests, as your remarks will not only be used against us, but will be twisted to suit the views of the other side. Any talk of the character to which you allude should be done, if at all, by our Attorney. While I am on the subject, I also wish to call your attention to the fact that while I was in New Mexico information came to me that statements had been made relative to the amount of stone which had been taken out of property, these statements being wild and absurd. The amount of stone taken out of the property since I have been connected with it has not realized sufficient to pay the expenses, and in Doty's time, I think probably the same condition prevailed. The misleading statement of the character I speak of have really in my judgement caused the other side to have an exalted opinion of the value of The American Turquoise Company's property, hence the bitter fight, and the absurd amount they place as damages. Now, Mac, be very careful what you say to any of your friends about this company, or about what has been taken out of the mines. ...It has yet to be demonstrated what are in the mines, and personally I am not so sanguine of results from them as I would like to be.

McNulty & Friends
Dialogs On Indians
1902 - 1903

McNulty to Parker, April 1, 1902

I have not got enough stone to ship you as it is very hard work but will do so as soon as I get a box filled. ...I am anxious to hear from you in answer to my last letter. I have been having considerable trouble with the Indians this last month, most of the time on the Castilian dump, which is about 600 yards from the house. When they see me coming to order them off, they run away, and then when I return to the house they come on again. I notified the agent in Santa Fe about them and he told me that he could do nothing about them, but to do the best I could myself.

On the 18th of March I fired a shotgun from the house to scare them off and they returned the fire with a rifle and it just missed me by about 2 ft, then I took the rifle and fired after them when they ran away and I have not seen them since but they may come around at any time. I intend to get a man to stay here while I go to Santa Fe to notify the Governor and the attorney for the Indians and also General Bartlett as my life is in danger here. When the mine was working, they did not trouble me much as they knew I had help, but now they know I am all alone they take advantage and one man cannot arrest half a dozen of them when they are armed.

The only satisfaction the Indian agent gave me was to arrest them for stealing and that I cannot do by myself and not knowing their names I could not get a warrant. They have shot at me many a time within the last ten years.

McNulty to Parker, April 25, 1902

In regard to the Indians I have not had much trouble with them since I last wrote you. I went to Santa Fe and had a talk with Governor Otero and he said he would have the District Attorney look into the matter and I also saw the attorney for the Indians and he wrote to the Chief of the tribes.

McNulty to Judge Abbott, November 30, 1903

I informed you some time ago about the trouble I had with the San Domingo Indians. They have been giving me lots of trouble this last month and doing great damage to the turquoise property, sorting over the dump and carrying away all they could find, and when they are ordered away, they won't go. Three of them were here yesterday the 29th inst, with rifles and bows and arrows, and I wish you would give this matter your earliest attention as my life is in danger here. Kindly let me know at your earliest convenience what steps can be taken to prevent them coming around here. I have enclosed you a copy of the letter that Judge Pope wrote to them after they had shot at me with a rifle.

McNulty to Parker, December 2, 1903

I have been having considerable trouble with the Indians coming around sorting the dumps for turquoise and they are so stubborn that they will not go away when ordered. Myself and wife went over to the Castilian on Sunday last to order the Indians off the property, and they would not go until I called for the man who is working for me to come with his rifle, then they got on their horses and went away before the man got up to me.

Parker to McNulty, December 10, 1903

I have your letter of the 2nd inst., and regret very much to learn that you have been put to any trouble through prowling Indians. ...You will be amused to hear that after all our travels together in the wild region of Hachita, and coming out unscathed, I was robbed on my way home, within 100 miles from New York, and in a Pullman car, of some $85. So you see, your country is a peaceful and law abiding one, where men can travel for days without seeing a policemen; can go among cowboys and others whose past probably will not bear inspections, and yet find himself in the midst of honesty and honor, and can carry his money about with him in safety. I presume you were happy to have Mrs. McNulty return, as I notice her handwriting in the letters.

128 • Patricia McGraw

McNulty & Friends
Dialogs On Home Life
1902 - 1903

Bartlett [ATC attorney] to Emma McNulty, August 7, 1902

Dear Madam [Mrs. J.P. McNulty] ...with reference to your further troubles with Mr. McNulty... Mr. McNulty was in to see me this morning, and opened the subject of your troubles. He talked very freely, and is equally positive as you in his statements, and that it is absolutely impossible for you to live together any longer. ...He said that there must be a separation and there was no use your trying to live together any longer. He did not want to bring any action against you and that he would divide with you what there is now in the house, and pay you a monthly sum for a reasonable time until you could make some other arrangements. ...if he should go to Arizona as you think, you could not get at him at all. So under all these circumstances, it is my opinion that the very best thing for you both is to make an agreement of separation without any expense for lawyers.

McNulty to Parker, April 1, 1903

I have been prospecting the property off and on but have found nothing but small stone. ...I am very hard up for money. My wife has been under Dr. treatment for some time, and I would send her to England this week if I had the money. The Doctor said she must take a trip somewhere from here, so I wish you would send me at least two month's salary. ...as she intends to leave here by the 14th inst.

McNulty to Emma, May 21, 1903

My Dear Emma, I received your letter and postal card and you can bet your bottom dollar if you have one. That I was to hear that you arrived there all ok, but sorry to hear that you were not feeling well. But as long as you were not in the trunk, I may see you again. Now in regards to the trunk you have no one to blame but yourself you should have seen that it went to the dock and have the No of your berth on it. Then you could come on to the steam boat company but now you cannot. You have placed too much confidence in the hotel man or the buggy man. You say you had no trouble at the custom house. But I think you had the worst kind of trouble. You lost everything but yourself so it is all right when you are safe with your sisters. My opinion is that your trunk is still in the hotel or at the dock in New York. If the buggy man has not taken it home. So I hope all our misfortune has gone with the trunk and I hope you have a little money to get you some clothes with until I hear from you when you get this. Let me know the nearest telegraph office that takes money orders or post office that will take money orders.

Here's the young, lovely high-spirited animal McNulty bought for his buggy hitch and for riding. The Tiffany mine sits in the background. (Photo courtesy Doug Magnus.)

Mariano F. Sena
Influence & Power in Territorial New Mexico

A chronology reconstructed from McNulty's letters of the efforts of seemingly different groups all working to drive the American Turquoise Company and J.P. McNulty off the Tiffany turquoise mining claims.

1896 — Sena visits mines - files ownership suit in wrong court

1899 — Sena files ownership case in Land Court

1900 — Sena loses case in Land Claims Court

1901 — Sena loses in Territorial Supreme Court

1901 — Sena protests ownership of the Tiffany mine which blocks all applications for mine patents in the area - even those not part of the suit

1903 — Pueblos and McNulty exchange gun fire.

1903 — Sena loses in U.S. Supreme Court - is denied ownership

1903 - 1911 most intense Indian activity

1905 — Sena loses suit of ejectment vs. ATC in Land Claims Court

1905 - 1911 Sena, New Mexico politicians and cohorts inflict maximum financial damage on the New Yorkers, all in an effort to acquire the Tiffany mine.

1907 — Tax assessor refuses tax payment

1907 - 1909 — Heavy Pueblo Indian activity. Shots fired. Governor says no protection for property or residents.

1908 — Tax records forged in assessor's office Taxes raised from $500 to $5000

1909 — Sena loses ejectment case in Territorial Supreme Court

Pattern of forgeries in the assessor's office, unjust tax rates, lost paperwork continues until 1919

1911 — Yearlong raids intensify at assessment time

1911 — Sena loses ejectment case in U.S. Supreme Court

Chapter 5

The Devil and Mariano F. Sena

September 29, 1899, Mariano F. Sena, filed a protest against said application alleging ownership...
      Quasi Contest No. 1851 by Edward L. Bartlett, attorney

HOW MUCH MORE?

When Mariano Sena filed his lawsuit against the American Turquoise Company and McNulty, his family and friends were on familiar ground. Jose D. Sena, Mariano's father and sheriff of Santa Fe County beginning in 1870, had been named in 1881 by Elias Brevoort, a territorial official in the Land office, as one of the most corrupt in New Mexico. Also, a surveyor general of New Mexico in 1889, George W. Julian, named Sena as one of those engaged in land stealing: Sena's family friend, Tom Catron, made the infamous list, too. So, when the dawning of 1899 presented Mariano Sena with an opportunity for quick wealth, he chose a familiar ploy. Mariano's plan was to show he was the owner of Turquoise Hill by means of an old Spanish Land Grant. This meant finding suitable heirs to show the validity of the land grant, and it meant turning those 4-to-8 acres of questionable pedigree into 18,000 acres.

  The practice of creative interpretation of Spanish or Mexican land grants had worked well in the past — and combined with buying pur-

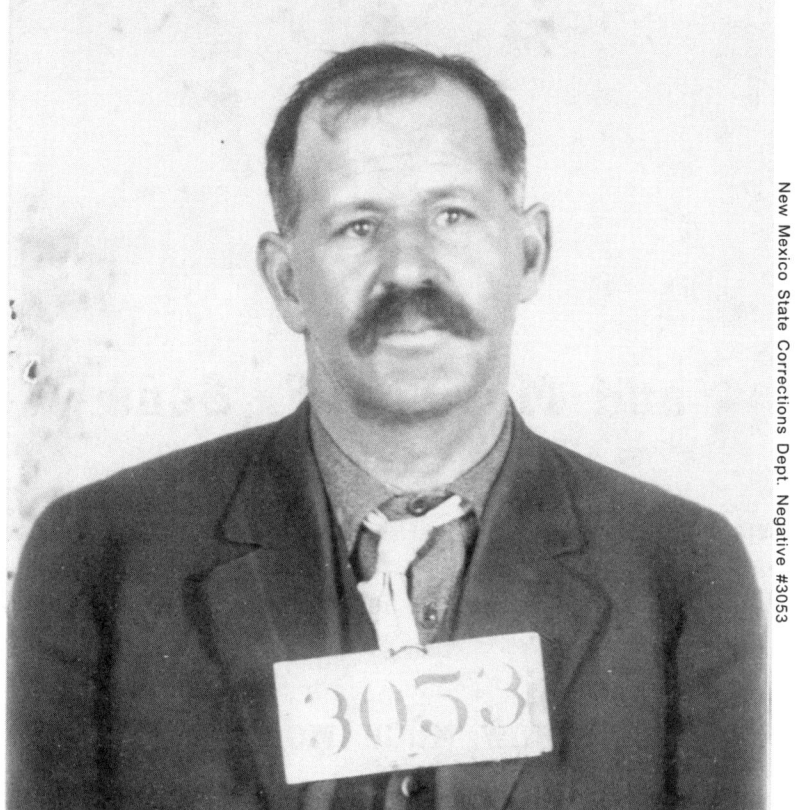

Mariano F. Sena, son of former county sheriff Jose D. Sena, became the source of endless trouble to the American Turquoise Company. He served as the front man of Solomon Luna, who was later known as the father of the New Mexico State Constitution. Eventually, Sena was convicted of forgery and served time in prison. This is his prison mug shot. Land wheeler-dealer Thomas Catron, member of the infamous Santa Fe Ring, served as Sena's attorney in the forgery case.

ported "shares" from possible "heirs", many New Mexican politicos had accumulated a land wealth, of sorts.

Sena's plans began with a simple visit to the Tiffany Mines in November of 1896 while McNulty was absent hunting. Sena, along with his friends Purdy, Vroom and Jones, nosed around the mines until McNulty appeared and forced them to leave.

Three years later Sena had generated a list of heirs to the Jose de Leyba Land Grant, as well as signed "deeds", and he had some witnesses who said the land grant covered the Turquoise Hill. At the same time he filed a suit of ejectment with the New Mexico Court to order the American Turquoise Company and McNulty off the property, AND to pay him $50,000 in damages. The court informed Sena that lacking confirmed proof of ownership of the land, it was rejecting his claim.

Sena then turned to the Court of Private Land Claims to prove he owned the land because he had purchased "interests" from purported direct descendents of Jose de Leyba. Unfortunately for Sena, the time had long passed when land grant challenges could be made under United States law. In order to prove an individual owned a land grant specific criteria had to be met:

• The grantee had to show clearly defined boundaries to the grant, boundaries that could be surveyed.

• The grantee had to show how he came to obtain the grant by tracing the previous owners' deeds (or wills).

• The grantee had to show that the land was not abandoned under Spanish Law. (The United States obtained New Mexico in the Treaty of Guadalupe Hidalgo and agreed to honor land grants provided the above criteria were met by the grantee.)

Because the time had passed for Sena to file paperwork for an outright land grant, he instead had to prove he owned the land by showing he purchased the land, or bought out the interests in it, or purchased all the shares in the grant.

In the meantime any attempt by the American Turquoise Company to obtain a patent — a Federally sanctioned clear deed to all rights, surface and mineral, on the property — was held up by the registrar of the Land Claims office, in part because of Sena's connections there, and later because of the cloud of litigation.

The first legal battle around the Jose de Leyba Land Grant commenced September 29, 1899, with Sena's filing. The Court of Private Land claims listened to testimony and determined that the Jose de Leyba Land Grant did not include the mines, and indeed, the grant had long been abandoned.

Four years later, Sena had dragged the American Turquoise Company into the United States Supreme Court, which also found in favor of the company.

Sena wanted the courts to confirm that he was the current owner of 18,000 acres, including the Muñiz mine, and he was faced with some fundamental obstacles. One was that his Jose de Leyba Grant contained portions of several other land grants that had all ready been confirmed by the governments of Mexico and of the United States.

The next courtroom battle stemmed from the refusal of the Land Claims office to grant patents to the ATC. Edward Bartlett, attorney for the American Turquoise Company, filed an appeal in the United States General Land Office, Quasi Contest No. 1851, arguing that the Land Claims office should allow the patents for the mining claims to move forward. Bartlett's effort stalled, pending completion of the first case to prove ownership.

The U.S. Supreme Court was brought into the fray in 1902. John K. Richards, Solicitor-General for the United States Government, Matthew G. Reynolds, Special Assistant to the Attorney-General of the United States, William H. Pope, Special Assistant to the Attorney-General of the United States, and Edward L. Bartlett, counsel for the American Turquoise Company and James Patrick McNulty, presented two briefs to the United States Supreme Court. Both briefs appear to have been written by Bartlett.

According to the briefs, Sena alleged he was the owner of a "certain grant and tract of land ...in the county of Santa Fe, in the Territory of New Mexico, known as the 'Jose de Leyba grant,' and bounded and described as follows: On the east by the San Marcos road; on the south by an arroyo called Cuesta del Oregano; on the west by lands of Juan Garcia de las Rivas; and on the north by the lands of Capt. Sebastian de Vargas." The land was never surveyed and Sena obtained title to the land by buying conveyances of the land from possible heirs, the brief states.

Sena had to prove that the people who sold him those conveyances were actual heirs to the grant; he had to prove that the boundaries to the land actually existed; he had to prove that the land covered 16,000 to 18,000 acres; he had to prove that the Leyba descendants had not abandoned the property and had passed it through the families through deeds or wills; he had to prove that the land was cultivated and contained woodlands (since that was a requirement in the grant); and he had to prove that half a "fanega" of corn planting land really equaled thousands of acres. (A "fanega" equaled 8.82 acres, and half a "fanega" therefore about 4.2 acres.)

Against this seemingly daunting task Sena had some powerful weapons. His relatives and cohorts peopled the court system, and he had many of the most powerful New Mexico politicos with him, eager for their share of the spoils.

The arguments by the lawyers for the U.S., the American Turquoise Company, and McNulty, on the other hand, were that the boundaries were not exact enough to locate the grant; the grant did not cover 18,000 acres; the Leyba descendants had abandoned the property; and Sena had applied for recognition of the grant too late.

Sena produced several witnesses to prove his claim. One of them, Antonio Jose Campos, 69, tried to identify the landmarks in the area that were named in the grant, but he was unable to place the landmarks in the proper location. In addition, under questioning, Campos first said he never met Sena, but by the end of his testimony Campos said he knew Sena and that Sena had paid him to testify. Campos was fairly representative of the witnesses Sena produced. None were clear about the landmarks named in the grant, and most of the Sena witnesses remembered the area as being open grazing land held in common for all members of the community. The most recent apparent mention of the grant in an 1839 will suggested that the land had been abandoned for possibly 50 years before the ATC became active in the Turquoise Hill.

As Sena's witnesses could not locate landmarks, and one particular arroyo kept changing location throughout the testimony, the defendants' attorneys argued that the grant could never be properly surveyed nor defined. The American Turquoise Company produced more than six witnesses, all of whom lived in the immediate area and many of whom were well over 70 years of age. All stated that they had never heard of the Jose de Leyba Land Grant and that the land in question was considered common land and open pasture.

Sena testified that he had purchased the interests in the land grant from two individuals. One of those individuals didn't even have his mother's name correct. As the testimony proceeded it became increasingly clear that the land grant had not been passed down in the family, since no family will mentioned it. One will listed what the family owned and passed down in minute detail, and there was no mention on that list of 18,000 acres or a 1/2 fanega piece of land.

Then the Sena lawyers argued that the ATC had not produced in court the witnesses who testified that the Leyba Grant did not exist. Those witnesses had been present in the court room but had given written statements. Bartlett's brief noted that the Sena group appeared to be trying to manufacture an error in the case, and Bartlett then offered to bring the witnesses in for cross-examination. The Sena lawyers declined to question them.

"This manner of attempting to make error, and complaining of the denial of rights prejudicial to his client's case, scarcely appeals to the indulgence of an appellate tribunal dealing with a record according to justice and right," Bartlett's brief noted.

He continued, "The depositions were taken before one of the justices upon proper application and due notice to appellant's counsel, and if he desired to cross-examine these witnesses, it was simple enough to call them and ask permission to cross-examine, which would, no doubt, have been granted. At least he should have made the attempt."

The U.S. Supreme Court agreed with Bartlett's brief. The court stated that the land appeared to have been abandoned; that boundaries for the grant could not be determined; that the time had long past when any grants could be filed; and that the land in question did not contain any cultivated lands or wood.

Justice Brown wrote the decision for the court: "...the government offered in evidence the depositions of several residents of that neighborhood, who swore that they had never heard of the Jose de Leyba grant, or its boundaries. Objection was made to the reading of these depositions upon the ground that the witnesses named were present in court, and might be sworn orally. It is unnecessary to determine whether the court erred in admitting the depositions under such circumstances, in view of the vague and unsatisfactory evidence on behalf of the claimant of the boundaries and possession of the tract. Admitting that the documents introduced afforded a sufficient presumption of continued possession from 1783 to 1834, there was no evidence of the occupation of the land by any member of the Leyba family subsequent to 1839. This fact of a total absence of any claim to the land made by the last heirs of the occupant, and that the house was allowed to fall into ruins, is strong evidence either that the land was abandoned as not worth cultivating or that a residence there became too dangerous by reason of the presence of hostile Indians. As there is no testimony tending to show that the Leybas ever sought to resume possession of the land after the death of Juan Angel, in 1839, there was, at least, a presumption of abandonment."

For 60 years the land lay unclaimed, and just because Sena came up with "interests" in the land did not make those "interests" valid.

Not even the adverse Supreme Court decision stopped Sena, though. Once his case was denied he reinstituted his case to eject the American Turquoise Company and McNulty from the turquoise mines. Apparently, he thought he could drag out the court process a lot longer — especially since his brother was clerk of the territorial Supreme Court, and as such he scheduled the cases.

Once again, there were court expenses for the company; court testimony, witnesses, more paperwork, and lawyers' demands. Sena's primary backer, Solomon Luna, fared little better. The Sena group attempted a financial settlement, but the American Turquoise Company was not interested. This second round of court cases also appeared to be destined for the Supreme Court. When it came time to put the case on the territorial docket the court clerk seemed deliberately slow settng a date. Eventually heard, the lower court sided with the American Turquoise Company, and once again the case wound its way to the Supreme Court of the United States.

On May 1, 1911, the U.S. Supreme Court passed down a second decision. The introduction to the brief noted: "This is an action of ejectment for about 50 acres in section 21, township 15 north, range 8 east, in the county of Santa Fe, New Mexico, which the defendant holds under mining claims dating from 1885 to 1892, and located under the laws of the United States. It was brought after the plaintiff's failure to establish title, under a Mexican grant, to a large tract of which this land is alleged to be a part, in the court of private claims, and in this court on appeal...the plaintiff claims were not proved to include the land in dispute. ...and the evidence of possession, etc., was too vague to raise a presumption in place of proof."

Sena had announced that new evidence of his ownership would be introduced, but by 1911 no such evidence had appeared.

Testimony from August 1905 in the land claims court illustrated Sena's difficulty, as the testimony of his witnesses did not make much sense. And, it was revealed, they were being paid to testify. On the other hand McNulty and others had no trouble reciting a chronological history of the area. Under cross examination by Frank Clancy, Sena's attorney, McNulty carefully answered each question.

Clancy: "Now you say that there was a great deal of money spent on the property outside of the assessment work?"
McNulty: "Yes, sir."

Clancy: "How much was the value of that work?"

McNulty: "I really cannot tell, considerable though — thousands of dollars."

Clancy: "Do you think you have done ten thousand dollars' worth of work there?"

McNulty: "I have."

Clancy: "That is about as much as you have done?"

McNulty: "More."

Clancy: "How much more?"

McNulty: "I cannot state now until I look over the records. I have done more."

Clancy: "You don't know how much more?"

McNulty: "No, sir."

Clancy: "Do you think as much as fifteen thousand dollars' worth of work has been done there by you?"

McNulty: "Yes, sir."

Clancy: "More than that?"

McNulty: "Yes, sir."

Clancy: "You know what I want — you can save time by answering me and tell me to the best of your knowledge how much it is."

McNulty: "To the best of my knowledge there is over twenty-five thousand dollars' worth of work on one mine."

Clancy: "Now what has been the value of the output of the property?"

McNulty: "That I know not. I ship stone when I take them out, but I don't know what they get for them in New York."

Clancy: "You don't know anything about the value of the stones you take out?"

McNulty: "No, sir, I have not sold any."

Clancy: "I did not ask you whether you had sold any."

McNulty: "Then, I do not know the value."

Clancy: "With all your years of experience there, you have no idea of the value of a piece of turquoise?"

McNulty: "I have not, only by hearsay, that is all."

Clancy: "Well, you have from what you have heard from other people — you have learned what the value of turquoise is?"

McNulty: "Some say they buy for 25 cents a carat, some say $5.00 per carat, but I don't know what my company gets for them."

Clancy: "I don't care what your company gets them, I want to know what the value of the output is when it comes out of the ground."

McNulty: "I don't know about that. I ship the stones in the rough and I could not tell you what they are worth."

Clancy: "At the time Sena and Purdy were down there, at the time you spoke of — didn't you tell Mr. Purdy that you were getting two hundred thousand dollars out of the mine?"

McNulty: "I did, and I have told others besides, anybody who will ask me — How much did you get out of here, I says, I will not put it under two hundred thousand dollars."

Clancy: "Don't you think now that since the time you went there to work that you have taken out and shipped away about five hundred thousand dollars' worth of stones?"

McNulty: "That I do not say. I do not know anything about it. I am under oath now."

Clancy: "I am not asking your opinion."

McNulty: "I cannot say."

Clancy: "You have no opinion at all?"

McNulty: "Not the moneys' worth; No sir."

Clancy: "How much in quantity have you shipped from the mine?"

McNulty: "That I know not."

Clancy: "Never kept any record of it."

McNulty: "Never kept a record."

Clancy: "Don't you know how many pounds you shipped at any time?"

McNulty: "Oh, yes; sometimes three pounds in a cigar box; sometimes six pounds, but it would be rock and turquoise mixed in together."

Clancy: "Did you always ship small quantities?"

McNulty: "I ship out the rough stone and let them do what they please."

Clancy: "How large a shipment did you make at one time?"

McNulty: "I do not know."

Clancy: "Did you every ship a carload?"

McNulty: "No, sir. Nothing that I was not able to lift myself."

Mike O'Neil, the miner most instrumental in keeping the records of the mining district, also came to give testimony. O'Neil's testimony showed that the landmarks Sena based his lawsuit upon did not exist and that the land where the mines were located had been used as grazing land and was owned by no one.

Then Diego Mares, a local resident from childhood and a miner in the Cerrillos Hills since 1880, came in to testify.

> Reynolds: "How long have you known that country in and around the mines?"
>
> Mares: "I know the place since I was fifteen years of age."
>
> Reynolds: "How old are you know?"
>
> Mares: "Fifty-eight years."
>
> Reynolds: "Did you ever hear of the Arroyo de la Oregano?" [Key landmark for determining the land grant boundaries.]
>
> Mares: "No, sir."
>
> Reynolds: "Or the Arroyo Cuesta de la Oregano?"
>
> Mares: "No, sir. I have heard many who were very old there and I never heard that name mentioned of the Arroyo de la Oregano, or the Cuesta de la Oregano."

Pedro Muñiz, the locator of the Muñiz mine, testified for the turquoise company. S.B. Davis, ATC's lawyer, questioned Muñiz.

> Davis: "Now when did you first hear of a grant known as the Leyba Grant?"
>
> Muñiz: "I bought from an American there the right to mine, and I came to take Mr. White for the purpose of having some surveying, and when he arrived at the place he told me that there was a grant which was called the Jose de Leyba Grant."
>
> Davis: "Now when was that?"
>
> Muñiz: "In the year 1896." [Muñiz is confused about the year. He and his brother acquired the mine in early 1890, and sold it to the ATC in mid 1891.]
>
> Davis: "What, if anything, did you do after you heard that there was a Leyba Grant down there?"
>
> Muñiz: "I hunted up one of the heirs and I bought an interest in the grant."
>
> Davis: "From whom did you buy that interest?"
>
> Muñiz: "I bought it from Salvador Leyba. I gave him $175 for it."

As testimony continued, with different witnesses, it became clear that the "descendents" of Jose de Leyba had difficulty remembering their familial relationships, and in one case a witness did not remember his mother's legal name.

At the same time this case wound its way to the Supreme Court, Sena developed some legal difficulties of his own. He was sentenced to four years in prison because he forged a signature of a co-signer on one of his legal documents. Sena's laywer, Tom Catron, appealed, which delayed the start of Sena's sentence for four years.

Between 1907 and 1910 McNulty reported several trespasses and attacks by Pueblo Indians, and he repeatedly requested protection for himself and his wife. The sheriff suggested McNulty was imagining it all, and refused to investigate or offer assistance. Suspicions were that somehow Sena was involved in the Indian altercations, and the sheriff, too, was partial to Sena. But McNulty was too stubborn and too dedicated to let these difficulties drive him from the American Turquoise property.

In the end, the argument for the second case was very much like the argument for the first case: no provable boundaries existed, and without boundaries the cause required to eject the American Turquoise Company and McNulty from the mines did not exist.

The American Turquoise Company — with great financial burden — won this case too. There had been two Supreme Court judgments over a period of almost 15 years, and through both of them the persistent Easterners had outlasted the New Mexican schemers.

Emma and McNulty took time off from the mines to pose for a picture in Santa Fe.

Chapter 6
1904 - 1907

A Judicial Shell Game

As you are aware, my salary has been due & unpaid since the 1st of October. ...this oversight and neglect has been a very serious matter to us and cannot be longer endured.

McNulty to Parker, undated draft letter
probably around November 24, 1906

SUBTERFUGE

As per the instructions sent by Parker at the beginning of 1904, McNulty laid off the worker who only the previous month had come to live at the Turquoise Hill. Now, when either McNulty or his wife went to town the person left behind at the mines was all alone. At night the Indians from the Pueblos often came to take what turquoise they could find, including what McNulty may have left in the dumps or down in the shafts after his day's work. They could be heard in the darkness. Every day, to forstall this, the Irishman collected potentially valuable stones and carried them to his house, where by lamplight he and Emma sorted them.

This stressful life did not suit Emma, nor the loneliness, nor the confinement in the evenings. Emma began to resort to automatic writing, by which she believed she was able to communicate with the spirit world. All of this led to some tense arguments. And when McNulty's daughter, Fannie, was present, tensions regularly escalated into shouting matches, slamming doors, and bedroom lockouts. At one point Fannie, in her anger, compared Emma to Judas Iscariot, the betrayer of Jesus Christ. As the family was Roman Catholic, Emma more so, that epithet resulted in enduring antipathy.

In this poisoned family atmosphere the land grant case moved slowly forward. Well financed and carefully scheming, Mariano Sena and his cohorts worked to cause the maximum distress to the American Turquoise Company. Hearing dates were set and re-set. The Indians grew bolder. And McNulty knew he was the object, because at the mines he personified the company's right to operate.

McNulty re-contacted the residents of the area and reminded them their testimony was required whenever the case was finally heard. The two lawyers for the company and McNulty encountered difficulties. Both lawyers wanted to avoid trial in Santa Fe County, Las Vegas County, and Sandoval County where judges and court clerks were especially unpredictable.

McNulty worked the mine as best he could, all the while keeping his ear to the ground for any rumblings about the Sena case. Ever the optimist, McNulty said that he thought the case would never come to trial since Clancy, Sena's attorney, was using the same tactics he had used in the past. Clancy would file a district court case, then neither he nor Sena would show up, and the case would be automatically postponed. Through delay and rising legal costs Sena would ultimately get what he wanted. In the past, Clancy posted no bond for any of the cases he had filed. This time, however, Bartlett promised that Clancy would have bonds on file before the case went forward.

The day-to-day activities at the mine, running a household and running a business, continued. Although Emma helped with some dictation and housekeeping, her health remained fragile, and McNulty's wife acquired what was called a "nervous" condition. Emma's efforts to contact their son who had died years before, and others in the spiritual world, aggravated her condition.

McNulty, in the meantime, served the company as a guard, a detective, a witness gatherer, a legal agent, a personal representative, and a paper filer, but his salary was chronically in arrears, sometimes by as much as five months. Still, he had household expenses: a receipt from H.B. Cartwright & Bro., wholesale grocers, illustrates the goods McNulty and Emma needed for the month of February, 1904.

Invoice from H.B. Cartwright

    1 sack of wheat....$2.14
    1 sack of bran...$1.31
    4 sacks of oats...$6.77
    4 gallons of oil...$1.10
    50# Imperial Flour...$1.25
    50# Queen Flour...90¢
    1 pound mt. cream...$4
    8 40# hay, $5.67

    McNulty remarked the Sena case would be heard in Las Vegas in May of 1904, "So I expect we must await our time in patience until after May." That waiting extended to his salary, too. He wrote letter after letter, and no response came back. In spite of this, McNulty doggedly kept at his ATC duties, and when he had time, he worked on his own claims above the Tiffany mine.
    By May 3, 1905, McNulty's frustration over being ignored by the

American Turquoise Company and its lawyers appeared in his letters. The lawyers told McNulty to be ready for the Sena land grant trial by the 16th of May, but suddenly, Sena changed plans and the court date went to May 27. On May 26, the members of the court decided to wait until November to hear the case. No explanations came forth about this mysterious scheduling. The real problem came as McNulty had to travel the countryside to keep his witnesses informed. Many of them had paid workers to stay at their ranches or on their claims so they could attend the court.

With things clearly going nowhere in the Sena land grant case, McNulty undertook the back-breaking assessment work that had to be completed before the new year. McNulty hired two of the witnesses to work as he thought it best to keep them close at hand. This way they would have a job and be more inclined to stay in the area.

By September, McNulty had completed 45 feet of work and faced about ten feet of solid rock to go through before he reached a main tunnel.

McNulty's payroll and expense account checks usually came with odd amounts of change on them: three cents, four cents, one cent, and two cents. But when he tried to cash those checks, the odd change was dropped off. As McNulty put it, "As there is nothing less than five cents given in change in New Mexico, it is of no use putting the odd cents on the check."

The rains that October were unusually heavy. In one case they lasted for thirty straight hours. Roads washed out, which interfered with mail delivery. In the Muñiz, also known as the Tiffany, the timbers on one side gave way from the weight of the mud, and the timbers and loose earth fell to the bottom of the shaft and filled in about 45 feet of it.

On October 9, 1904, conditions were dire. Damaged property, filled in shafts, and more assessment work had to be attended to, and there was little time left in which to do it. Surely, it could get no worse for the American Turquoise Company? It could.

In the midst of the Sena court case the lead attorney for the ATC, the man with all the information, the man who was McNulty's attorney, was no longer there. Attorney E. L. Bartlett had died.

McNulty quickly wrote to Reynolds, who had just been elected to a federal judgeship in St. Louis, and explained what had happened.

McNulty expressed concern that Bartlett's papers might disappear, but the good news appeared on the horizon when R.J. Palen, the president of the First National Bank of Santa Fe, was appointed Bartlett's administrator. McNulty noted that the papers and documents belonging to Bartlett would most likely be safe. Reynolds, attorney for the United States government in the case, quickly scheduled a trip to Santa Fe, and the Sena case was further delayed until the court session that summer.

As 1904 wound down, McNulty gently reminded the New Yorkers that assessment work needed to be completed. Parker authorized an additional worker, and McNulty hustled about completing tunnels and shafts.

BUGGY WHIP APPLIED FREELY

With company matters in disarray McNulty's wages and payroll arrived late. He commented that workers quit if they did not receive their wages by the 15th of the month, and he hoped that the situation would be rectified quickly. Parker sent the money due the workers, but McNulty had to wait. His salary lagged three months behind.

The winter of 1905 was uncommonly harsh. Much snow covered the ground, and McNulty wrote the winter was the worst in 15 years. Horse teams and travellers found the road extremely difficult. It was almost impossible to bring feed, wood, coal and water to the mines. Fresh water couldn't be delivered to the mines, and they had to resort to melting snow.

The letterhead on American Turquoise Company stationery changed at this time — now it was typed in, not pre-printed. No money was wasted on the company's image. In fact, all monetary resources of the American Turquoise Company were funneled into legal fees. McNulty simply occupied the claims, and guarded them, occasionally venturing into them for turquoise. Then on April 3, 1905, McNulty received an ominous letter from the company treasurer: "We are under the necessity of delaying monthly remittance for a few days, but hope to be in a position to write you again shortly." This did not please McNulty. He kept detailed records for the company, records containing the names of all workers at the mine along with notes on their position or work. The sheet included the days, the rate of payment, and the total amount to be distributed to the workers. At the bottom of the page, bills for the month were recorded along with the amount of work on each claim. The sheets, signed by McNulty, were sent off to New York for payment, which always seemed to come late.

Summer, June 1905, did not begin well. McNulty fell ill and could not muster the strength to write, while Emma descended into screaming fits and was unable to help her sick husband. McNulty's daughter, Fannie, moved in, managing the mine and correspondence until her father could get back to business. Fannie did not expect much from her stepmother.

Finally, by July, McNulty was back on the job, and he travelled to Las Vegas, New Mexico, in an effort to catch up on the latest news about the Sena case. Regrettably, when McNulty returned to his house he found Emma severely "unbalanced". McNulty wrote, "I agreed with her in everything that week."

The situation worsened with Emma trying to run out of the house during a screaming rage. Fannie and McNulty restrained her, managing to pull her into the buggy so they could take her to a doctor. She screamed, she pummeled them with her fists, and at one point she grabbed the buggy whip, applying it freely to any who were near. Although McNulty drove the buggy at a brisk pace towards Santa Fe, Emma repeatedly tried to throw herself out. It was Fannie who kept her from falling. When they arrived at the hospital, she was taken inside, where she threw hysterical fits every time she saw either her husband or Fannie. The doctors recommended she go to the asylum in Las Vegas, and McNulty agreed to this since there was nothing else to be done. He paid the $90 in advance and awaited word as to when Emma could return home.

In a letter to McNulty, Matthews expressed concern about McNulty's wife and hoped that she would be able to rejoin her husband.

It wasn't until August 2, 1905, that McNulty was well enough to take over letter writing from Fannie.

Emma stayed in Las Vegas under a doctor's care where part of her treatment included writing long letters about her life and what happened when she was with McNulty. In one of her letters Emma described the scene as she was being whisked away to Santa Fe.

> Cerrillos N. Mex.
> July 2, 1915 -
>
> R. A. Parker, Esq.
>   52 Wall St.
>   New York.
>
> Dear Sir:-
>   In my telegram to you on June 10 I stated that I would write you full particulars later. I went to Las Vegas to enquire about the Grant Case and on my return on the twelvth Dr. I found my wife to be unbalanced or as I might say deranged. I agreed with her in everything for that week, and the following week

Fannie took dictation and described the recurring condition of McNulty's wife. The road to Emma's recovery was a long and hard one.

Filled with anger and venom, Emma clearly had difficulty dealing with the isolation of the mine, and her frustration came through in her letters. She took to criticizing McNulty and his daughters with a rhetoric that mirrored her unhinged state. Always nervous, and suffering from sicknesses almost on a monthly basis, she practiced automatic writing and thought she possessed exceptional "spiritual" powers.

Emma wrote about her automatic writing, her drawings, the swirling lights she saw, and her spiritual knowledge. Her letters revealed that several other individuals agreed with family members that she should have treatment. She admitted that she had spent some time in an asylum in "Tuskaloosa", after she had typhoid fever and before she ever married McNulty.

Her letters rambled and accused McNulty and Fannie of being cruel and unreasonable. Finally, after two weeks of treatment, Emma realized that McNulty would be the one to ask for her release and it might not be a good idea to accuse him of being unfair. In a subsequent letter to McNulty, Emma said that her condition had improved and she was happy and contented. McNulty had been able to get her thread and material for sewing as well as her hymn books. He even brought her the brown shawl their baby "was dying in," as well as his picture. Her next few letters demonstrated her lack of anger and her ability to re-enter the normal life. But, as the month progressed, she again relapsed.

Emma, writing from the Las Vegas asylum, recounted her memory of the day her baby died, and in the same letter she asked for some luxuries — cards and a cribbage board, scrapbooks, and water paints. In late August Emma asked her husband to allow her to enter the outside world on a probationary status. Neither the doctors nor McNulty thought the time right for Emma's release.

IN COURT, AGAIN

The Sena case headed to court and McNulty rounded up his witnesses: Mike O'Neil, Ed Bennett, Tom Whalen and Felipe Mares. All appeared on August 28, 1905, in the San Miguel County court room of Judge William J. Mills, Chief Justice of the Supreme Court of the Territory of New Mexico and District Court Judge, for depositions. By September 8 the district court handed down a decision favoring the American Turquoise Company. Sena asked for a retrial right on the

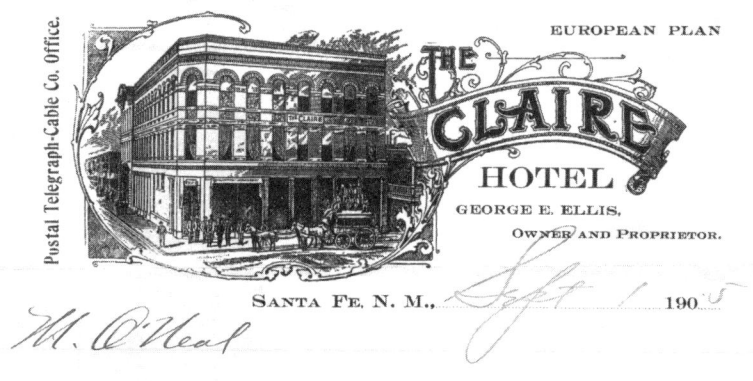

For the upcoming court case, Mike O'Neil's board and hotel bill covered five days. The Claire Hotel, owned by George E. Ellis, provided accommodations.

spot, but that was not granted. Apparently, Sena intended to go to the United States Supreme Court once more.

Back on the claims, mining work turned so difficult in October that McNulty's workers quit. Workers were hard to find, and low wages did nothing to help keep them on the site. It didn't help that payrolls arrived late.

At one point McNulty feared that the court expenses he incurred on behalf of the Turquoise Company would not be paid, plus he still had to complete the assessment work. Good, reliable miners seemed to have no trouble finding a job during the winter months, and it wasn't at the Tiffany. McNulty commented, "This place is so far from town that men do not like to come here on account of the accommodations of houses, wood and water."

The Territory of New Mexico,

To **E.F. Bennett**
Cerrillos, N.M.

Greeting:

You and each of you are hereby commanded to appear before the District Court of the Fourth Judicial District of said Territory, ~~at the term thereof now being held~~ within and for the County of **San Miguel**, ~~at the Court House of said County~~, forthwith at **Santa Fe, N.M. August 28th, 1905 at 9 o'clock A.M.** at Chambers of Hon. Wm. J. Mills, Chief Justice etc., then and there to testify in a certain cause in said Court pending, wherein **Mariano F. Sena** _plaintiff_ and **The American Turquoise Co.,** _defendant_ on the part of the **Defendant** ; and this do you under the penalty of the law. Witness, The Hon. WILLIAM J. MILLS, Chief Justice of the Supreme Court of the Territory of New Mexico, and Judge of the Fourth Judicial District Court thereof, and the Seal of said District Court, this **21st** day of **August**, A.D. 190**5**

The subpoena served by Sheriff A. J. Ortiz and Deputy Jas Coleman called E.F. Bennet to court to testify in the Sena Case. He testified for the ATC and said that no grant existed in the area of the mines as far as he knew. He had been in the area before 1889.

He still promised, "I will rustle and get men to do the assessment work."

When McNulty found a reliable worker he asked the company to promise the man winter employment. The company declined. By the end of the year it was obvious that the Sena shakedown was headed on to the territorial Supreme Court, then possibly to the United States Supreme Court. Again. Everyone knew that as legal expenses continued to grow mine work would diminish.

With his salary behind, McNulty's first letter of 1906 requested that Parker make sure that the checks for the workers, supplies, etc. arrived promptly by the 15th of the month. "I need money to pay up my bills," he wrote. With his wife in the asylum, more than half of his money went to her care, while the rest went to supplies. McNulty paid some of the bills for the mines out of his own pocket and trusted the company to send him what was owed. He shipped out an occasional box of stone, but nothing like what he had shipped two years earlier.

When the Sena case was decided in favor of ATC what was a little problem at the mine became a bigger problem. The Pueblo Indians began to appear almost every night and in greater numbers.

Sena had talked freely about his plans to appeal what he considered an unfair decision. No one except McNulty paid very much attention to that. But by then it was obvious that McNulty at the mine was the major impediment for Sena, and a decision had been made to attempt to remove him. It might be that the Pueblos were encouraged to confront and threaten McNulty in hopes that he would leave or end up dead. Sena's effort to remove McNulty and take control hadn't worked in the past, and it wasn't going to work in 1906.

To confuse things, Sena started another rumor. He said he had already filed an appeal with the United States Supreme Court. This rumor led to a flurry of letters running from Cerrillos to New York to Santa Fe to St. Louis as McNulty, Parker and Reynolds tried to gather more information. After multiple trips to Santa Fe, McNulty could uncover no information on the appeal. Of course, since Mariano Sena's brother controlled the announcement of the filings, McNulty was not eager to travel to the court offices and request any information of him.

COVER MY DAMN BACK

The year 1906 was marked by an increase in Pueblo Indian activity at the American Turquoise Company Mines. McNulty, now alone, was a target for turquoise takers who came to the mines in groups from six to fifteen. They came with rifles. Exchanges of rifle fire in the dark, all near misses, could easily have turned deadly.

"I have had some pretty bad struggles with the Indians. ...seven of them ...with rifles ...told me to cover my damn back," McNulty wrote. He ran back to his house, grabbed a rifle and returned fire.

When he reported the incident, the brother of the governor agreed to write a letter to Washington, D.C., but nothing came of it.

And it didn't help that McNulty's salary was four months behind and the bills for his wife at the asylum mounted.

The inauguration in February of the new governor of the territory, George Curry, gave McNulty a reason to visit with the Chief Justice of the Territorial court, W. J. Mills. McNulty wryly noted that Mills simply laughed when asked about the appeal date for the land grant case. Mills said the grant people could take as along as one year.

> BOARD OF DIRECTORS.
> JEFFERSON RAYNOLDS, President
> W. E. GORTNER, Secy and Treas.
> O. L. GREGORY
> D. C. WINTERS
> B. D. BLACK, M. D.
>
> DR. H. M. SMITH, Supt.
> GEO. W. WARD, Steward
> MRS. FLORA PRENTICE, Matron
>
> THE N. M. I. A. HOSPITAL
>
> Las Vegas, N. M., June 1st, 1906.
>
> Mr. J. P. Mc Nulty,
> Cerillos, N. M.
>
> Dear Sir:-
>
> In reply to your letter of the 29th ulto. will say that I shall be pleased to extend your wife's furlough sixty days. I hope that in that time her condition will have again improved.
>
> Yours very truly,
>
> [signature]
>
> Superintendent.

Dr. Smith of the New Mexico Insane Asylum Hospital expresses optimism that Emma is improving.

Good news arrived in the form of an announcement that Emma could soon return home in March. McNulty asked the doctor to let his wife come home for 60 days. Her letters lacked the anger and inflammatory accusations of previous letters, an indication that her mental state had improved. She even wished her husband good health.

Finally, by the end of March, McNulty received word that Emma's physical health had improved, and that her mental health seemed quite stable. Upon her arrival, their relationship remained strained, although both tried hard to avoid conflict. They did enjoy the comfort of each other's companionship, but past words and actions prevented them from being close again. Emma didn't take the dictation of letters from McNulty at the rate she had done before, but she

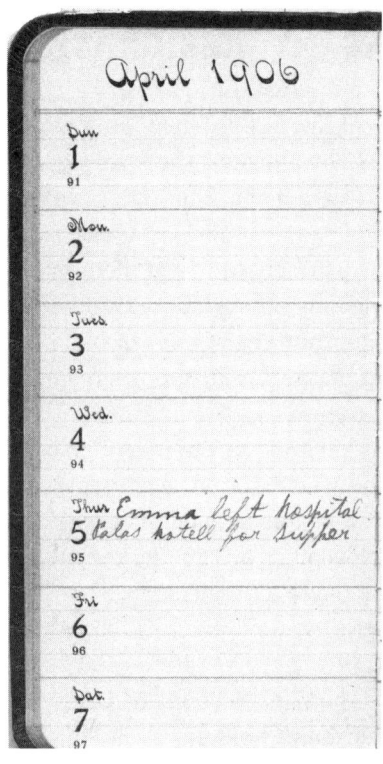

April 5 marks the day of Emma's freedom from the asylum. She returned home to an uneasy truce with her husband.

provided the home atmosphere, food, cleaning, companionship, and once again, help with guarding against the Pueblo Indians. Emma's recovery sped along so well that McNulty requested her furlough to be extended for an additional 60 days.

With nothing really happening on the legal front, McNulty requested instructions about assessment work. He thought five months of work would meet the assessment requirement until patents could be issued. The company withheld the issuance of any mining orders.

The company also had trouble getting McNulty's pay to him.

With his personal finances in a mess, McNulty decided to sell interests in his personal claim, and on September 3, 1906 he received a letter from West Branch, Iowa, from Eli Browning, a realtor and investor. Mr. Browning's letter reviewed the terms of McNulty's offer: "Has Turquoise Mines 900 X 1500 now show good colors, lay parallel to and adjoining the famous Tiffany mines. Offers 1/2 interest paid sum for $6500 or 3/4 for $16,500. Will take 1/2 down and balance on your own terms." No deal was made.

When November rolled around and McNulty's assessment orders still had not come from the company, the miner nagged the New Yorkers. It was an absolute necessity that the assessment work be completed. Still, no orders came for McNulty from the company.

ACCEPT THIS LETTER AS MY RESIGNATION

Although McNulty and several local lawyers thought Sena would never appeal his case, on November 23, Sena proved them wrong. He filed in the Territorial Supreme Court, where his brother was the clerk, and got a court date in January.

Life in Cerrillos took a sad turn, when Richard Green died on November 29, 1906, "after a long and lingering illness of paralysis, from which he had been afflicted for the past four years." Green had built the Palace Hotel in Cerrillos, a miner's favorite haunt, and where Emma had celebrated her release from the asylum.

Although McNulty faithfully represented the turquoise company in legal matters and served as the person who received legal papers on behalf of the company, the ATC was rarely able to send his salary in a timely fashion. Several times during November of 1907 he threatened Parker with a lien on the property if payroll didn't arrive. After a particularly scathing letter sent by McNulty, the New York banker responded.

Parker said that he was sorry but the bank account had run dry. He awaited the return of the wealthiest bond holder, James Stillman, so the bank account could be refreshed. He concluded that if McNulty were to place a lien on the property, things would become very complicated. He suggested that a week or two wait was not out of line.

In an uncharacteristically blunt letter, McNulty demanded payment so that he could buy provisions. "I am so financially fixed that I must do this [take a lien] to get money to buy provisions with. And Mr. Parker, you will please do me the favor in paying me up in full and accept this letter as my resignation as superintendent of this property." He added in a subsequent letter that he expected claim jumpers to move in if the assessment work was not completed soon.

Parker then urged McNulty to avoid taking in rash steps and encouraged him to start the assessment work with a promise to pay by the end of the month.

The dismal accounting for 1906 told the whole story. The mine records showed that only McNulty's salary was billed for January through November, and then in December, when assessment work was completed, the miner's salary and expenses added up to $130. Apparently, most of the investors' money went into legal fees, and

A PIONEER GONE.

RICHARD GREEN died at his home in Cerrillos, N. M., on the 29th day of November, A. D. 1906, after a long and lingering illness of paralysis, from which he had been afflicted for the past four years. Richard Green was born in Wautauga County, North Carolina, near Meat Camp, in the year A. D. 1847, on the 14th day of February. His father died when he was three years old, his grandfather, Richard Green, then took him to his home and raised him to manhood. Before he was grown, at the age of 19 years, while the Civil War was going on between the States, he became a member of the North Carolina militia, but the war closed in a few months after. He was married to Mary C. Lewis on the 31st of October, in A. D. 1867, at the home of her father, near Meat Camp, with whom he lived and raised a large family of children, twelve in number. Richard Green and his beloved wife resided near the old home in North Carolina, where they were born, until the year 1874, when they moved to Jack County, Texas, where he engaged in farming and stock raising until 1884, when he came to Santa Fe County, New Mexico, and finally settled at Cerrillos, where he opened up a coal mine, which he worked for a time with success. He then built the Palace Hotel in Cerrillos, which he and his wife have operated ever since. Hundreds of miners all over the Southwest have been the guest of this old hostelry, which was the home of many of them that were homeless. While living in Texas he joined the Baptist Church at Barton Springs, and also at Jacksboro, Texas. He became a member of the Masonic Fraternity and was a consistent and bright ornament to his profession, and when the time came for him to rest until the call of the Great Master of the Universe, his brethren laid his body away in the cemetery with loving hands, they cast the evergreen sprig on his coffin. Requiscat in Pace.

The wife remains in sorrow to mourn the loss of a husband, and the children the loss of an honorable and affectionate father, which can never be replaced.

One son, Calvin Green, was killed in a mine explosion near Las Cruces in 1895; another son, Clay Green, was killed at San Juan Hill while in discharge of his duty as a soldier under the Stars and Stripes. The command to which he belonged was called the Rough Riders, under the intrepid Col. Theo. Roosevelt.

Richard Green was a patient sufferer and never complained of his lot in life, and when his last days drew nigh, he prayed that he might be taken away to where there is no more suffering and where sorrow never comes.

A FRIEND.

Richard Green, a prominent businessman in Cerrillos, died in 1906. This page from an unknown source and written by A Friend serves as a testament to the world as to the quality of Green.

McNulty received payment for the months of January through March, with only a half salary received for April. His work for May through December remained unpaid.

McNulty's "resignation" as superintendent never materialized. Parker ignored the offer and conducted business as usual with a promise to pay up in the very near future.

McNulty's comment, "You say that in the future remittances will be made promptly which I hope will be so."

The market remained depressed for turquoise in 1907, and this coupled with the legal expenses of the mine, forced the American Turquoise Company to cut back on everything unnecessary to retain ownership of the mine.

By now the bond holders of the mines had changed somewhat, and the directors of the company were Allan Pinkerton, 57 Broadway, New York; Courtland Betts, 44 Wall Street, New York; John D. Bogert, Leonia, New Jersey; Robert A. Parker, 81 Fulton St.; and James Matthews, 52 Wall Street, New York. (Betts, a lawyer, had completed legal work for the company in the past.)

When McNulty tried to pay taxes for the company in 1907, the tax collector inexplicably refused to accept the payment. In the typical bureaucratic runaround, McNulty had to make several trips to Santa Fe to get the taxes paid. (Mariano Sena served as chief clerk in the assessor's office and most likely had friends in the treasurer's office, too, which might explain this.) In the end, McNulty had to take a city marshal with him to observe the attempt to pay the taxes. With a

This is the list of the board of directors of the American Turquoise Company, apparently recorded by Fannie, included addresses so that McNulty could write them about his back salary.

marshal at McNulty's side, the collector took the money. Of course, this happened two months before the scheduled March Territorial Supreme Court date for the land grant case.

The Indians increased their activity as Sena finally argued his case for the second time. Once again, the courts found in favor of ATC and said the company owned the mines. Again, Sena said he was headed to the United States Supreme Court. And again, McNulty finished the assessment work.

For the past four years the turquoise mines had not produced commercial turquoise, yet the county handed down tax assessments as if they had. McNulty found this very unfair, and in June determined to ask for a reduction of taxes. He pointed out that no assessor had visited the property in the last 10 years and the county commissioners had never been out either. McNulty expressed the opinion that taxation should occur only on property improvements, not on production when there was none. The turquoise company agreed with McNulty and urged him to continue efforts to get the taxes reduced.

In addition to battling the tax assessor, McNulty was troubled by more visits from the Indians. He carried around a small notebook, and in it every day, when he arrived at the mines' entrances, he listed the damage done. McNulty offered a reward, using his own money, since the sheriff and the captain of the mounted police needed incentive to come to the remote area to investigate. The reward would accomplish that. During one event, August 16, 1907, the captain of the Mounted Police observed the mines for two consecutive nights. Apparently, the captain determined that his Mounted Police were outnumbered, and they waited until the morning to track the Indians who had been there at night. They left McNulty with instructions to telegraph them should the Indians return. Of course, that would require a ride to the telegraph office in Cerrillos miles away.

Matthews, acting for Parker, told McNulty that it "is very unfortunate indeed that property protection cannot be afforded by the authorities." He then asked for the names of the people in charge in New Mexico so that letters could be written to people in Washington, D.C. and in New Mexico to register complaints.

McNulty sent a letter back to Matthews and commented that the proper authority began with the territorial governor who was the only one to give orders to the Mounted Police. At the same time, Matthews took up the matter with Judge Abbott, special attorney for the Pueblo

Indians of New Mexico, and he wished McNulty better luck in dealing with the Indians. Abbott seems to have had no better luck than McNulty. The record of the Indian trespasses was told in a list McNulty wrote: "August 2nd-New door on Castilian; broke it open night of the 5th; hasp broke on the night of 7th; broke open on night of the 12th; broke open night of the 14th; mounted police 15th and 16th; Indians broke door on night of the 29th, 30th and 31st; Indians came on Sept 1st, 2nd, 3rd, 4th, 5th, 5-7th, 8th..."

While Indian visits to the mines persisted, McNulty prepared to go back before the tax board to request a reduction in the tax assessment. He found a mining law that applied to the company situation: McNulty quoted the law that said "... no mining claims are taxed until patented, except the improvements and the output thereof." That winning argument brought the tax assessment down.

A broadsheet announcing the results of the September 11, 1907, hearing stated, "In the matter of the appeal of the American Turquoise Company, Santa Fe County, the Board having had the same under consideration and being fully advised in the matter, sustains the appeal and it is ordered that the action of the county board be and it is hereby vacated and set aside." The written document to this effect circulated throughout Santa Fe County.

McNulty carried memo books constantly as he made notes on the day's activities.

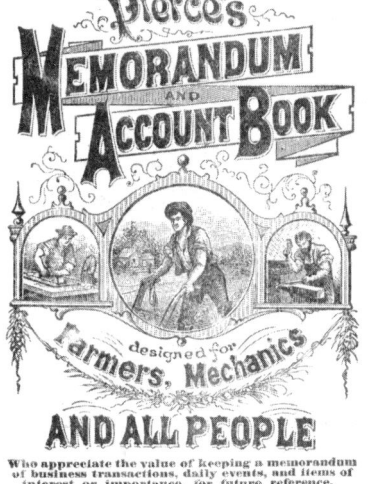

FORGERY

McNulty offered a reward to Sheriff Closson to help capture the Indians. "It is the only way I can see to have the Indians captured, which must be done on the property as lives will be in great danger," McNulty said.

For a while, the Pueblo Indians ceased trespassing, and that allowed McNulty the time to do the assessment work. The tunneling and shaft driving went through such hard rock that the miners quit, and the replacement McNulty managed to hire suffered from malaria and also had to quit.

In 1907 there was a shortage of cash in the local banks, which made it difficult to get company checks cashed in Santa Fe. McNulty asked Parker to send only cash — the Santa Fe Bank did not have a lot of money on hand and did not honor checks during the last few weeks of 1907.

Once again, at the end of the year, the county tax assessor couldn't remember making the tax adjustment earlier in the year, he couldn't find a record of it, and he didn't have access to the official publication stating the adjustment given to the American Turquoise Company. In fact, the assessor declined to accept the collector's notes about the tax reduction. The ATC papers in the assessor's office went missing. When the paperwork reappeared a few days later, the amount of assessment had been crossed out and a larger amount written in. When McNulty wrote back to Parker he said that it would not be worthwhile to take the case to the Santa Fe County District Attorney since the DA ran in the same crowd as the assessor. The company paid a reduced amount and did not call the forgery to anyone else's attention. Sena had been convicted of forgery several years earlier, so McNulty thought him the likely perpetrator of these problems in the assessor's office.

McNulty & Friends
Dialogs On Mariano Sena &
the Jose de Leyba Land Grant
1904 - 1907

McNulty to Parker, January 4, 1904

...we were very glad to hear from you and to know that you recovered the stolen money. ...I was in Santa Fe on the 30th ...and I had a talk with Mr. Bartlett. He told me that Mr. Reynolds had barred out three counties where the case could not be tried, and that Judge McFie had notified Mr. Clancy to that effect. He asked him to decide in which of the other counties he is willing to have the case tried, but Mr. Clancy has not replied to his letter as yet.

McNulty to Parker, April 2, 1904

I went to Santa Fe about two weeks ago to see Mr. Reynolds, and he was glad that I called to see him for he was just about to telephone to Cerrillos for me to come and see him. He wanted to know some important points about the property, and to give me instructions what papers to have with me to take to court. He told me that Mr. Bartlett would let me know what witnesses I would need to take to Las Vegas.

Mr. Reynolds said he would try and have the case tried on or about the 16th inst. I will see Mr. Bartlett as soon as he returns from the East and find out what witnesses I will need, as all witnesses that worked for me 10 or 12 years ago have moved away. I will have some trouble to locate them. I do hope you will be out here when the case is tried. I would like you to please have Mr. Matthews to send me my month's salary a few days earlier so that I can get it here about the 12th before I go to Las Vegas.

McNulty to Reynolds, May 3, 1905

Will you please give me some information about

the Sena case if it is to be tried this term of Court or not, as I am very much worried, not hearing anything from you or Mr. Parker concerning the case. I do not consider that I am being treated rightly in the matter, by the Company, as they owe me five month's salary up to date and cannot get any satisfactory answer from them. When I was in Santa Fe two weeks ago, I met Frank Delgado and he told me that he was trying to find out all he could from Sena. He also said you had appointed Mr. Charles Spiess and Sena told Delgado that Mr. Spiess was working the case for him and they expected to win the case by default. If not, that he had some good pointers now and more documents.

McNulty to Parker, May 7, 1904

I went to Santa Fe last Saturday to see Mr. Bartlett and he informed me that the case was set for the 27th instead of the 16th, so I had to make a flying trip back home so as to notify my witnesses that I would not need them till the 27th as some of them had to engage men in their place to look after their work while they are away.

McNulty to Parker, May 26, 1904

I went to Santa Fe on the 24th inst. and Mr. Bartlett told me that Mr. Reynolds and Mr. Clancy went to Las Vegas, but that he did not go himself. He said that Judge Mills told them the case was the last on the docket and could not be tried till the next term of court in November which I am very sorry. When I talked with Mr. Reynolds a month ago, he was very anxious to have the case tried and said he was going forthwith to Washington to obtain the patents for the property. Now that we cannot get the patent in time, it will cause me to have to do the assessment work on the claims. I am very glad we have Mr. Reynolds to look after the case as all of my confidence is placed in him alone.

McNulty to Parker, October 22, 1904

I am very sorry to have to write you on this occasion about the death of our attorney, General wrote me that he received a letter from Mr J. M. Vroom, asking him to meet him in Chicago, which he declined.

Mr Vroom was one of the party who came here 8 years ago & tried to get up to the mine when I ordered them down, carrying the gun with me. I have not seen him since that time. He afterwards went to New York & demanded money from the Farmers Loan & Trust Company.

If the case should be tried this month I do hope you will be here.

Hoping to hear from you soon. With best wishes.

Yours very truly,
J. P. McNulty.

McNulty went through multiple drafts before sending a letter. Many of his letters show crossouts and rewordings of text. In this letter, he discusses the time a lawyer named Vroom tried to get money from the ATC with the promise he would make the Sena Land Grant Case disappear.

E.L. Bartlett. I did not hear of it until I wired you yesterday. I regret very much his death happening at this time, as I have written Mr. Reynolds today that if Mr. Bartlett had any papers that he would need in the grant case that some of the Senas might get possession of them as some of them were always in his office whenever I called. He having a Mexican typewriter and clerk, she might be induced to show where the papers are. I also wrote him to please give me all instructions and advice concerning the grant case which Mr. Bartlett told me three weeks ago that he would inform me in due time if anything new would come up. I also write you to please give me full instructions as there will be an agent needed. I am going to Santa Fe this afternoon to attend the funeral of Mr. Bartlett tomorrow and will inquire from the Mexican clerk if the papers are safe. ...owing to more washouts the mail has been very irregular...

Parker to McNulty, October 24, 1904

I fear the death of the General will complicate our law suit. I had written him some time ago asking the condition of affairs, but received no reply, in fact not a letter was received by me from him since last April. We have written Mr. Matt Reynolds for a report on the condition of affairs.

Reynolds to McNulty, October 25, 1904

I wrote him [Parker] very promptly last night, and will forward to him today a report upon the condition of the case, and also stated that I would write you relative to the matter, but that I did not deem it necessary to employ local counsel until I should arrive in New Mexico immediately after the election. On last Saturday, I received a long letter from Mr. J.W. Vroom, asking me to meet him in Chicago on Wednesday or Thursday of this week, and informing me that he had placed his deed on record at Santa Fe, and that he proposed to assert his rights against Sena and everybody else who might get in his way. ...I telegraphed Mr. Vroom at his request, declining to meet him in Chicago, and

informing him that I would write him there.
I am satisfied the row between Vroom, Sena
and others will result in uncovering or exposing the general arrangement these people
have had to acquire the property of the American Turquoise Company without consideration
if they could. The only thing I have to
suggest to you is to keep possession of the
property as you have in the past, and I will
write Frank Delgado to be on the look-out
for these people until I can get to Santa
Fe. I shall write to Mr. L.A. Hughes with a
view of finding out who is liable to administer upon Gen. Bartlett's estate. This will
enable us to get possession of all of the
papers and documents belonging to the American Turquoise Company.

McNulty to Parker, November 3, 1904

The same day I received your letter, I also received one from Mr. Matt G. Reynolds, in which he stated that he would be here shortly after the election. When I wrote to him on the 22nd last month, I enclosed him a clipping from the Santa Fe paper showing where James W. Vroom had recorded, an individual one fourth interest in the Jose de Leyba Grant, conveyed to him by Sena, and Mr. Reynolds wrote me that he received a letter from Mr. J.W. Vroom, asking him to meet him in Chicago, which he declined. Mr. Vroom was one of this party who came here eight years ago and tried to get up to the mine when I ordered them down carrying the gun with me. He afterwards went to New York and demanded money from the Farmer's Loan and Trust Company.

McNulty to Parker, May 4, 1905

I must say that this state of affairs is very unsatisfactory to me as living in this isolated place and not getting my salary for the month of December yet. I have written to Mr. Reynolds telling him the news that I heard from his friend Frank Delgado about Mariano Sena, saying that he had extra attorneys working on the case for him and that they expected to win the case by default.

Parker to McNulty, May 11, 1905

    I am very much surprised to learn report has become current that the Sena case is likely to go by default. I instructed Mr. Spiess over a month ago to take the necessary action to guard our interests, and the matter has been in the hands of Judge Reynolds ever since I saw you, now two years ago. Do you think we are getting a square deal?

McNulty to Parker, August 2, 1905

    I have been to see Judge M. G. Reynolds two weeks ago in Santa Fe and will see him again on Friday or Saturday if I get a man to work as I may have to go to Las Vegas on the seventh inst. Mr. Reynolds was well pleased when I told him the abuse I gave Charles Spiess last June when I had called him everything but a gentleman. Reynolds told me that Mr. Spiess would have nothing to do what so ever in the grant case.

McNulty to Parker, August 22, 1905

    I thank you very much for your sympathy for me but I regret to have to say that my wife's condition is no better. I went to Las Vegas last Friday night to see S.B. Davis and I accompanied him to Judge Mills' office on Saturday morning. Judge Mills set the date for the 24th inst. Davis wired Matt G. Reynolds and he could not reach here by that date, so we went to Judge Mills again and he set the date for the 28th and it happened that Frank Clancy the attorney for the land grant was in Las Vegas on Saturday. He agreed to the date so I expect Judge Reynolds in Santa Fe next Sunday. While I was in Judge Mills' office looking over the matter I told Judge Mills that I expected the Sena party to have me in the Justice of the Peace Court next and he laughed at it. All I can say now about the case is I am confident we will win.

McNulty to Parker, September 5, 1905

    I know you must be as pleased over the victory of the Sena Case as I am and I congratulate you. It was a tedious case as they had so many witnesses

168 • Patricia McGraw

to examine. ...by the fourth and fifth day we knew we had the case won and Mr. Reynolds did not call there any of my witnesses. ...the Sena attorney called for a new trial, but my opinion is they will not take it to court again but they will drag along so long as they possibly can for meanness.

McNulty to Parker, October 5, 1905

I have considerable trouble to keep men here to do the assessment work as the rock in the tunnel is hard and they want more pay, but that I would not give them. I have been to Las Vegas a few weeks ago to see S.B. Davis in regards to the grant case. If the other parties did not take our appeal I would not have to do the assessment work as I have talking to Mr. Easely to see if he is getting the patents. But he said he could not do it if they took an appeal. Davis told me he understands they have undertaken the appeal and I was also told of ones to see about the expenses of our witnesses which was supposed to come from the other side when we won the case.

McNulty to Matthews, June 25, 1906

I have not heard anything about the grant case since my last letter, but will try and find out soon. I do not like to go to the court house as M. Sena's brother is clerk in the Supreme Court.

Stephen B. Davis [potential attorney for the ATC] to McNulty, November 23, 1906

I have your favor of the 21st. An appeal has been taken in the Sena case but I do not know certainly as to whether or not I will represent the company in the Supreme Court. I expect to hear definitely from Mr. Parker or Mr. Reynolds within a few days. The case may possibly come up in Janaury.

McNulty to Parker, July 3, 1906.

I went to Santa Fe last week while the Supreme Court was in session and I had a talk with Chief Justice Mills and Judge Pope. Judge Pope told me

to notify Mr Davis, ~~the word~~
notify ~~Judge Reynolds~~ him.
Enclosed is a clipping taken from
the New Mexican of July 28, 1906
where Mariano Sena ~~whose~~
sentenced four years ago for
forgery, but had taken an appeal
& the case is still in court.
Hoping to hear from you
soon with instructions.
With best wishes
Yours very truly.
J. P. McNulty.

This note reminds Parker of the forgery charge against Sena. At bottom of the letter, practice strokes demonstrate how Emma most likely drew the letters for the final draft.

that M. Sena did not have his appeal on the books yet.

McNulty & Friends
Dialogs On Finances
1904 - 1907

Matthews to McNulty, August 27, 1906

We hand you herewith check for $65.00, being half of your salary for April, and ask that you make it go as far as you can, as we may be delayed a little while in sending you the next remittance. Money is scarce at the present time and the parties interested are still away from the city.

Parker to McNulty, December 3, 1906

I note what you state in the postscript that unless you receive some money by 10th of December you will have to take a lien on the property of the American Turquoise Company. I am very sorry indeed there has been any delay in sending you a check for wages, but the fund which was subscribed by the stockholders of the company has been exhausted temporarily. I am negotiating with two of the wealthiest of them with a view to having more money supplied to carry us along for a while and hope to have the matter consummated this week. I ask, therefore, that you do not take this lien you speak of as it will only complicate matters and retard plans which would result to our mutual advantage. Having waited so long you can certainly stand an extra delay of a week or so.

Matthews to McNulty, January 8, 1907

We are sorry there has been a delay through the formalities referred to in Mr. Parker's last letter, but they have extended a little further than we expected. We hope, however, to have everything settled satisfactorily in a few days, and to send you check not later than the end of this coming week.

Matthews to McNulty, February 16, 1907

...we do not wish to have you continue

operations at the mines after the assessment work is complete, at least for the present time, and we would like to have you get this assessment work done with the least possible expense, both in the matter of labor and in supplies, as we do not care to spend any more money at this time than is absolutely necessary. There is no market at present for stone, and being unable to dispose of that which we have on hand, we feel that it is useless to make expenditures which are not warranted by business conditions.

McNulty & Friends Dialogs On Taxes 1904 - 1907

.McNulty to Parker, January 16, 1907

I was advised to tender to the collector the full amount of taxes that the Board of Equalization had agreed to, and the collector would not accept any of it only in part payments; so I went to the capital and informed the Board of Equalization of his actions. They told me to go again to the collector and take someone with me as witness and offer him the money again. ...if he refused to take it, they would have to take it court to protect me and the company. I then took the city Marshall with me for a witness and handed him the money which he finally took and gave me a full tax receipt for same.

Matthews to McNulty, June 7, 1907

We feel that the heavy taxation to which we have been subjected for several years past has been severe upon us, in view of the fact that we have not operated the mines for so long, and are not in receipt of any income from it.

McNulty to Parker, June 14, 1907

I am glad to know that you were pleased with the action I have taken in trying to have the taxes reduced on the property. I was in Santa Fe and had over an hour argument before the County Commissioners, two of them being Mexicans and one American, who is the chairman. They had an interpreter. They gave me great praise for the part I had taken in the matter but they decided to sustain the Assessor's report on the grounds that the Company had paid that amount of taxes heretofore without complaining. They also said that they were raising the taxes on all property whether they were producing or not. I told them that I had complained to the old County Commissioners but did not take it before the Territory Board of Equalization, so I notified them that I should take an appeal this time to the Territory Board.

My pleas with the County Commissioners was that this property was not patented and therefore was not real estate and being in litigation for over 10 years and had not been producing for four years; furthermore, there has not been any of the assessors out to see the property for over 10 years.

I also told the County Commissioners that the man who handed him the assessor's report is the one who has the property in litigation. Mariano Sena is the chief clerk in the assessor's office. ...about 12 years ago, the County Commissioners raised the valuation on this property from $5,000 to $25,000 and I went to Santa Fe and pleaded before the County Commissioners for a whole day and got it reduced to $4,000 and Mr. Doty happened to be here the same time and complained because it was not exempt from taxation altogether.

McNulty to Matthews, November 28, 1907

I have been to Santa Fe and seen the tax collector Lopez about the taxes and am very glad that you notified me about the taxes not being reduced. Mr. Lopez informed me that he had the publication where the Board of Equalization had sustained my appeal but that the assessor and the County com-

missioners did not make any change in the assessment roll. So I hunted up the deputy assessor and demanded of him the blank that I had filled out and signed. He looked over his papers and told me he could not find it and that he had not received it from the assessor [Ortiz] who is sick and not in town. So I told him that it looked to me as if they had done away with it and tried to collect money that was not due them and that if they did not produce the blank that I had filled out that I would have them prosecuted.

Then I went to see the President of the First National Bank, who is Secretary of the Board of Equalization and told him about my blank not being produced. He told me to offer the collector the amount that I had the blank filled out with and if they would not accept it that I not pay them anything. The next morning I called at the collector's office and he told me that the assessor had just handed him the blank that I had made out and showed it to me and drew attention that the figures being scratched and made out for $1750.

I told him that I had it filled out for $1500 and no more so he told me that he would see the District Attorney and have his advice about the matter. I told him that the District attorney was just as bad as the assessor. Mr. Lopez said that he would write to you as soon as he consulted with the attorney. My opinion is that it would not be worth while going to court over the figures being changed should he not take off the $250.

McNulty & Friends
Dialogs On Indians
1904 - 1907

McNulty to Parker, January 3, 1906

...as I have had some pretty bad struggles with the Indians. The 2nd of the last month, I went towards the Castilian with a shot gun and three dogs to drive the Indians off but seven of them stood up with rifles and told me to cover my damn back. So I returned but when I got home I opened on them with a rifle at 100 yards. So you must know that the danger here by myself. I have notified all parties in Santa Fe that is in charge of the Indians here, but they are no good. The Governor's brother has written to Washington about my trouble with the Indians but there, it will be "the poor Indian".

McNulty to Abbott, March 13, 1907

I am writing to you these few lines to inform you again of the damage that has been and is being done by the Santo Domingo Indians on the American Turquoise Company property. When the Indians got through sorting the dump over then they broke the hinges and the lock of the two inch plank door that covered the mine and have done much work in the mine and have taken out several hundred dollars worth of stone and carried it away. I have nailed the planks over the shaft several times. Still they come at night and break it open again, and do their work and steal at night.

I caught three of them one time and when I demanded them to give up the turquoise that they had stolen they wanted me to fight them; but of course, I did not want to shoot them so I had to let them go. They generally have one watching while the others are doing the work in the mine. Now, Mr. Abbott if you cannot do something to keep them away from here and let me know to this effect within a week, I will be compelled to see the Governor and have him send the mounted police out here and arrest them. I regret having to take any severe steps, but something must be done to protect myself and the property.

McNulty to Parker, July 1, 1907

I don't like to be always writing to you about the trouble I am having with the Indians, but they are getting so troublesome that something must be done to keep them away from here. A week after the men had got through with the assessment work,

> *1907*
> *Aug 2nd New door on Castillian*
> *Broke it open Indians night of the 5th*
> *Hasp broke on the night of 7th*
> *Broke open on night of the 11th*
> *Broke open night of the 12th*
> *night of the 14th*
> *Mounted Police 15th and 16th*
> *Indians broke door on night of the 29th*
> *" " " " " night of 30 and 31st*
> *Sept Indians 1st, 2nd, 3rd, 4th, 5th, 6 - 7th*

McNulty kept notes on every event, large or small. Here he catalogs 17 break-ins over a 38-day period

the Indians came at night time and broke the lock and hinges off the double door I had on the Castilian mine and went into it. At the risk of my life, I went down into the mine and found they had a scaffold built to climb up on to where they could pick out some green stone. It is a dangerous shaft to go down into as the timbers are partly rotten, still they go down at the risk of their own lives. As they broke the door, I have been nailing the planks solid on the top and still they come repeatedly at night time and take off the planks.

 They generally come several together so that some can watch on top while the others are inside. I have been there many times until dark to see if I could catch them; but they manage to hide themselves and watch me and when I go there early the next morning, I have found the mine had been opened and this last two weeks they have been three times and got into the mine, although I have nailed it solid each time. I have notified the Indian attorney and also have told the Captain of the Mounted Police, and he wants me to get a warrant for them, but I do not know their names and have not caught them in the mine, but I know they go there.

The only suggestion I can make to you is to let me engage the Mounted Police to watch and capture them when they get into the mine. I cannot capture them myself as there must be several of them that come to do the work. I don't think that we would have to pay much for the Mounted Police as they are paid by the territory. ...I have to get the warrant made out for ficlitious names as I do not know their names. If we do capture them it is a penitentiary offense. ...I do wish that you would give me permission to put on one or two men to do the assessment work soon as I want to have it done for four claims in the one tunnel which will be to the best advantage to the property. ....besides when the men are working we would have a better chance to capture the Indians at night. ...the Indians coming for five nights in secession, breaking into the mine, I was compelled to go to Santa Fe on the 15th inst and have the Mounted Police come out here.

I had a talk with the new Governor [Curry] and he said he wanted to protect life and property. He advised me to see the District Attorney [Mr. Gorntner], Mr. Abbott, attorney for the Indians, and also the Indian Agent and have them all to meet together in his office in the afternoon. So I managed to see all of them and made arrangements for them to meet me at the Governor's office at 8 p.m. After consultation, they all agreed to have the Mounted Police sent out and the Governor gave orders to the Captain of the Mounted Police. He and one of his men followed me out the same evening and stayed at my house for two days and nights. On the night of the 15th inst. the two police and the man there is working hid themselves near the mine but no Indians came that night. On the night of the 16th

THE AMERICAN TURQUOISE COMPANY,
52 WALL STREET,
NEW YORK.

May 10th, 1904.

J. P. McNulty, Esq., Supt.,
 Cerrillos, N. M.

Dear Sir:—

I enclose a letter from Mrs. Cordelia S. Kay in which she says that we are throwing our ore on her ground, claiming that her property is next to ours. Does she mean that she owns property near the Castillian Group, or is she under the impression that we own mines in Mineral Park, which I always understood belonged to Doty.

Please let me hear from you and oblige,

Yours very truly,

President.

(Enc.)

Mining could be a confusing business, as this letter shows. A lady in Arizona mistook the mining near her claim as the work of the American Turquoise Company. The company possessed no mines in Arizona and suspected that Doty was the owner of the mines in question.

the three went out watching again and about 11 o'clock the Captain spoke to one of the men, when all at once they heard someone whistle and the man working here saw Indians running from behind a bush.

So the Captain made up his mind that the whistle

was a signal given by the Indian hiding behind the bush to the other Indians to go back and they got away without being caught. The next morning we all went out and traced their tracks after which the Mounted Police returned to Santa Fe. They gave me orders that if the Indians came again for me to telegraph them from Cerrillos and they would come out.

Matthews to McNulty, September 13, 1907

We wrote Mr. George Curry, Governor of New Mexico, in regard to the Indian raids, and received a letter from him under date of August 31st, in which he states that he will be very glad indeed to take whatever steps may be deemed proper to protect our property and that he had sent the Captain of Mounted Police force to the mines to make an investigation and to render you any assistance necessary. We trust that this will put a quietus on the trouble you have been experiencing, but if in the future you should have any further difficulty, please let us know, in order that any steps which might be necessary to take can be proceeded with.

McNulty to Parker, September 14, 1907

Now in regards to the Indians, they are giving me lots of trouble and ruining the Castilian property. Inside the mine there is likely to be a cave in at any time. For two weeks they have been in the mine every night, until this last three nights. I sent two telegrams to the Mounted Police during the two weeks but they did not come out until I went to Santa Fe last Monday. Then two of the police came out on Tuesday night, but the Indians did not show up that night so the Police went home the next morning and claimed that they are under too much expense in hiring a conveyance to come out here. I intend to inform the Governor what the Mounted Police said about their expenses, although they are receiving their salary from the Territory.

McNulty & Friends
Dialogs On Mining
1904 - 1907

McNulty to Parker, August 3, 1904

 I am progressing very nicely with the assessment work. I have started an open cut for a tunnel at the side line of the Gem claim, to go under the dump at No. 2 shaft, which I showed you when you were here. I intend to do the assessment work in this tunnel for three claims, the Gem, Muniz, and Morning Star as they are running parallel with one another, and will also improve the property. This will give me a chance of getting nearer the shaft where I hope to get stone. When I reach the shaft, I will be about 40 feet under the surface where the Spaniards left off working.

Matthews to McNulty, December 17, 1904

 We trust you have been able to complete the assessment work before this, I presume there will, therefore, be no necessity of employing any help until you receive instructions to do so.

McNulty & Friends
Dialogs On Personal Matters
1904 - 1907

Matthews to Fannie McNulty, July 3, 1905

 We beg to acknowledge receipt of your letter of the 28th ult., addressed to Mr. R.A. Parker, who is absent from the city at this time, and regret exceedingly to hear of the trouble that has overtaken your father, which we hope is not as serious as might appear.

P.S. You cannot expect me to address you as my dear Husband after such cruelty & injustice & the false report you & others your Daughter have given to others & Dr. Gordon about me.
Your Lawful Wife
Emma J. P. McNulty.

Las Vegas Asylum
Las Vegas,
New Mexico.
July 21st 1905

James P. McNulty:—
Los Cerrillos,
New Mexico.

As you have deceived every one about my sickness in order to disguise your past cruelty to me; when you have been under the influence of adulterated liquor, and Absinthe, also that disgusting stuff you bought in Santa Fe from that Saloon Keeper in Judge Laughlin's building, called "Invigorating Tonic", with the picture of a naked woman on it, to be taken to make you passionate; because you

James P. McNulty (Superintendent)
Los Cerrillos,
New Mexico.

Emma's first letters in 1905 were filled with anger although her writing showed a calmness and attention to accurate penmanship.

If Mr. McNulty's son is at liberty to take charge of the property at Cerrillos while his father is indisposed, we would like to have him do so. Kindly let us know by return mail if he will do this, as we feel at the present time someone should be there to protect the property against any trespassers. We are also very sorry to hear of Mrs. McNulty's illness, and trust she will soon be on the road to speedy recovery.

McNulty to Parker, July 8, 1905

I went to Las Vegas to inquire about the grant case and on my return on the twelfth, I found my wife to be unbalanced or as I might say deranged. I agreed with her in everything for that week. The following week I was obliged to take her to the Sanitarium in Santa Fe which cost me about eighty dollars paid in advance. They kept her for two weeks and on July fourth I was compelled to take her to the asylum at Las Vegas where I had to pay in advance the amount of ninety dollars. No one was allowed to see her after she entered the institution. I fear she will never recover.

Emma to McNulty, July 21, 1905

As you have deceived every one about my sickness in order to disguise your past cruelty to me, when you have been under the influence of adulterated liquor and absinthe, also that disgusting stuff you bought in Santa Fe from that saloon keeper in Judge Laughlin's building, called "Invigorating Tonic," with the picture of a naked woman on it to be taken to make you passionate; because you have almost lost your manhood vitality. ...You drank, gambled, and took absinthe and "Invigorating Tonic" very often, about every month or two, and sometimes you would keep sober for three months at a time. ...Before you came to Las Vegas ...you and I had some wonderful, spiritual knowledge and experience, and you were guided where to work on your property for coal, water, turquoise, gold, copper, lead, and a hidden treasure.

Emma to McNulty, August 2, 1905

I have prayed earnestly that Almighty God would teach me how to forgive your cruelty and unkindness to me ...and also Fanny for interfering and holding my body firm, when I was so weak and sick and prevented me from going out of my house. ...When I tried to get out of the buggy [on the way to Santa Fe], the only word you said to me in the buggy was that you wanted to find a doctor on the road. The only way that I can try to forget Fannie's interfering is by prayer and giving away everything that she has made for me, or even given to me.

Emma to McNulty, August 15, 1905

On account of your repeated cruelty to me I have lost every confidence in you ...and Fannie not holding me down and interfering with me like she did on the 18th June when Baby was dying, such cruelty & unkindness I never can forget and how you went to Santa Fe three days after Baby was born and stayed two days on a drunken spree and I was so sick. ...After Baby was buried you left me all alone and remained in Cerrillos nearly two days on another drunken spree. ...Do you remember how you frightened me a few months before Baby was born and how he always threw his head back and his little arms up? This was caused by the fright you gave me, and the picture I drew by automatic drawing represented the way poor Baby always did. ...I will ask the Court to give you a divorce.

Emma to McNulty, January 20, 1906

I write these few lines to let you know that Dr. Lucus came today to dress my ear and he said that it is doing nicely and it will be perfectly well in six weeks from the time he operated on it Jan. 2nd. He said that Miss Payson or the attendants would be able to dress it for me soon. He is very kind and does not hesitate to tell me the truth and answer any question I ask him for which quality he is very much to be admired.

Whether I have to remain here four weeks longer or not rests entirely with yourself as you have it in your power to either take me out of here or to remove me to a more congenial place. It is very hard and trying for a convalescent patient to be so closely confined among Insane and partially insane people. ...One has to try to be contented in here, but as for being happy ...is a very trying ordeal and quite out of the question. After Dr. Lucus has discharged me, it would be quite an easy matter for you to take me out of here; unless you are still of the opinion and believe me to be Insane. ...if you believe me to be sane and in mind perfectly normal, why keep me in here longer than is necessary, or after my ear is healed? I get up at 5:15 a.m. and work from eight to ten hours every day, either crocheting or sewing, which becomes very dreary and monotonous, but I do it to keep my mind off myself and it gives me some pleasure to do for others. I have just finished crocheting a lovely shawl for my sister.

Dr. Tipton told me when he came from Santa Fe that he received a nice letter from you, I wished I was able to say that I had received a nice, encouraging satisfactory letter, and I that I was going to be taken out of here soon, but I have never had one yet, and it will be seven long dreary months since I have been here on the 4th of February. Am I to remain here for my 39th birthday because you refuse to take me out of here. ...All I can do is to pray that Almighty God will one day soften your heart and that he will give me grace and strength to bear my cross and disappointments until it shall please Him to release me from this unhappy existence when you yourself can do it if you like or care to. Still I wish you no harm, but that you may continue to be perfectly well, happy, and contented.

Parker to McNutly, April 30, 1906
```
     I  am  very  pleased  to  hear  that  the  health
of   your   wife  has  improved  and  that  she  is
now   home   with  you  again.   I  sincerely  hope
that  her  recovery  may  be  permanent  and  that
you  also  are  enjoying  good  health.
```

Tom DiLallo's store on Main Street near First in Cerrillos, is one of the places Emma accused McNulty of conducting gambling business.

Chapter 7
1908 - 1909

More Politics & Corruption

I can plainly see that I can get no protection from the county officers or territory...
                                        McNulty to Parker, November 23, 1908

WHO'S GOT THE TROUSERS?

Since the territorial officials, the sheriff and the governor, ignored his requests for protection from raiding Indians, McNulty had no illusions about the dangers he faced in 1908. Almost every night in November and December Pueblo Indians came to the mines, tore down the planks, doors, and locks protecting the Castilian mine and took what they could find. Always, by early morning they were gone, with the damage apparent to McNulty, but not to territorial officials. The Pueblos developed sophisticated techniques for getting into the mine. They cut the heads off thick screws, removed the hinges, then pried off the thick planks that McNulty had nailed down. One night they broke three heavy locks, but the locks had slowed their entry into the Castilian mine.

When McNulty entered the mine, he found scaffolding and ladders, which the Indians brought along with them, as well as multiple tools. The evidence left behind, including a torn pair of trousers, were of no interest to the authorities. In addition, he found an eyewit-

> REMEMBER♪♪
> **W. H. GOEBEL,**
> The Hardware Dealer,
> ❧❧TO-DAY.
>
> Jany. month 25th 1908
> the Indians broke in
> or got in to the Castillian
> mine 25 26 27 28 29 30 31st
> February month 1908
> up to the 10th they carried
> one lock away or through
> it away and broke an
> other lock had put on the
> door - and left it
>
> REMEMBER♪♪
> **W. H. GOEBEL,**
> The Hardware Dealer,
> ❧❧TO-DAY.
>
> February th
> 1 2 3 4 5 6 7 8 9 10.11.12
> 17 18 19 20.21.22.23.24.25. 29
> on the 25th I went in the
> mine and took all the
> tools they left in the
> mine 12 in all
>
> March 22
> 1st 7th 8.10.11.12 23.24.25.29.31.
> April
> 1st 2 3.4. 6.8
> may 10.11. 25.26

McNulty kept track of the Indian raids on the mines in his ever present memo books.

ness to the attacks, but that witness, too, was ignored, and of course, the witness hesitated to be identified for fear of retaliation. A witness accompanied the Indians to mines during the attack nights and said that he went along to protect McNulty's life. Of course, he also bought the stolen gems from the Indians.

Even McNulty's three big dogs could not find the Indians, especially when the wind blew from the wrong direction. The dogs, of course, were a threat to the Indians, as the dogs would scent them and raise the alarm. The six to twelve Indians who raided the mines, were of sufficient number to keep McNulty from directly approaching them. Most of the time he left his rifle inside since he didn't want bloodshed. Shots rang out many nights and kept his wife inside for fear of being hit. McNulty only shot to scare, not to kill.

In true detective fashion McNulty scouted around Cerrillos and found shop keepers and residents who had bought turquoise from Pueblos who had been at the mine. The ringleaders of the thefts

> Cerrillos,
> New Mexico.
> Feb 26th 1908.
>
> James Matthews Esq
> New York City.
> Dear Sir:—
>
> Your letter of the 19th inst, with check to pay my salary for the month of September 1907 has been received & many thanks for it, & enclosed you will please find receipts for same.
>
> The Indians are still coming a nights & working in the Cas-tillian mine. I traced the tracks of four Indians on the road yesterday going from the mine. Yesterday I went down into the mine & took a man with me & we tore down the ladder & scaffold the[y] they had fixed to stand on. It shows a large seam about ¼ inch thick of green turquoise, where they have been working. I took up twelve tools in all, chissels, file, hatchets & hammer, that they had left in the mine; but I expect they took their best tools with them, as they must have some sharp instrument to cut the heads of the nails off & raise the harp.
>
> I am anxiously looking forward to a letter with instructions what to do about this matter.
>
> Judge Pope told me last week that he thought the Judge of the Supreme Court would give the decision in the Grant lease this week, as the Court is now in session.

Emma took the dictation for this letter describing the scaffolding in the mine.

bragged openly about how they had recovered the turquoise, but they also laughed that old man McNulty, alone, couldn't stop them at night. McNulty even learned from a shop keeper that one Indian who had lost his trousers when the dog attacked him had arrived in Cerrillos the following morning, bought new trousers, and talked about the event.

From February onward, McNulty repeatedly asked Parker to offer a reward because the sheriff and Mounted Police worked only for rewards, even though their salaries came from the territorial government. McNulty figured that maybe the reason for the lack of attention to the attacks on private property was that most politicians wanted New Mexico to become a state, and news of Indian troubles or attacks on private property could derail the statehood effort. Politicians wanted to keep such news out of the papers.

One news story appearing in the Santa Fe *New Mexican* said

> New Mexican 7th of November 1908.
>
> Appeals To Governor Curry For Protection.
>
> Governor Curry was in receipt of a telegram this morning from J. P. McNulty, who resides at Turquesa, near Cerrillos in the southern part of this county, where he is in charge of the mines of the American Turquoise company, saying the Indians had attacked him & asking the governor to send the Mounted Police there to protect him. According to Mr. McNulty, the Indians fired several shots at him sometime last night. Governor Curry at once informed Sheriff Charles C Closson & ordered him to investigate the affair, thoroughly & if there was any foundation for Mr. McNulty's story to see that he was offered every protection. So far as could be learned, to-day nothing of the kind occurred there & it is believed that Mr. McNulty probably had a bad dream last night in which he imagined the Indians were after him.

This handwritten copy of the news story was part of the McNulty files.

McNulty's Indian raids were no more than bad dreams, and this infuriated McNulty.

The real event, described by McNulty, came nowhere near the story planted in the press. He referred to the event as "quite an exciting time." One of his dogs grabbed an Indian and tore his trousers off. The other dogs attacked, but the Indians drove them off with rocks. McNulty raced back to his house, grabbed his rifle and shot in the air. They immediately returned fire. When McNulty arrived in Cerrillos he sent a telegram to the sheriff to ask for an investigation, but no one came. Now that everyone knew the sheriff and the governor provided no protection, it became open season on McNulty and his wife at the mines.

He explained the dangers to the New York banker:

> So now you can see the danger of us being alone, should we get killed or wounded, we might lay here for several weeks before anyone would come around here to find out what was the matter...Should I happen to kill one of them then I would have to leave here at once as they would come back in force and do away with all of us.
>
> McNulty to Parker, November 8, 1908.

The banker responded, and informed McNulty that a letter to the Governor of New Mexico would take care of everything. If further trouble appeared on the horizon, McNulty should let the banker know immediately. Parker commented that the governor had promised an inquiry, but that McNulty had simply been frightened.

In private, Governor Curry agreed with McNulty that the news story was unfair, and the governor said he would talk to the sheriff about placing untrue stories in the newspaper. He said that he would ask the sheriff to correct the facts. But nothing ever came of that. And McNulty, one to never put all his eggs in one basket, had already written a correct rendition of the altercation at the mines, and he presented it to the editor of the *New Mexican*. Unfortunately, the editor, after a two hour consideration, decided not to run the correction, and as McNulty explained to Parker, "I think it was on account of politics."

SHENANIGANS

To add insult to injury, while Governor Curry visited Washington to drum up support for statehood, the acting governor of New Mexico wrote to Matthews that the government would not protect the mine property.

> Replying to your letter of the 19th instant, in which you state that your representative, Mr. McNulty, alleges that he is being troubled by Indians in and about Turquesa. I beg to inform you that both County and territorial peace officers have on different occasions investigated the situation, and are unable to secure tangible evidence on which to base arrests. I take this occasion to suggest that you appoint a competent guard to take care of your mine. The territory does not furnish permanent guards for private property, in fact, I know of no commonwealth in the union that does so.
> Nathan Jaffa, Acting Governor, territory of New Mexico, to Matthews, November 30, 1908.

McNulty listed the dates the Indians had visited the property and taken turquoise. He commented, "It seems to me that the company cares very little about the property when they don't give me power to offer a reward." McNulty again said he was of a mind to leave the property since it was too dangerous and the authorities chose not to stop the thieves.

McNulty connected the Indian incursions with the Sena case, as it was obvious to him they were all intended to drive him off the mines. The Sena parties managed delay after delay, so it had now been 18 months since the territorial Supreme Court had heard the case, and still no decision had been handed down. He figured that the Senas hoped the delays would convince the American Turquoise Company to sell out. After all, the long battle drove up costs, and the company would not welcome another long, expensive, lengthy battle. With the conniving of Solomon Luna, the case could drag on forever.

Finally, in 1908, it seemed the Sena land grant decision might be near — maybe. McNulty knew that sufficient shenanigans had gone on to warrant a federal inquiry, and he suggested that Parker look to the federal authorities for help. But McNulty knew if the decision went against the Senas, the case would probably be carried to the United States Supreme Court.

It had by now become evident to the American Turquoise Company that an array of politicians, lawyers, judges, and appointed officials had conspired to take the mines away from them.

AMERICAN TURQUOISE COMPANY,
52 WALL STREET,
NEW YORK.

May 14, 1908.

Mr. J. P. McNulty,
    Las Cerrillos,
        New Mexico.

Dear Mr. McNulty:-

    Your telegram of April 29th and letter of May 6th duly reached my hands. I am very sorry to say that we are rather short of funds at the present time and have been unavoidably obliged to delay sending you your money. Inasmuch, however, as we have paid you a good salary for several years now, and your work has not been of a hard character, I trust you will not feel it amiss, if I say that the tone of your last letter and your telegram were both a surprise to me.

    Whatever money is owing to you will be paid in due course, but the amounts put up by the stockholders have been depleted, but I expect to get some more money in the very near future, when you will receive remittances as before.

    I cannot understand why a decision on this appeal suit has not been handed down. There must be some local reason for it, as it is now going on eighteen months since the case was brought up for a final decision.

    I enclose check for fifty dollars ($50.00) on account, and, as stated above, I hope to be in a position to send you some more money soon. In the meantime, however, inasmuch as your expenses cannot have been as much as your salary, which, allow me to say, has been a very good one and is considerably more than you could have got from any other company, the short delay should not cause you any hardship.

    With best wishes, I am,

        Very truly yours,

                        President.

Encl.
G

This is one of many letters about the fund shortage at the ATC. Usually the company secretary, Matthews sent the letters, but this one was signed by Parker.

192 • Patricia McGraw

We are very much surprised and disappointed at the turn matters have taken in conjunction with our suit, as we had fully expected that the decision of the courts of New Mexico would be final.

McNulty to Matthews, October 15, 1908.

On the financial end, 1908 began with more or less good news. McNulty managed to get the tax assessment on the mines reduced, and his salary was paid up to September of 1907 — just five months behind. At least the company sent him his arrears checks more or less regularly.

McNulty received this telegram at the last minute and had to push forward with the assessment work to get it completed quickly.

By the end of the year the New Mexico tax assessor had again raised the assessments against the mine and charged the company for capital goods that did not exist. McNulty's original document listing the capital improvements on hand had been ignored, and the assessor had just arbitrarily attributed a steam engine to the American Turquoise Company, which raised the assessment value by $4500. Most likely, Mariano Sena had a hand in the redo of the assessment. In between the Indian raids and the trips to the assessor's office, McNulty figured out ways to get the assessment work going. He knew the law, and he took the time to write the company and remind them of the absolute necessity to complete assessment work. He cleverly pointed out that the work could be done on all four claims by careful planning. This would decrease the cost to the company.

[Handwritten lease document dated June 17, 1908 between J.P. McNulty and Mike Koury for a store building, Lot 1, Block 10, in the town of Cerrillos, County of Santa Fe, T. of N. Mex., at $10 per month payable in advance.]

Any extra money McNulty had went into buying real estate in Cerrillos. This is the agreement between McNulty and shop owner Mike Koury showing Koury paying $10 in advance for rent.

...the mining law says distinctly that there must be $100 worth of work or improvements done on each claim every year and the year ends on the 31st of December; otherwise it [the claim] is jumpable. But where claims are in a group joining each other the amount of expenditure can be done on the one claim providing it will benefit the other claims. That is the reason why I have been urging you to start the work sooner in order to do all the work in the tunnel as it would benefit the property.

McNulty to Parker, October 16, 1908.

It wasn't until December 8 that Parker went ahead and gave the okay to do the work to keep the claim. He had waited, optimistic that the Sena case decision would come down and he would be able to patent the claim.

Still, even at that late hour, McNulty managed to pull off most of the assessment work: the Muñiz tunnel was extended by 15 feet; the Castilian shaft and tunnel gained an additional 14 feet; and the Gem open cut crossed 27 feet. The Morning Star tunnel, Sky Blue tunnel, and Agnes P tunnel were extended by more than 12 feet, the latter being completed in January, February and March of 1909. The properties' value had been improved, and they were protected against claim jumpers.

INDIAN RAIDS

For McNulty, 1909 was one year that he could have done without. In between the Indian raids, the gunfire, threats of death, legal maneuvering, and politics, McNulty had to complete the mining work required by law. Top that off with a reluctance on the part of the company to pay for assessment work, and the year shaped up as trouble.

His days filled with detective work, trips to Santa Fe and meetings with elected officials who tried mightily to keep any news of Indian raids out of the newspapers — or if a story appeared in the paper, some unknown person planted "facts" that minimized the impact of the raids or placed the blame for the raids directly on McNulty. Many political leaders and residents wanted New Mexico to become a state, and a territory out of control could derail that effort and slow development.

One of Sena's key financiers was Solomon Luna, the Republican Committee chairman and the chief architect of the New Mexico State Constitution. It was Luna's support and money, along with that of Sena, Purdy and others, that was the life blood of the protracted effort to wrest the control of the turquoise mines from the New Yorkers.

As the mine raids picked up, the Sena appeal headed to the United States Supreme Court, which, of course, drained more resources from the company. Cash flow problems and expenses associated with protecting the mine, dealing with territorial officials, and high tax assessments, all challenged the finances of the company.

Indian raids resumed on New Year's Eve and brought out as many

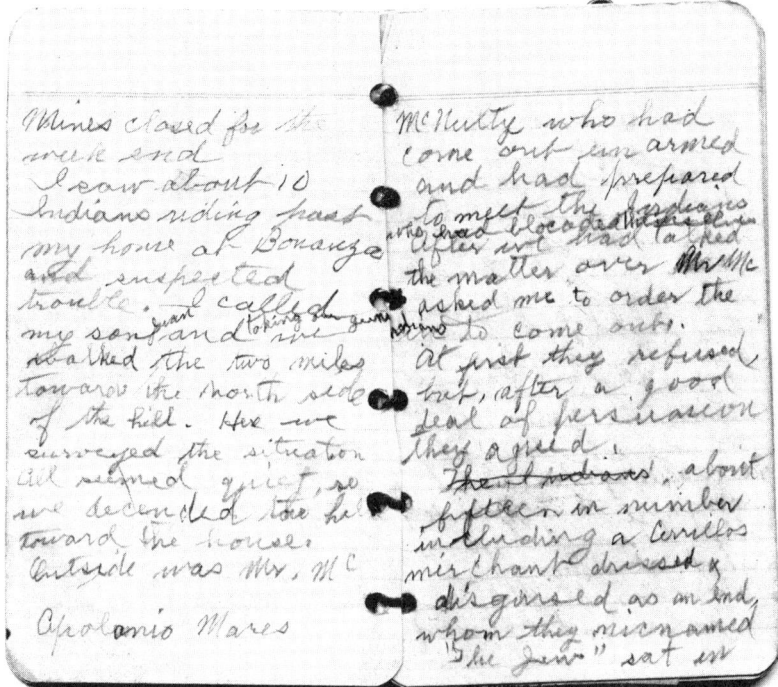

Right after the marauders shot at McNulty, his daughter Fannie took the statement from eyewitness Apolanio Mares, who later testified to this in court.

as 30 Santo Domingo Indians, who threatened McNulty and took turquoise from the mine. From 600 yards away McNulty, alone at first, watched the Indians enter the mine. When Apolanio Mares and his son, Juan, showed up to find out what was happening, McNulty asked Mares to tell the Indians that he had already sent a man to Cerrillos to bring out the deputy sheriff. Mares also asked them to leave the mines.

Mares spoke to the marauders, who said they would take McNulty away. They finally came out of the shaft to sit around a burning fire. Mares immediately recognized a merchant from Cerrillos — The Jew, Isidore Lazard — who had disguised himself as a Santo Domingo Indian. Mares realized that he himself, his son, McNulty, and McNulty's wife faced death. He hoped the man McNulty had sent to Cerrillos would arrive soon with the deputy, but the town lay eight miles away.

Under his breath Mares said to Juan, "Take a shot at him just above his head." It was the shot not fired. Indians hidden in the

> [Lease document image]
>
> LEASE. Printed and for sale by the New Mexican Printing Company, Santa Fe. N. M.
>
> **This Indenture,** Made this 9th day of September, in the year of our Lord nine hundred and 1908, between J. P. McNulty of the first part, and Isidore Lazard & Co of the second part.
>
> **Witnesseth,** That the said party of the first part for and in consideration of the covenants and agreements hereinafter mentioned to be kept and performed by the said party of the second part his executors and administrators, has demised and leased to the said party of the second part, all the premises, situate, lying and being in Cerrillos in the County of Santa Fe, and Territory of New Mexico, known and described as follows, to-wit: Store Building & Shelvings, Lot 2, Block 10, in the Town of Cerrillos, County of Santa Fe, Territory of N. Mexico
>
> **To Have and to Hold,** The above described premises, with the appurtenances, unto the said party of the second part, his executors, administrators and assigns from the 1st day of September, in the year of our Lord one thousand nine hundred and 8 for and during and until the 31st day of August, in the year of our Lord one thousand nine hundred and 9. And the said party of the second part, in consideration of the leasing of the premises aforesaid by the said party of the first part to the said party of the second part, do covenant and agree with the said party of the first part, his heirs, executors, administrators and assigns, to pay the said party of the first part, as rent for the said demised premises the sum of $10.00 per month, payable in advance, on the first of each month.

Isidore Lazard rented a store building from McNulty. Lazard also dressed up as an Indian and joined in the raids on the mines. He said later he had gone along to protect McNulty.

surrounding area appeared, waving guns and forced McNulty, Mares, and his son to run for the house. The Indians told McNulty he would die if anyone came out.

McNulty's wife and friends hid behind the thick adobe walls of the house and waited for the daylight, which usually signalled the Indians' retreat. Daylight made it easier to recognize the assailants, and apparently they had no wish to be seen. Then, McNulty raced to Cerrillos and sent a telegram to the American Turquoise Company.

Not one to wait for the next attack or to even wait for the sheriff to arrive, McNulty took his witnesses to the territorial governor. The sheriff also attended that meeting. Governor Curry assured McNulty that protection would be provided. It became clear to McNulty that Curry tried to backtrack on past news reports that downplayed the danger of guarding the mines. Curry, in fact, stated that he had been misled by comments made by people who had not even witnessed the attack in November of the previous year. The sheriff said he didn't know who had published the false reports in the local papers. He blamed the falsehoods on the newspaper editor.

But that was in the past. Now the authorities had to deal with a very real threat, a threat that could prove how dangerous New Mexico had become and its inability to protect citizens and residents from harm. The news media had a field day, embellishing the story until it verged on a massacre: six Indians had been killed by McNulty and the sheriff and his deputies had heroically stopped the massacre.

With his usual self-reliance and distrust of prompt action from the authorities, McNulty conducted his own investigation. He discovered that it was not a crime to enter a mine and take turquoise. He asked the political leaders to correct that oversight, and within two months the territorial legislature passed a law that made breaking, entering, and stealing from mines a burglary. But as it was now, the Indians could only be charged with trespassing and threatening McNulty.

Lazard said he would help McNulty find the perpretrators of the crimes, and of course, he expected a big reward, which McNulty himself had agreed to pay upon convictions being passed down in court. For McNulty, the money was well spent if it protected him from further troubles.

Mares and Lazard pointed out the Indians who visited the mines and threatened McNulty, and the sheriff made three arrests. But when the grand jury convened only one suspect present was the correct one. The others answered

Isidore Lazard rented his shop from McNulty, who had invested money in real estate in Cerrillos. Lazard also accompanied the Pueblo Indians on their raids to the mine. Although Lazard said he dressed as an Indian and participated in the raids, he said he really joined them to protect McNulty.

198 • Patricia McGraw

to the names Lazard had given, but they were not the Indians who had committed the trespassing. With one person indicted and convicted, McNulty had no choice but to wait for the others to be arrested. The stalling game started. For months the sheriff and the district attorney declined to deal with the warrants.

Finally, at McNulty's insistence, a meeting between the Indian agent, the district attorney, and the chief of Santo Domingo was convened. Immediately following that meeting Santo Domingo Indians broke into the mines, on that night and the next one, too.

By December Parker felt sure that acting governor Jaffa would take action to "put a stop to the raids..." and McNulty could then rest easy. That same month Parker said that the American Turquoise

New York, January 8, 1909

J. P. McNulty, Esq.,
    Cerrillos, New Mexico.

My dear Mr. McNulty:

    Your letter of the 2nd inst., came duly to hand and on reading same I was very much gratified to learn the Governor of New Mexico had taken matters in hand looking to the security of yourselves and the company's property. Shortly afterwards, however, I read a dispatch in the newspapers here, as from Santa Fe, under date of 6th inst., in which it was reported an attack had been made last Sunday night resulting in you and your men killing six indians and wounding several others. Furthermore the Rangers had captured three men. I trust this report is untrue and that I shall hear from you in a short time that you are receiving proper protection from the authorities. I cannot say how sorry I am that you should have been harassed and that your lives were in danger and it has caused me very much concern.

    Hoping to hear from you favorably in the course of a few days, I am

Yours very truly,

Parker sent this urgent message to McNulty. The banker, alarmed at news reports, was relieved to find out the media had lied about the story and no one had been shot.

Company's bank account had been depleted, and the price of turquoise did not make it profitable to operate the mines.

McNulty figured that the raids, staged to slow his assessment process for the mines, were geared to drive him off the property. As the end of the year rolled around, other miners watched with an eye towards jumping the claim. Everytime McNulty went to Cerrillos, people asked him if he intended to continue the mining, but he kept his plans secret.

As usual, Parker withheld permission to begin assessment work until the very end of the year, and, as usual, McNulty scrambled frantically to complete the work in time. And for a second year he pulled it off, and he prevented the mines from becoming fair game for any claim jumper who came along.

McNulty & Friends Dialogs On Mariano Sena & the Jose De Leyba Land Grant 1908 - 1909

McNulty to Matthews, February 26, 1908

> Judge Pope told me last week that he thought the Judge of the Supreme Court would give the decision in the grant case this week as the Court is now in session.

Parker to McNulty, May 14, 1908

> I cannot understand why a decision on this appeal suit has not been handed down. There must be some local reason for it, as it is now going on eighteen months since the case was brought up for a final decision.

McNulty to Parker, May 20, 1908

> In regards to the decision of the Sena Case not being handed down at the last term of court, it is my opinion that the Judge who is to give the decision is very friendly with Solomon Luna, who is put-

ting up the money for Mariano Sena to fight the company and that they are trying to keep the decision back to see if the company will compromise. ...At the hearing of the case a year ago last February, Chief Justice Mills and Judge Pope were barred from sitting on the case by Sena's attorney. Judge Parker acted as Chief Justice at that hearing on the case. I understand by good authority from one of the Judges that Judge Parker is the one to give the decision. If I had a say about this matter I would report the matter to the right authorities in Washington and have them come to town.

McNulty to Parker, September 3, 1908

Enclosed you will please find a clipping taken from the Santa Fe paper containing the Supreme Court's decision in the Grant Case which I have marked.

McNulty to Parker, October 6, 1908

I am very much surprised that your attorney or agent in the grant case did not inform you at the time that the case was argued in the Supreme Court a year ago last February as it was understood that day in court while I was there that the attorney for Mariano Sena would take the case to the Supreme Court of the United States if the decision went against them.

Matthews to McNulty, October 15, 1908

We are very much surprised and disappointed at the turn matters have taken in conjunction with our suit, as we had fully expected that the decision of the courts of New Mexico would be final.

McNulty's Letters on Mining Matters
1908

McNulty to Parker, April 4, 1900

    I have filled out a blank form for this year's taxes which includes as follows — 1 house, 2 small cabins, whim, wire rope, 2 buckets, bellows, anvil, tools and tram car for a total valuation of $500. I expect I will have some trouble with the County Commissioners and assessor as it is $125 less than it was last year but I think I will succeed in getting it taxed for that amount. ...I wish you would give me permission to put on a man or two to do the assessment work for this year as I would like to do the assessment for all of the claims in the tunnel if I have the time to do it in.

Parker to McNulty, May 14, 1908

    I am very sorry to say that we are rather short of funds at the present time and have been unavoidably obliged to delay sending you your money. ...as we have paid you a good salary for several years now, and your work has not been of a hard character, I trust you will not feel it amiss, if I say that the tone of your last letter and your telegram were both a surprise to me. ...I hope to be in a position to send you some more money soon. ...inasmuch as your expenses cannot have been as much as your salary, which, allow me to say, has been a very good one and is considerably more than you could have got from any other company. The short delay should not cause you any hardship.

McNulty to Parker, June 4, 1908

    In the Santa Fe paper of June 2nd, I see that the assessor and County Commissioners has raised the taxes on the property. I filled out the blank for $500 and they have raised it to $5,000 more than I had put it in at. You will see by the enclosed clipping that they have assessed for what we have not got.

Matthews to McNulty, June 19, 1906

...we would like very much to have you protest to the Assessors and County Commissioners against increasing the assessment on this company $4,500, as we feel this is unreasonable and entirely unwarranted upon the conditions at present existing. We trust you will spare no efforts in emphasizing the necessity for reducing this taxation to at least not more than the amount originally filed for, and hope, therefore, that you will be fully successful in this.

McNulty to Parker, July 2, 1908

The County Commissioners will meet on the 6th and the 8th inst. so I will be there to protest and do the best I can to have the taxes reduced to the amount I filled out on the blanks which is $500. They have raised it $4500 for ore on hand, $500 for a steam engine which would make it $5,500 in all. If they don't agree with my terms, I will take an appeal. ...I would send you the notice they have served on me about the taxes being raised, but I need it to present to the Territory Board of Equalization when they meet to let them see that they are assessing the Company for a steam engine and ore on hand which we have not got. I also intend to report matters to the attorney general as neither the assessor or county commissioners has ever been here to look at the property for twelve years; it is only imagination on their part to think that we have a steam engine and ore on hand.

McNulty to Parker, July 11, 1908

I was in Santa Fe... before the County Commissioners about having the taxes reduced and gained my points which you will see from the clipping taken from the paper that I have enclosed. I had quite a long argument with them and offered to pay their expenses if they would come out here and see for themselves as they said that they did not want to put any expense on the county but they finally submitted to the returns that I filled out which is $500.

Now, I think I did just as well as if an attorney was employed to plead for me.

Matthews to McNulty, July 16, 1908

We realize the impressive argument you must have set forth before the commissioners, and congratulate you upon your splendid success.

Matthews to McNulty, August 21, 1908

We note your request to commence the assessment work but we prefer for the present to await the decision of the court before proceeding with this work.

McNulty to Parker, October 7, 1908

I have been anxiously awaiting to hear from you in regards to having the assessment work started as it will take some time for me to be able to get men and material after I do hear from you as all the idle men in the district are being employed by a company that has started to pen up two lead mines between here to Cerrillos.

McNulty to Matthews, December 7, 1908

...as you did not heed my letter, it will be impossible to get the work done by the end of the year unless I have a big force of men to work and even so it will be very hard to get miners as they are all working doing other people's assessment. If you want to hold the property from being jumpable, you had better wire me at once.

McNulty & Friends
Dialogs On Indians
1908 - 1909

McNulty to Parker, February 3, 1908

I am having the same trouble with the Indians again, especially this last week, having been here three times. I put on a new lock and hasp on the door of the mine a month ago, and I put four long screws into the piece that holds the staple. They cut the heads off the screws and opened the door. I also put long nails in and they did them the same way. They have not broken the woodwork of the door lately, but they are expert in cutting of the heads of the screws and nails and getting into the Castilian mine, but when they have finished their work there, they will be coming to the big mine at the house. I would suggest that something must be done to prevent them from coming here. It being seven miles to Santa Fe from here, the mounted police say that they are under great expense to come out here. As I said before I would suggest to you that a reward be offered to them or the sheriff to have the Indians captured.

McNulty to Matthews, February 13, 1908

...they broke one lock and took it away, and the second one they broke the spring, but left it on the door so as to disguise it from me, and today I am putting on the third lock. I went to Santa Fe today... I saw the Captain of the mounted police and the Lieutenant and told them about the Indians, but they seem to pay no attention.

McNulty to Matthews, February 26, 1908

The Indians are still coming at night and working in the Castilian mine. I traced the tracks of four Indians on the road yesterday going from the mine. Yesterday I went down into the mine and took a man with me and we tore down the ladder and scaffold that they had fixed to stand on. It shows a large seam about 1/2 inch thick of green turquoise where they have been working. I took up twelve tools in all, chisels, file, hatchets and hammer, that they had left in the mine, but I expect they took their best tools with them as they must have some sharp instrument to cut the heads of the nails off and raise the hasp.

McNulty to Parker, November 4, 1908

I have not written you about the trouble I am having with the Indians for some time; but I assure you I am having it worse than I have ever had as they have been coming to the Muniz mine these last two months as often as twice a week and we are really worried not knowing what to do. They have broken into the mine each time, although we have three big dogs, they cannot scent them unless the wind is blowing in the right direction. I have gone up to the mine in the night with the dogs and gun several times but they manage to get away before I can get to the top. They seem to have given up coming to the Castilian mine and are very daring to come here.

I have heard that they have sold stone in Cerrillos and other places. It is equally as dangerous to go into the Muniz mine as it is into the Castilian for the timbers are nearly all rotten and where I had it planked at the first level are all caved in and fallen to the bottom. Very true that they cannot find but very little in the mine to the first level, but they are too daring coming so near the house and we being all alone away from any help in case of emergency.

McNulty to Parker, November 8, 1908

Since I last wrote you about the Indians, we have had quite an exciting time. When the Indians were here in the 2nd inst. the dogs had bitten one of the Indians and tore his trousers off him. He got a new pair in town to put on. Last Friday, the 6th, I tied one of the dogs at the mine, and the Indians came about 9 p.m., and had been either throwing rocks or something at the dog, and the other two *dogs who had bitten them on the 2nd seemed afraid to go up to them and looking out I seen two Indians on the dump, it being a very bright moonlight night so I got the rifle and shot in the air to scare them off.*

They immediately returned the fire by shooting at me three times in succession, the distance being less than 200 yards. But as God was with me, they missed their mark. We both saw the blaze from their gun when they fired, so I filled the rifle with cartridges and went around the hill of the mine, as I dare not go up to the top that night, there being so many places they could hide.

They did not open the door of the mine that night. I went to Cerrillos early the next morning and telephoned the sheriff and asked to please come out here with the blood hounds so as to scent the trail and to catch the Indians, who did the shooting. I also told him to notify the mounted police and I asked him when he would leave Santa Fe. He said in an hour's time, then he called up the deputy sheriff in Cerrillos through the telephone and told him the blood hounds were no good, and it would be no use for him to come out. When the deputy sheriff told me that, I sent a telegram to the governor telling him what I had telephoned to the sheriff and what the sheriff had said the deputy sheriff. I asked the Governor to also notify the mounted police, but none of them have come out and the Indians came again last night and broke into the mine.

note written by McNulty itemizing 23 days of raids

Nov. 2nd the dogs bit the Indians; Nov. 6th shot at me three times; Nov 7th, 11th, 14th, 15th, 18th, 19th, 20th, 24th, 25th, 26th: came again to the mines; 12 days. Dec. 2nd, 10th, 19th, 20th, 21st 24th, 26th 28th, 29th, 30th, 31st 11 days.

Parker to McNulty, November 19, 1908

```
     I can assure you that I regret exceedingly
the trouble you are having with the Indians
again.  I realize how necessary it is for
you to have protection, and I have again
```

written the Governor of New Mexico, making a very strong complaint and at the same time sending him copies of your letters, which will serve to emphasize the necessity of speedy action being taken to afford you full protection against the raiders. Let me know if you have any further annoyances from them, and I shall insist upon having our rights respected.

Parker to McNulty, November 27, 1908

I trust... matters are much better than you suppose and that the lives of yourself and Mrs. McNulty are not endangered by the Indians. Immediately on receipt of your letter. ...I had Mr. Matthews send an extract from it to the Governor New Mexico urging on him the necessity of having a thorough investigation made. In a previous letter we received from his excellency he had stated that inquiries had been instituted and it would appear that you had become frightened unwarrantably.

McNulty to Parker, November 23, 1908

I went to Cerrillos and received a telegram from the Governor in answer to mine, which I have enclosed you. As I told you in my last letter that no sheriff, mounted police or peace officer has come out here to investigate the matter and when I got the Saturday's New Mexican, I saw a piece in the paper which I will enclose for you to read and will also enclose you a copy of the piece I wrote in reply which I took with me to Santa Fe on the 10th inst, and gave it to Governor Curry to read. He said that he did not blame me to have it printed for the sheriff did not do right and that he would have a personal talk with the sheriff to have it corrected but nothing has been done in regards to it.

I went to the editor's office of the New Mexican to have the piece printed and he took it from me and told me to call in an hour or two which I did. He decided not to print it. He would not give me his reason for not doing it, but I think it was on account of politics. I had a talk with the governor and he told me that he and only a limited amount of officers and they were scattered all over the territory. They could not be under the expenses to stay out here to capture them and he also said that it was the Company's place to have armed guards to arrest the Indians whenever they came to the mines and that then he would send out the mounted police to take them into Santa Fe. He also said that if the legislation had provided more money, in order to have a larger force of officers that he would willingly send them out here to try to capture them.

It is understood in this territory that the sheriff will not come out or send deputies unless there is a large reward. Since I last wrote you, the Indians have come here on the 11th, 14th, 15, 18th, 19th, and 20th, and have worked in both of the mines each night. I am powerless to do anything but to guard the house. So you see there must be quite a few of them to be working in both of the mines at the same time and have a guard to watch on the outside.

I went to Santa Fe again on the 19th and had a talk with the governor and district attorney. The governor repeated the same again that he told me on the 10th. The district attorney said that he could do nothing unless I swore out a warrant and had them arrested. Then he would prosecute them to the full extent of the law. I told him I have the name of the Indian who shot at me on the 6th inst. which I got from a store keeper in Cerrillos whom an Indian told him about the shooting and were laughing about it. The attorney said that unless I could recognize the Indian he might deny it in court. I can plainly see that I get no protection from the county officers or the territory. ...as I am here without any protection or money, so I hope you will please attend to this matter.

McNulty to Parker, December 2, 1908

...it seems to me that you doubt the truthfulness of my letters to you the same way that the Governor has misrepresented my complaint to him by his reply to you saying he had stated that inquiries had been situated and it would appear that I had become frightened unwarrantably, which I can say to prove this he has stated to you falsely. I intend to meet him on the matter, when he returns from Washington.

I am perfectly convinced that owing to the false way that the governor has acted towards me and yourself that he is in sympathy with Solomon Luna (who is the National Republican Committee man) who is putting up the money for Mariano Sena to beat the grant case. My candid opinion is that we will never get any protection from the governor, sheriff, or mounted police as I have heard the sheriff and mounted police remark several times, that the Company had better give up the property if they cannot give a reward. My belief is that they are also in sympathy with the grantees.

I understood while in Santa Fe that the officials are keeping the Indian matter quiet for fear it would interfere with the passing of the Statehood Bill where they are now in Washington working to get it passed at the short session. If I had the means I would appeal myself to the authorities in Washington, and would suggest you should do it if you think it advisable. If the Pinkertons have an interest in this property, why not acquaint them of this trouble and have one of their men to come out here and investigate the matter as I will not stay out here without protection or money any longer than a reasonable length of time for you to decide what you intend to do.

The Indians broke into both of the mines on the 24th, 25th, 26th of November since I last wrote you and owing to a heavy snow storm they have not been since. I have also the names of two of the Indians that came to the mines on those dates from the storekeeper whom the Indians trade with and sell stone to, but he doesn't not want his name mentioned. They always ask him to accompany them to the mines but he does not want his name mentioned for fear of having any trouble with the Indians and his partner in business. This storekeeper is the man who gave me the name of the Indian

> Turquoise Mines.
> Cerrillos,
> Jan 1st 1909.
>
> R. A. Parker,
> 52 Wall Street,
> New York.
>
> We caught nine Indians in big mine last night. Had them closed in, and sent to Cerrillos for Deputy Sheriff. In the mean-time eleven more came and overpowered my men and let the nine Indians out of the mine. Fifteen rushed to the house with guns and swore to kill me if I came out, and would lay wait for me next night. Before Deputy arrived they all went down in the mine leaving ten Indians on top to guard. Before Deputy could get up to them they all ran away but he saw ten of them at the fire they had burning. Have men guarding and I and Deputy are going to Santa Fe to report to all authorities. Act immediately lives and property in danger.
>
> J P McNulty

Emma took one of many dictated letters discussing the danger of the two of them being on the mine alone without protection from any interested government agency in the territory.

who shot at me so I think if one of the Pinkertons men would come here we could capture all of the Indians that steal from here.

Matthews to McNulty, December 4, 1908
    Referring to the trouble with the Indians, beg to state we are today in receipt of a letter from the Governor of New Mexico and

hand you herewith for your information copy of same. It is very unfortunate that a situation of this kind should exist, but there appears to be no help for it under the circumstances.

McNulty to Matthews, December 7, 1908

...*as you did not heed my letter, it will be impossible to get the* [assessment] *work done by the end of the year unless I have a big force of men to work. ...The chances are the Indians may hold the property by force as nothing is being done to keep them away, but they have not been for a week owing to the very heavy snow storm. And another reason is many have been asking me why I am not having the assessment work done, which looks very suspicious.*

McNulty to Matthews, December 30, 1908

You say in your letter that "you trust we are free from further trouble with the Indians," and in reply will say that they have been here since I last wrote you on the 10th, 19th, 20th, 21st, 24th, 26th, 28th, 29th. I took men to the Castilian mine yesterday and took out two long ladders that the Indians had placed in there to work. Last night, the 29th, they came again and put in another long ladder and as we went over take it out, there was an Indian hidden in a hole near the dump as a spy.

The men chased him but he outran them. They were also in the big mine last night as we could see their tracks between the house and cabin. It seems to me that company cares very little about the property when they don't give me the power to offer a reward to have the Indians captured and sent to the penitentiary or have your agent as an attorney to give me instructions what to do.

McNulty to Parker, January 1, 1909 (Most likely sent as a telegram and not as a letter.)

We caught nine Indians in big mine last night. Had them closed in, and sent to Cerrillos for deputy sheriff. In the mean time, eleven more came and overpowered my men and let the nine Indians out of the mine. Fifteen rushed to the house with guns and swore to kill me if I came out, and would lay wait for me next night. ...Before deputy could get up to them, they all ran away but he saw ten of them at the fire they had burning. Have men guarding and I and deputy are going to Santa Fe to report to all authorities. Act immediately, lives and property in danger.

Parker to McNulty, January 2, 1909

I deeply regret this state of affairs and I have today instituted an investigation through private sources which I feel confident will put an end to these raids and restore peace and quietness to you.

McNulty to Parker, January 2, 1909

....after hearing what the deputy and myself had to say about the terrible time we had at the mine with the Indians, he [Governor Curry] acknowledged to me that he had been misinformed about the former shooting on November 6th by conflicting stories from different people. He then told me that he would give me all the protection that he could, but that he first wanted to have a consultation with the county sheriff, district attorney, and the attorney for the Indians, and told me to come at 2 p.m.

When I was called in the governor told me that he would send the mounted police with the sheriff to the mine if he needed them but the sheriff said he would attend to it himself with his deputy and the men I had at the mine. Then I said to the Governor, "You have written untruthfully to my company about the shooting on November 6th," and that I wanted matters straightened out.

He then replied, "Mr. McNulty this meeting will straighten matters aright and as I have before said, I was misinformed." The sheriff also said that he never gave anything to the papers to be published and that someone at the printing office must have done it. ...I...swore out a warrant and then

TIFFANY BLUE • 213

returned with the deputy... to Cerrillos. ...But before leaving Cerrillos, I had a talk with the storekeeper, whom I have written to you about, giving me information at different times when the Indians were coming up here. He acknowledged that he was with the Indians in the mine that night and that there were thirty Indians instead of twenty and nearly every one was armed and that he would give me all of their names that he knew.

...the sheriff and his deputies... drove out from Santa Fe... but when they reached here there were no Indians. We talked matters over and I gave him all the information I had from the storekeeper and he said that was all he needed to make the arrest. ...he [the storekeeper] gave the same information to the Sheriff and several of the Indian names, but he did not want to go with the sheriff to identify the men so the sheriff took one of my men who was deputized and said he could recognize most of the Indians and the one who threatened to kill me and said he had shot at me three times before and this time he would kill me if I came up to the mine.

The storekeeper told the sheriff and myself the reason that he came with the Indians was that they told him that they were going to tie me with ropes and put me away some distance off from the property and leave me there. He wanted to come with them so as to inform me but they would not let him come near the house. This information to my estimation is doubtful but nevertheless, I told him that I would not prosecute him if he would turn state's evidence in court. And another reason one of the Indians told one of my men that he was with them and in the mine and that it was also reported in Cerrillos before I returned from Santa Fe.

Dictated statement by Apolanio Mares

I saw about 10 Indians riding past my house at Bonanza and suspected trouble. I called my son, Juan, and taking my gun, we walked the two miles towards the north side of the hill. Here we surveyed the situation. All seemed quiet, so we descended the hill toward the house. Outside was Mr. Mc.

INDIANS BATTLE FOR MINE WHICH ANCESTORS OWNED

New Mexico Authorities Arrest Reds After Rangers Prevent Massacre.

Santa Fe, N. M., Jan. 6.—Repeated attempts to murder John P. McNulty and his wife in charge of the mines of the American Turquoise company owned by the Tiffanys of New York, has resulted in the arrest of three Indians of the Santo Domingo pueblo. The Indians were taken into custody by Sheriff C. C. Closson of this county yesterday, and brought to Santa Fe and lodged in the county jail.

At various times for several months past Indians from this pueblo have fired upon the mine headquarters, fourteen miles south of Santa Fe, at night. Recently McNulty appealed to Governor Curry for protection and a detail of rangers was sent to the mine. This had a quieting effect for a time.

A few nights ago a band of about fifty Indians made an attack on the mine, but McNulty and several Mexicans stood their ground until daylight came, when the Indians fled after they had broken into the mine and robbed it of considerable valuable ore.

The Indians worked these mines years ago, before white people gained possession of them, and they do not seem to understand that they now have no right to them.

The Indians arrested will be prosecuted for trespass. In the meantime a special guard has been placed at the mine to prevent further violence, as the arrest of the three Indians has further aroused the hostility of the other members of the tribe. McNulty declares that had the Indians been able to gain possession of the mine headquarters, they would have murdered him, his family and Mexican employes. They were heavily armed and bombarded the place at intervals during the night.

The Denver Post carried inaccurate articles about the raids and mines. Many times, McNulty had to correct stories carried locally as well since the papers of the time sensationalized almost every raid.

McNulty who had come out unarmed and had prepared to meet the Indians who had blockaded in the mine. After we had talked the matter over, Mr. Mc asked me to order the Indians to come out. At first they refused, but after a good deal of persuasion, they agreed. About fifteen in number including a Cerrillos merchant dressed and disguised as an Indian whom they nicknamed "The Jew" sat in a circle to an open shaft. Their spokesman demanded that I turn Mr. Mc over to them. I tried to reason with him but he said they would take him any way. I said, "You take him over my dead body." Just then I recognized The Jew. I told my son to look and see if he could recognize the man. He did. I said, "Take a shot at him just above his head." Juan did not need to.

McNulty to Parker, January 7, 1909

....the sheriff and deputies and the one I sent with him made three arrests and took the Indians to Santa Fe on Sunday night the 3rd. I went to Cerrillos on the

4th and telephoned to the sheriff what I should do. He told me to come to Santa Fe on the night train with my witness, So I took Apolanio Mares and the storekeeper (Isidore Lazard) with me to identify the Indians. ...when the case was called my witness could only identify one of the Indians.

...the storekeeper gave me the name of the Indian who shot at me on the 4 of November and who threatened to kill me on the 31st December. He has not been arrested, another Indian, of the same name, was given in his place. Before leaving Santa Fe, the district attorney and myself had a talk about making more arrests and he said that if the storekeeper would give all of their names or could identify those that were there on the 31st of December that he would do his utmost to have them all arrested, especially the one who shot before and threatened to take my life that night. ...the Indian agent abused my witness, the storekeeper, shamefully, for giving such damaging evidence against the Indians. ...In regards to the laws of New Mexico, there is nothing in the statutes to prosecute any person from breaking into a mine, breaking locks, hinges or doors on a mine, or mining property, so the only complaints I could bring against them was the trespass and stealing and threatening me.

Parker to McNulty, January 8, 1909

I was very much gratified to learn the governor of New Mexico had taken matters in hand looking to the security of yourselves and the company's property. Shortly afterwards, however, I read a dispatch in the newspapers here, as from Santa Fe, under date of 6th inst., in which it was reported an attack had been made last Sunday night resulting in you and your men killing six Indians and wounding several others. ...Furthermore the Rangers had captured three men. I trust this report is untrue and that I shall hear from you in a short time that you are receiving proper protection from the authorities. I cannot say how sorry I am that you should have been harassed and that your lives were in danger and it has caused me very much concern.

McNulty to Parker, January 14, 1909

I... regret very much to hear that such untruthful reports have been sent from Santa Fe to the newspapers about myself and men killing six Indians etc., as no shooting has been done and no Indians have been seen around here since they have been arrested. How such a report was given to the papers I do not know unless it was some spite work to injure me and the company as the Santa Fe papers have not even printed the [previous] *attack the Indians made on the mine and the house and threatening our lives.*

They seem to be keeping everything secret and I have not heard that it was printed in any paper in the territory. Mr. Carver, the detective from Denver called here about ten minutes on Monday and I directed him to call on the storekeeper, [Isidore Lazard] *who was in the mine that night. ...I have on several occasions doubted him as being implicated with the Indians, but as he was giving me the names of the Indians and the nights they were coming to the mine. ...I had to give him the benefit of the doubt. ...The Indians did not come to the Muniz mine for several years until after The Jew and his partner located in Cerrillos. They came here from* [Santo] *Domingo. ... and he can talk their language well. ...I told Mr. Carver about the Indian's attorney,* [Mr. Abbott] *being the Father of the district attorney and they practice law together. ...I thought it advisable to have another attorney to assist in the case. ...Should the Indians not come any more to the mines, my life is still in danger, by the threats they have made and they may lay in ambush and shoot at me at any time. Still I am not scared, but I would not want to get ambushed.*

McNulty to Parker, February 1, 1909

The Indian who was confined in jail is out on bond. The governor of the tribe furnished it.

TIFFANY BLUE • 217

McNulty to A.E. Carver, Pinkerton Detective Agency, February 24, 1909

Mr Charles Siringo called to see me last Friday, and not being at home, I went to Santa Fe to meet him on the 22nd; he informed me that he was instructed by the Pinkerton's Agency in Denver to assist me in the Indian case. I have known Mr. Siringo for about twelve years and never knew before that he was on the force. His not showing his card or letter of introduction from your agency... would like very much to hear from you if he is the right party sent by your agency?

Parker to McNulty, January 22, 1909

I am very happy to learn of the lack of foundation for the lurid reports I read in the newspaper and am very glad to see that you have no Indian blood on your hands. ...It looks to me as if that storekeeper has been playing fast and loose, and if there is any way by which we could give him his just deserts, I would like to see it done.

McNulty to Parker, February 25, 1909

I... had a talk with the district attorney about having a bill passed to punish anyone for breaking into a mine and stealing therefrom. He said he would make one out. Then I had a talk with the leaders of the council and House of Representatives and they said that they would try to have the bill pass at this session

McNulty to Parker, March 1, 1909

Mr. Abbott... set my case before the Grand Jury for trial March 10th. ...I learned that the Indian agent and the attorney for the Indians has told some people that they could beat me in court and that turquoise was not classed a mineral, but I will take some specimens in with me that will convince the court that it is mineral... please get an analysis of the turquoise from the Tiffany experts which I expect you can do and let me know the results as soon as possible that it will assist me if they fetch the matter up in court.

218 • Patricia McGraw

Matthews to McNulty, March 12, 1909

....we were pleased to hear of the progress you are making in regard to the prosecution of the Indians, and we sincerely hope that your efforts will be successful.

McNulty to Matthews, March 18, 1909

....by our testimony given the grand jury, there were four Indians indicted and they are to be arraigned on the 20th inst for them to plead either guilty or not guilty.

McNulty to Parker, April 2, 1909

The bill that I had introduced at the legislature has passed on the 15th of last month and became a law from the date that breaking into or entering a mine without permission is burglary.

McNulty to Parker, April 9, 1909

....the case came up for trial... When the Indians were called into court my witnesses saw at once that they did not answer to the names that were given at the grand jury, only the first one that was indicted, and he pleaded not guilty. The judge then set the case for 2 p.m. to be tried. When the case was called, the Indian withdrew his plea of not guilty and entered his plea of guilty and said that he was in the mine that night.

The judge gave him a great reprimand and said that if ever he or any of the Indians came near the mine again, they would be put in the penitentiary. For the offense he would fine him $100 and costs but for the present he would not sentence him until the others who were indicted be taken to court. The indictment for the others is for bombarding the house and threatening our lives. So I don't know when the Indians will be arrested. I believe The Jew is expected to go along with the officers to identify the Indians when they make the arrest as they give the wrong Indians for the names every time.

McNulty to Parker, September 2, 1909

The district court will convene on the 6th inst.

> Coyote
> New Mexico
> Oct 25th 1909
>
> To E. C. Abbott Esq.
> Santa Fe. N.M.
>
> Dear Sir:—
>
> After my Husband wrote you on the 13th inst. about the Indians, I visited a Mexican Family (Mrs. Nathan) at Bonanza about 2½ miles from the mine; & she told me that her Husband had seen the Indians @ the mine on the 11th inst, & tho two of the Indians came to the house, & tho one of the Indians with grey hair told her tho they were coming again & tho if Mr. McNulty came to the mine with a gun to order them away, tho some one from the Pueblo would lay in hiding & shoot him. When the Indian made the remark to kill Mr. McNulty she told the Indians tho it would not be right to take his life tho it was the Company's property & tho he is here to protect it. The Indian then replied

Emma dictated her discovery of a plot to kill McNulty to his daughter. Since the Pueblo Indian mentioned Mariano Sena, the McNultys thought this proved a direct connection between the pueblo and Sena.

and the sheriff has not made any effort as yet to arrest the three Indians he has warrants for; I have not rushed matters myself as long as they are keeping away from here. ...The district attorney's father who was the Indian's attorney sent in his resignation after we had the Indians indicted. ...Mr. Wilson has been appointed by the government to succeed him.

McNulty to Parker, October 2, 1909

...*nothing has been done this term of court* [about the warrants] *It seems to me that the sheriff does not want to act on the warrants so as to keep in with the Indian agent as the agent does not want to have the Indians arrested.*

McNulty to E.C. Abbott, October 13, 1909

The Indians were here last night and broke the shaft door open of the Castilian mine. They drew the nails out of the hasp and went into the mine and put up scaffolding to work upon to get at the turquoise. ...The Castilian mine is about 600 yards from the house so they have a good chance to escape before I could reach them. ...I write you this so you will please see to the warrants being served or have something else done so as to keep them away from here.

E.C. Abbott, district attorney, to McNulty, October 21, 1909

I have requested that the warrants against the Indians be placed in the hands of a deputy at your place so that the Indians may be brought in. I think it would be well for you to have your men deputized so as to capture the next Indians visiting your mines for the purpose of stealing turquoise. I hope that you can have the Indians identified so that you can have them arrested. It is my opinion that Lazard is more friendly towards the Indians than he is to you or he would have identified them while at Cerrillos. As he is the only one able to identify the Indians named and does not seem to care to do so, it will perhaps be necessary for us to commence all over again and capture the Indians that may come to the mine in the future. I would therefore lay quiet and not let the Indians know that I knew they were returning until

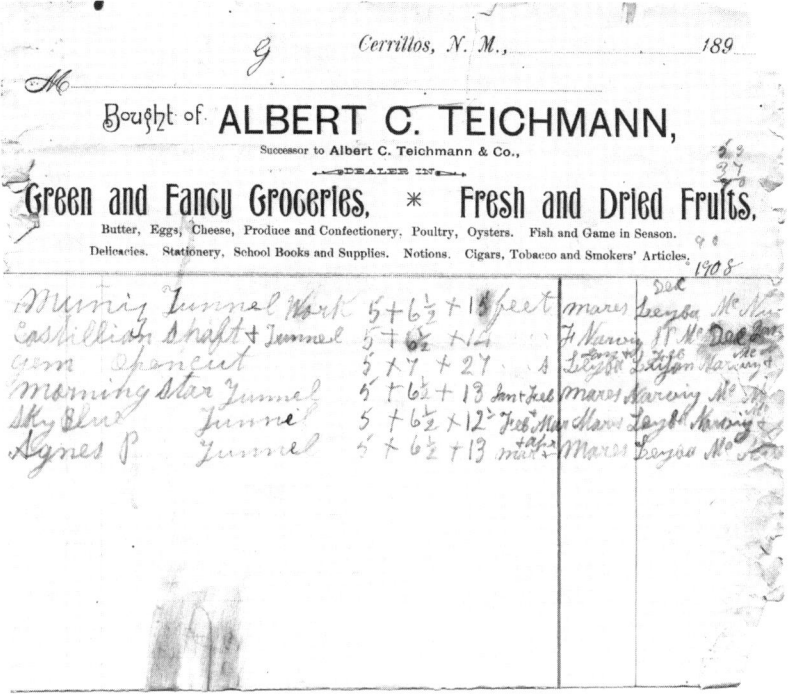

A ledger sheet from shopkeeper Albert C. Teichmann provided the paper for McNulty's records on assessment work.

you are prepared to capture them with sufficient force.

Emma McNulty to C.G. Abbott, October 25, 1909

I visited a Mexican family (Mrs. Navarez) at Bonanza about 2 1/4 miles from the mine. She told me that her husband had seen the Indians at the mine on the 11th inst. ...Two of the Indians came to the house and... one of the Indians with grey hair told her they were coming again and that if Mr. McNulty came to the mine with a gun to order them away, that some one from the Pueblo would lay in hiding and shoot him. When the Indian made the remark to kill Mr. McNulty she told the Indian that it would not be right to take his life that it was the Company's property and he is here to protect it. The Indian then replied that the property belonged to them and also to Mariano Sena.

222 • Patricia McGraw

McNulty to E.C. Abbott, October 25, 1909

I went to Albuquerque last week. ...I had a talk with Mr. Lazard abut the Indians and he said that if the warrants had been in Cerrillos when he was living there, that he could have had some of them arrested. ...he pledges himself willingly to go at any time with the sheriff to Santo Domingo Pueblo that he would identify to the sheriff the three Indians that the warrants are against if the Indian Chief will have all the tribe brought forward, but that the Chief might keep the guilty ones hidden as was done before as the one who did the shooting at the mine is the son of a former Indian Chief. Mr. Abbott, if there is not something done to make the Indians obey the law soon, I shall instruct my company in New York to take the matter up with the authorities at Washington. This action I have been holding back for fear it would interfere with statehood, ...my life is now again threatened by the Indians.

E.C. Abbot to McNulty, October 28, 1909

I have instructed the sheriff to have the warrants for the Indians placed in the hands of his deputy at Cerrillos with instructions to communicate with you. I have stated that you would assist by having Mr. Lazard come from Albuquerque and if necessary go with him to the Pueblo and identify the Indians. Please let me know whether the deputy communicates with you the fact that he has the warrants in his possession.

McNulty to Parker, November 4, 1909

...the district attorney does not want to have the Indians arrested.

McNulty to Parker, November 4, 1909

...the district attorney, sheriff and authorities do not want to take any active part to have the Indians arrested, but leave it all to me as you will see by their letters.

McNulty to Parker, December 1, 1909

I had a talk with the attorney and he told me that he had a talk with the Indian agent and they agreed to have the Indian Chief to come to Santa Fe which they did...the same day they held the conference and the day after the Indians did more digging and sorting on the Castilian dump, than they have done in previous trips, but did not go into the mine. I am mighty glad that Judge Mills is appointed governor as he is a friend of mine for many years and when he takes office I shall have a talk with him about the captain of the mounted police who tries to make out that the Indians do not come here.

Parker to McNulty, December 10, 1909

I have received word from the acting governor and also from attorney Wilson stating that they have taken up the matter with regard to the Indian trouble and they assure us that action will be taken to put a stop to the raids.

McNulty & Friends
Dialogs On Mining Matters
1908 - 1909

McNulty to Parker, April 4, 1908

I have filled out a blank form for this year's taxes which includes as follows — 1 house, 2 small cabins, whim, wire rope, 2 buckets, bellows, anvil, tools and tram car for a total valuation of $500. I expect I will have some trouble with the County Commissioners and assessor as it is $125 less than it was last year but I think I will succeed in getting it taxed for that amount. ...I wish you would give me permission to put on a man or two to do the assessment work for this year as I would like to do the *assessment for all of the claims in the tunnel if I have the time to do it in.*

Parker to McNulty, May 14, 1908

I am very sorry to say that we are rather short of funds at the present time and have been unavoidably obliged to delay sending you your money. ...as we have paid you a good salary for several years now, and your work has not been of a hard character, I trust you will not feel it amiss, if I say that the tone of your last letter and your telegram were both a surprise to me. ...I hope to be in a position to send you some more money soon. ...inasmuch as your expenses cannot have been as much as your salary, which, allow me to say, has been a very good one and is considerably more than you could have got from any other company, the short delay should not cause you any hardship.

McNulty to Parker, June 4, 1908

In the Santa Fe paper of June 2nd, I see that the assessor and County Commissioners has raised the taxes on the property. I filled out the blank for $500 and they have raised it to $5,000 more than I had put it in at. You will see by the enclosed clipping that they have assessed for what we have not got.

Matthews to McNulty, June 19, 1908

...we would like very much to have you protest to the Assessors and County Commissioners against increasing the assessment on this company $4,500, as we feel this is unreasonable and entirely unwarranted upon the conditions at present existing. We trust you will spare no efforts in emphasizing the necessity for reducing this taxation to at least not more than the amount originally filed for, and hope, therefore, that you will be fully successful in this.

McNulty to Parker, July 2, 1908

The County Commissioners will meet on the 6th

Bureau Of Pensions.

No 1. Yes. Present Wife Emma McNulty, maiden name Emma Hawley, Married Dec 18th 1898, by the Catholic Priest in Santa Fe N. M.)

No 3 No family.

No 4. Yes. My first Wife, Agnes Dunn married April 1873. in Saint Mary's Church Chicago Ill, who died August 1882 in Leadville Colorado, No 5 Three Children living by first Wife, Edward James Born the 9th day of February 1874 @ Pittston, Pa. Jennie Born October 31st 1876, Pa. Sarah, Agnes, Born the 15th day of April 1879 @ Central City, Colorado.

While I was @ Little Rock Arkansas in the Summer of 1866. I had the Ague with chills & also @ the time of the Epidemic of the Asiatic Cholera, I was sent to the Hospital with the Cholera & the medicine that was given me to the best of my knowledge sulivated my mouth

Once McNulty reached the age where he could request a government pension for his army work, he did so. The questions he answered tell the entire story of his life.

and the 8th inst. so I will be there to protest and do the best I can to have the taxes reduced to the amount I filled out on the blanks which is $500. They have raised it $4500 for ore on hand, $500 for a steam engine which would make it $5,500 in all. If they don't agree with my terms, I will take an appeal. ...I would send you the notice they have served on me about the taxes being raised, but I need it to present to the Territory Board of Equalization when they meet to let them see that they are assessing the Company for a steam engine and ore on hand which we have not got. I also intend to report matters to the attorney general as neither the assessor or county commissioners has ever been here to look at the property for twelve years; it is only imagination on their part to think that we have a steam engine and ore on hand.

McNulty to Parker, July 11, 1908

I was in Santa Fe...before the County Commissioners about having the taxes reduced and gained my points which you will see from the clipping taken from the paper that I have enclosed. I had quite a long argument with them and offered to pay their expenses if they would come out here and see for themselves as they said that they did not want to put any expense on the county but they finally submitted to the returns that I filled out which is $500. Now, I think I did just as well as if an attorney was employed to plead for me.

Matthews to McNulty, July 16, 1908

We realize the impressive argument you must have set forth before the commissioners, and congratulate you upon your splendid success.

Matthews to McNulty, August 21, 1908

We note your request to commence the assessment work but we prefer for the present to await the decision of the court before proceeding with this work.

McNulty to Parker, October 7, 1908

I have been anxiously awaiting to hear from you in regards to having the assessment work started as it will take some time for me to be able to get men and material after I do hear from you as all the idle men in the district are being employed by a company that has started to pen up two lead mines between here to Cerrillos.

McNulty to Matthews, December 7, 1908

...as you did not heed my letter, it will be impossible to get the work done by the end of the year unless I have a big force of men to work and even so it will be very hard to get miners as they are all working doing other people's assessment. If you want to hold the property from being jumpable, you had better wire me at once.

McNulty to Parker, February 25, 1909

In regard to the assessment work for last year, it will be done about the middle of next month and I would like very much to keep one or two miners to do the assessment for this year. By doing the assessment for this year I will be able to get the tunnel through to the big mine. In regards to the stoping, there could be none done until the tunnel was complete.

Parker to McNulty, March 12, 1909

...we have given the matter of assessment work for the coming year serious consideration, but have decided, in view of the present financial situation, not to do the coming year's assessment work until next fall.

McNulty to Matthews, March 18, 1909

I was glad to hear from you but very much am disappointed at not being allowed to keep at least one man on to do this year's assessment. ...I am going to keep my principal witness to work here until the case is tried as he might go a distance off or leave the territory to hunt up other work.

Parker to McNulty, March 23, 1909
> ...your suggestion as to keeping the principal witness to work on the assessment until the case is tried is satisfactory.

McNulty to Parker, April 2, 1909
> I am glad that I kept one man on (my witness). I kept him to work in the tunnel running to the No. 2 shaft and yesterday as we got to the left side of the shaft, we struck some good colors, which I will enclose you the largest stones. ...It looks very encouraging and I may strike some good stone by driving the tunnel further in the hill.

McNulty to Matthews, July 22, 1909
> I would like very much for you to please give me permission to put on two or three men by the first of September so as to have the assessment work finished by the end of the year and not be left in the lurch like I was for last year's assessment.

Matthews to McNulty, August 18, 1909
> Mr. Parker has considered your suggestion of having the assessment work done by the end of the year, but for obvious reasons he prefers that nothing should be done in the matter for the present.

Parker to McNulty, December 10, 1909
> In regard to the assessment work, I presume there is nothing to do but proceed with the work, although I would have been very much pleased if you could have done the work yourself without the employment of others as in that way it would have kept down the expenses which are already quite large in considering the fact that we are not selling any turquoise. However, I trust you will make the expenses as light as possible and let me know when you are through with the work. With regard to your salary will say that as I have written you on several occasions in the past, the company is not doing any business and is thereby dependent for support upon the private means of a few of

our principal stockholders. The long drawn out suits have been a severe drain upon these gentlemen and we have had to apply the funds obtained from them in several ways, and this has consequently interfered with sending your salary as promptly as we should like to have done. We would ask you to kindly bear with us for the present for your back salary, until we are in receipt of funds which will enable us to remit you in full.

230 • Patricia McGraw

The unlucky four, captured at the mines in December 1910. At the booking they identified themselves as Cochitis, Santo Domingo's neighbor and rival. Were they, or was that just to shift the blame?
New Mexico State Corrections Department Negative Nos. 2772, 2773, 2774, 2775 (all partials)

Chapter 8
1910 - 1911

It Is The Decision of This Court

It appears to me that the company has misdoubted my honest and truthful reports about the Indians stealing from the mines and coming so often to the mine, but a smart detective can find out who is telling the truth and where honor and justice belongs.

McNulty to Parker, December 21, 1910

NO TRESPASSING PENITENTIARY OFFENSE

Patents and Indian raids — two things that sum up the years of 1910 and 1911 in McNulty's life. If a patent arrived it meant that McNulty's assessment work would no longer need to be done, and the company would hold clear title to the mines. But each year the patents were not issued because of the pending land grant case. As October rolled around McNulty reminded the New Yorkers of the necessity of of performing the assessment labor, and at the last minute the bankers told McNulty to proceed. Unfortunately, Indian raids slowed the work and kept many of the miners away.

With his salary in 1910 a year or more in arrears, McNulty and his wife stayed on the job. The small sum from his rental properties in Cerrillos kept him in provisions and necessities. Although McNulty usually went without his salary, he made sure his workers received theirs as soon as possible. He even signed letters of credit for his miners, guaranteeing payment personally, when the company lagged behind. Of course, once word got out about the slow payment workers became even more scarce. Add to that the lack of accommodations at the mines and the dangerous raids, and mining never moved at more than a snail's crawl. Work also suffered when McNulty had to spend hours rounding up witnesses and dealing with authorities who didn't want to provide protection for residents of the area.

On many a moonlit night McNulty and Emma must have feared the worst — an aggressive attack that would take their lives. When he could hear that the trespassers had arrived, McNulty would leave Emma and the thick adobe walls of the house and confront the Indians and order them off the company property. He usually approached them unarmed, and those times when the situation seemed to be escalating he would rush back to his home and take cover. Even though the governor and the district attorney told him to shoot to kill, McNulty never considered it a real option. He knew bloodshed would beget bloodshed, and death would likely result in his death as well as that of his wife and any workers who happened to be nearby. He personally believed that legal remedies provided a better way to solve the trespassing problem, provided he could get the sheriff and territorial officials to do their jobs.

McNulty wrote, "It is certainly not an enviable position for me and my wife to be in, surrounded nearly every night by the Indians watching every move we make and threatening to take our lives and to get no protection from the company, territory, or the government."

McNulty kept track of almost all incidents of trespass with personal notes and a notebook. His notes for 1910 show: The American Turquoise mines — Indians went in the mines the following nights: September 12, 16, 20, 22, 24, 25 (I found claw hammer), 26, 28, October 2, 3, 5, 6, 7, 8, 9, 10, 22, 25, (Sheriff here on October 12 and 13) November 6, 10, 15, 19, 21, 22, 24, 25, 25 (in Castilian and sheriff here), 27, 28, 29, December 1, 2, 3, 4, 5, 7, 8, 11, 14, 16, 17 (caught by deputy sheriff in Castilian mine), 18 (Castilian mine), and 19. These dates coincided with McNulty's efforts to get the assessment work going.

For 1911: January, Tuesday, 17, Indians pried open the door on Castilian Mine; 17th, 18th, 24th in the mine, 25th; February 4th, March night of the 3rd, 4th, 5th and Indians stole drills; April some party or some one broke into the Castilian on the nights of 4th, 5th, 8th, 20th; May 12, 19, and 20th; 24th; June 3rd, 9th, 10th, 24th and blasted; July 11st, 14th, blast, 15th, 16th, 20th, 22nd, 29th. (April was the expected date for the United States Supreme Court to hand down its second decision on the Mariano Sena land grant case.)

McNulty made complaint after complaint and report after report. He wrote letter after letter. He posted signs stating "No Trespassing: Penitentiary Offense", and the raids continued. Even McNulty's advice to the sheriff went unheeded. He told the peace officer how and when to arrive at the mines so that the Indians would not see the officers coming. Instead, the officials arrived on moonlit nights with much fanfare and noise — any person on lookout could see them and give warning to his friends. Because of this lack of concern and lack of attention to detail, the Indians disappeared most of the time before the sheriff ever arrived. On top of that, McNulty noted that the Indians seemed to know when the sheriff or deputies were to appear, and they would not show up on that night.

Trip after trip to Santa Fe resulted in little or no help for the mine raids. Witnesses identified the men who had raided the mines — sometimes Cochiti Pueblo Indians, but most times Indians from Santo Domingo Pueblo. Even when the sheriff had warrants in hand the sheriff seemed unable to serve them and lacked the gumption to bring in the accused. And Isidore Lazard, "The Jew", who could identify the criminals, dragged his feet when asked to identify them. Finally, the territorial Governor Mills hinted that the sheriff Closson might lose his job if nothing happened soon. McNulty concluded that only officials in Washington could straighten things out in the territory, so he urged Parker to pursue contacts there. McNulty began to think of the Santa Fe politicians as a "gang."

"In regards to politics," McNulty commented, "I do not agree with him [the district attorney], for they have given us enough trouble and now I am working for the Progressives Republican Infusion with the Democrat Party to see to break up the gang in Santa Fe."

"New Mexico officials have never done anything to stop them [the Indian raids]," McNulty wrote.

A news article appeared in Los Angeles with a dateline in El Paso which described one of the raids.

Indians Seize Rich Tiffany Mine and Use Turquoise for Beads

Threaten Manager With Death, Then Gather Up Gems; Posse Now in Pursuit

EL PASO, Texas, Oct. 17.—Tiffany's turquoise mine in New Mexico is the scene of an Indian outbreak. The San Domingo tribe of Indians seized the valuable mine from which the Tiffany Company gets its supply of turquoise and mined enough of the stones to make beads and jewelry for their annual festival of thanksgiving. They threatened Manager J. P. McNulty with death if he interfered.

After doing a war dance at the mine, they placed a guard of sixteen braves at the mouth of the shaft and went into the mine, where they took all of the precious stones they wished. The red men escaped to the hills and are now being pursued by mounted Territorial police and deputy sheriffs.

The San Domingos claim the mine by right of possession from their tribal ancestors, who worked there before the advent of the white men in New Mexico. The mine is located fourteen miles from Santa Fe and is owned by the American Turquoise Company, a Tiffany corporation.

The news papers always picked up stories of Indian raids. Papers of the time rarely checked their sources, and at the end of this story is the statement that the American Turquoise Company was subsidiary of Tiffany of New York.

E.J, McNulty's son, weighed in on the lack of protection. He advised his dad to leave the company since the ATC didn't send money to hire more workers or even put up a reward. "You ought to set a trap with Giant Powder for them and blow them all the H...next time they come up."

McNulty ignored the advice. He worked through the legal system and expected political officials to do their part. He called the sheriff who failed to show when the Cochitis were on the premises. So on his own McNulty posted a reward, and he managed to arrange to have deputies at the mine one Sunday morning at 2:30 a.m. when some Cochitis, who had been working with some Santo Domingos, were finally captured. The reward had aroused the interest of the sheriff and deputies, and perhaps the territorial governor had supplied some motivation, too.

Captured!

With the Indians in custody the deputies proceeded to Santa Fe, and McNulty was left behind to secure the mines. Two hours after the deputies departed McNulty found more Indians hiding in a tunnel. They "hollered and swore" at him, then scampered away. McNulty hightailed it to make another report to the sheriff, and with his new report McNulty beat the deputies and their prisoners to town.

In late December 1910 the sheriff had managed to arrest some of the Cochiti raiders. The Cochitis were immediately bonded out when the governor of the pueblo along with several businessmen provided the cash. At the trial the Indians received a reprimand and 6-to-9 months of hard labor in the state penitentiary. The judge informed the Cochitis that they best tell their friends to leave the mines alone.

Matthews congratulated McNulty, and commented that the directors of the company had discussed a course of action that could be taken in the event that "extreme measures" became necessary. "We are very glad to see that you have succeeded in having some of them arrested and sincerely hope now that you have secured a line on the miscreants. We will soon have a satisfactory termination of this whole trouble. We congratulate you upon the success you have attained, and hope that you will be entirely successful in having the guilty ones properly punished."

Even with those trespassers in prison the nighttime raids continued, obviously in an effort to pressure McNulty. At the very least if McNulty didn't leave the mines he might be convinced to ask the governor to release the Indians who were in jail. On one of the evening raids the miscreants took some mining tools — drills, necessary for assessment work — but McNulty stepped in and provided his own personal tools so that the work could be completed.

McNulty promised Matthews, "I will try to have them captured by the men as I did before as it is of no use to depend on the authorities in Santa Fe, as I have written you before."

The raids became more interesting and dangerous when unidentified Mexicans joined in. McNulty came to this conclusion because the trespassers were now blasting, and the foot tracks he found nearby were made by a high boot. Most of the time the thieves outnumbered McNulty many times over, and during their forays he made sure his wife remained hidden.

During daylight hours some friends of the imprisoned Indians approached McNulty and demanded he do something to get their friends released. McNulty told them to write to Parker in New York as Parker was the one to answer their request. Apparently, the Indians did write, but their friends stayed in prison.

Success in Court; Tragedy in Life

Finally, by May of 1911, the Sena Land grant case decision was rendered by the U.S. Supreme Court. The court determined that the company owned the land and Sena had no right to it. The American Turquoise Company could begin it operations again. For the last eleven years little or no production had occurred at the mines because the company had waited, all their resources going for legal expenses. By May the company bank account had been so depleted that it, together with what money investors were willing to put in, was not sufficient to resume full-scale mining operations. Only the assessment work was funded, and that only at a marginal level.

In both 1910 and 1911 McNulty warned the company that claim jumpers, including Mariano Sena, eyed the mines and waited for a lapse in the assessment work. McNulty requested orders to begin that work, but the company withheld instructions until the very last minute, thereby putting the claims at risk. The only good news for 1911 was that the company could proceed with the process to patent the claims by the end of 1912. So once again — the last time he hoped — McNulty scrambled to finish the assessment work. He rounded up materials and workers, and in spite of bad weather he completed the job.

In July 1911 word arrived that E.J. had died. McNulty had to borrow money to attend the funeral in Arizona, (since his salary was months behind), and he also had to hire a man to watch the mines. The doctor diagnosed E.J.'s demise as due to ptomaine poisoning.

After the funeral, McNulty returned to the mines and faced the same troubles: late paychecks, Indian raids, forged tax documents. In October, McNulty noted that the taxes on the mine were way out of line — it was said that the mine's output reached $25,000 for 1901-1911 per year — those same years the mine's output stalled because of the numerous lawsuits on the part of Mariano Sena. As McNulty put it, the intention of territorial officials was to keep the company in constant litigation, and now he had to fight the tax raise, again. He sued the treasurer and his collectors to get the tax bill set aside and a tax rate that reflected the actual output of the mines.

The disarrayed finances of the company put McNulty's salary behind by a year, at the same time that McNulty was facing financial difficulties on his own. "I have fought the company's battles in court and at the mine for many years without assistance or money to work with," McNulty wrote to Matthews, "and I do think it is imposing upon me a little too much [to do without my salary]."

                            Chloride, Arizona. 10/22/1910.

Mr. J. P. McNulty,
    Cerrillos, New Mex.

My Dear Father:-

        As it is some time since I wrote to you and have not heard from you I thought I would write again to find out how you are getting a long.

        Am incloseing clipping and letter received from a friend of mine, U. S. Marshal at Kingman, he was just up in Taos Co., N.M. on some Indian trouble and he means what he says about wishing to be up there and get after them.

        Why dont you leave there if the Co., dont furnish you some-body to help you, they wont thank any for scraping for them, You ought to set a trap with Giant Powder for them and blow them all to H*** next time they come up.

        Fannie went through here last week on her way to California, where she is going to stay a couple of months she stoped off here one day, but that was as long as we could get her to stay as she was anxious to get into the Sullivan bunch.

        WellI guess that is all for this time hopeing to hear from you soon, Laura and the children join in sending love,   From your loveing son,

McNulty ignored Eddie's suggestion that he set a trap "and blow them all to H***". It is a tribute to the intelligence of both McNulty and the Santo Domingos that there was never any blood shed over the mines.

The troubles compounded in December when a group of people sunk a shaft barely 30 feet from the property line of the Castilian mine. McNulty jumped into action and sunk his own shaft about 40 or 50 feet to block the tunnel he suspected was coming underneath the company's property line. He knew that the people planned to complete a drift or slanted tunnel toward the Castilian. "When I started to sink the shaft, they notified me not to sink there, but I merely laughed at them and I told them that one of the tunnels [was] opening up new ground."

McNulty & Friends Dialogs On Indian Raids 1910 - 1911

McNulty to Parker, September 2, 1910

The Indians broke the staple on the shaft door at the big mine [Muñiz] *on the night of August 31st, and they went down below the 45 foot level and took a ladder down with them. ...I would not get down to see what work they had done for it is not safe to go down there, the timbers being rotten. ...I must say they are very daring to venture in the mine, and of course, they have someone to watch on top all the time, and my being all alone I can do nothing. ...I shall notify the officials on Monday about the Indians.*

McNulty to Matthews, September 21, 1910

I wrote to Mr. Parker ...about the Indians giving us trouble again and my being subpoenaed on the Grand Jury; but I was excused from serving on account of the Indian trouble. ...I had a quick talk with the sheriff and the district attorney in regards to the Indians, and we had the judge renew the three warrants that were out before for the three Indians. It may help to keep them away when the Indians hear of it. I really don't think the authorities want to have the warrants served as I have offered to pay the sheriff or the deputy's ex-

pense if they will go to Santa Domingo and get the Indians and take the Jew with them to identify them. I still have reason to believe the Jew is still backing the Indians and encouraging them to come to the mine. If they don't do something soon I will see the new governor [Mills] who is a friend of mine.

McNulty to Matthews, October 14, 1910

I been to Santa Fe twice to see the governor and the district attorney. I think by the governor having a talk with the Indian agent [Mr. Crandel] the Indians have not been here these last three nights. The district attorney also got after the sheriff to see to the capture of the Indians, so the sheriff with his deputy came out here in his automobile on the 12th and 13th inst. If the Indians were on the hills watching as they always do, they could hear the noise of the auto and see them also walking on the road as it is moonlit, and they could be seen for a long distance. I cautioned the sheriff in Santa Fe on the route he had best come to the mine and the hour, but he did not heed. The governor hinted to me to the effect that if the sheriff did not do his duty in serving the warrants etc. that he would be liable to lose his office.

McNulty to Parker, November 23, 1910

I have done all I can with the authorities in Santa Fe and they don't seem to want to give us any assistance or protection. ...All they tell me to do, even the district attorney, was to shoot to kill the Indians. ...Mr. Crandel, the Indian agent, said he had not been notified [about the Indian raids] and three days previous to that date I was in the governor's office with Mr. Crandel, and the governor told him in my presence that he had better do something to stop the Indians from coming to the mine.

Parker to McNulty, November 30, 1910

I... express my regret at the annoyance you are occasioned by the depredations of the Indians. I have written by this mail to the special attorney, Mr. Francis S. Wilson, requesting that he take the matter in hand with a view to your protection at once.

McNulty to Parker, December 6, 1910

>I hope that some protection and justice will be given to us soon as the Indians have been here and bothering the mines eleven nights. ...I had the sheriff out and hired two men to assist him on the 12th of last month, but they did not see any Indians at the big mine, but the same night the Castilian mine door was broken open, but they had time to skip before the men could get over there. ...It does seem to me that every time I ask the sheriff to come out that the Indians have a clue and keep away, as they have only mined one night since he was here.

McNulty to Parker, December 21, 1910

>As I have written you many times that I could get no assistance from the Authorities in Santa Fe to capture the Indians, I offered a reward of $25 two weeks ago to Apolonia Marez and for him to get some one to assist him to capture the Indians, so he got another deputy sheriff to come with him. I was in Cerrillos on Saturday and paid for a telephone message to Sheriff Closson to meet the two deputies at Bonanza (two miles from the mines). He failed to come; but through my instructions the two deputies caught four of the Cochiti Indians in the Castilian mine about 2:30 at night Saturday night [really Sunday morning].
>
>There were six Santo Domingo Indians in the mine with the Cochiti Indians up to ten o'clock but they left [and] ...came to the Muniz mine. The Cochiti Indians gave us that information on Sunday. I found it to be true. I told the deputies ...to hire a team at Bonanza and take them in to Santa Fe ...and I would overtake them. At 5 a.m., I went to feed my horse and then went to the Muniz mine to see if there were any Indians there. There were one or two Indians on the top watching, and they ran across the hill. My dog followed them. Having no gun with me, I returned down the hill towards the

tunnel and five Indians ran out of the tunnel.

That was two hours after the deputy left with the four Indians. As the Indians ran they hollered and swore at me in English. My wife hearing the noise and it being a bright moonlit night, she ran out of the door saw them run. I drove to Santa Fe and got in ahead of the deputies with the Indians and found the district attorney. In the afternoon he wrote out the complaint.

The Indians we captured had quite a quantity of matrix, I did not examine the stone very much as the deputies turned them over to the district attorney. The district attorney said that it was a burglary case and that they would not get off with a $10 fine, and would not let them out on bail. The Castilian mine door has been broken open twice since then — Sunday night and Monday night. From information that I have these last few days, there are several Mexicans assisting the Indians. The company has lost several hundred dollars of stone or matrix these last few months by the company not giving me assistance or permission to offer a suitable reward. As they are still coming, I think you should give me permission to offer another reward and see if we can capture the worst ones [Santo Domingo Indians]...

Copied from Unknown Newspaper, December 28, 1910

The four Cochiti Indians who have a hankering after Tiffany Turquoise, despite the warnings issued by J.P. McNulty, the veteran and efficient manager of the mines and who is prominent in Masonic Circles were brought before Justice Alarid today on the charge of stealing turquoise and were held on $1,000 bond for the action of the grand jury. The bond was furnished by the governor of Cochiti and several business men.

McNulty to Matthews, January 3, 1911

Since the four Indians were arrested the mines have been broken into three times on the 18th, 19th and 29th, of December, but [they] have not been since then.

Matthews to McNulty, January 7, 1911

Mr. Parker has requested me to write and state to you that he has received your several letters with regard to the Indian trouble and will write you with reference thereto as soon as he has been able to reach a satisfactory decision with some of our directors as to the plan of action to be taken in the event that we have to resort to extreme measures. He has, however, communicated with the Special Attorney for the Pueblo Indians of New Mexico at Santa Fe and has received his assurance that he would do everything in his power to assist in the prosecution of the Indians.

McNulty to Matthews, March 6, 1911

The Indians broke into the two mines the nights of the 3rd, 4th and 5th inst. and even went into the tunnel where the men work. ...[They] carried off all the drills that were of any value, but fortunately, I had some drills of mine own which may do the men till the assessment work is finished. The Indians seem to pay no attention to the notices that we have printed on the mine door. ...I had ...boxes nailed on the door with printed notices. They break the boxes off just the same as if there was no notices there, and the same notices are placed at the mouth of the tunnels. The tunnel is only about 50 yards from the house. I received a later notice to appear before the Grand Jury on the 9th inst and will have to leave here on the 8th inst so as to be in time. Of course, I will report the stealing of the tools to the grand jury and also the men will but do not know if it will do any good in this case.

McNulty to Parker, March 10, 1911

I have been successful in getting the four Indians prosecuted. We were called before the grand jury on the 9th inst. After my witnesses gave their testimony, I had them to go home. I stayed over till today. At 11 a.m., the grand jury turned in a true indictment against the Indians. Then the case was brought up in court. They pleaded guilty through their Attorney Mr. F. C. Wilson who made a hard plea for over half an hour to have them liberated, and [he] wanted to have them pay a small fine as he claimed it was their first offense and that they would not do it again.

But Mr. Abbott (the district attorney) brought up the last law that was put into effect two years ago where the case was burglary ...they could not be let off with a fine. He showed the statues to Judge McFie told the Indians that the penalty was three years, but as they said ...if they were the San Domingo Indians they would get the full term, but as they were the Cochiti Indians and not having broken into the mines as often and pleading guilty as the others he would only sentence them from 6 to 9 Months in the ...[territorial] penitentiary at hard labor. Then he gave them a great reprimand, and told them to notify all the other Indians through their friends, if any of them were caught again in the mines they would get the full penalty of the law. I hope this will keep the other Indians away from here, and that peace will be restored.

McNulty to Parker, April 18, 1911

The Castilian mine was... [broken] into on the nights of the 4th, 5 and 8th inst. I traced their tracks but I cannot say whether they were Indians or Mexicans as they were large boot prints and some of the Indians wear high boots.

McNulty to Matthews, June 3, 1911

Some friends of the Indians have been after me for two months to sign a petition to have the four Indians out of the penitentiary on parole and I told them that I would not do so. In order to get rid of them, I gave them your address and told them that it was the company's business and not mine. I understand that they have written you, which I hope will be of no avail, for they have given me enough trouble. Either the Indians or Mexicans are still coming. The Castilian mine was broke open last month on the 12th, 19th 20th, and 24th.

McNulty to Matthews, June 21, 1911

I wish you would appoint an agent in Santa Fe to assist me with the Indians and the taxes as Mr. S.P. Davis is in Las Vegas one hundred miles from here and is of no assistance to me here, being so far away. Governor Mills and [his] family were out here on the 11th, and we had a long talk about the Indians. Before he reached here, he was told on his way out about the Indians being here on the 9th and there were seven all armed with rifles. The mine was opened on the 9th and 10th.

McNulty to Matthews, July 1, 1911

The Castilian mine is still being opened by Indians or Mexicans, I think, but this time...by Mexicans, and at midnight the 24th of June they blasted. We heard it quite plain, and it being 600 yds away. The next morning we found on top half a stick of powder and a piece of candle.

McNulty & Friends
Dialogs On the Land Grant Case
1910 - 1911

McNulty to Parker, March 4, 1910

I met the company's agent, Mr. S.B. Davis, and he told me that he expected the grant case to be heard in Washington in October of this year. I was in hopes that it would have been settled this spring that we might start up work.

McNulty to Parker, April 3, 1911

I see by the New Mexican that the grant case is to be argued in Washington D.C. this week, and when the decision is given I do hope you will come here or send someone who will understand what will be needed to start up the property in proper

> Cerrillos
> New Mexico
> Feb 3d 1910.
>
> R. A. Parker Esq
> New York City.
>
> Dear Sir:—
> I am sending you to-day the Pay Roll & bill for the Month of January.
> I have laid off one of the men I had to work, & will finish up the assessment work this Month with the one I have, & there will be no more supplies got for this Month.
> I have been very successful in surveying my tunnels site all by myself with one of the men, & I am glad to be able to tell you that I have just broke through the tunnel that I was running in to the big mine, into the long drift at the 457 foot level, & I did not miss the drift on one side top & bottom one inch; but the drift inside being a little too narrow to push a can through I will be obliged later on when we will start to work to start down widen a little on one side, so as to lay the track for the tram car, & run all the rock out at th.

McNulty sent letters back East so that the investors could follow along with the work he completed.

shape. I wish you would see to getting your patent for the property. Attorney (Mr. Easley) says he is ready at any time to see to the patent papers..

McNulty to Matthews, May 5, 1911
Now that the case has been decided which I see

in the paper in favor of the company I do hope that you or Mr. Parker will come here as soon as you can, or that you will send some one who will understand what will be needed to put the mine into shape to resume work.

McNulty & Friends
Dialogs On Mining
1910 - 1911

McNulty to Parker, February 3, 1910
I have been very successful in surveying my tunnels...all by myself with one of the men. I am glad to be able to tell you that I have just broke[n] through the tunnel that I was running to the big mine. ...Unless you were here to see for yourself, you can not imagine the amount of work I have had done to develop the property where we will get the best results in course of time.

McNulty to Parker, September 21, 1910
Hoping to hear from you. ...with instructions to start the assessment work. Even should the grant case be settled this or next month, we have to do the assessment work for this year as we would not get the patent in time.

Matthews to McNulty, October 7, 1910
So far as the assessment work is concerned, will write you about this shortly, but for the present would prefer that you do not do anything so long as we are within the limit of the time allowed to do this work.

McNulty to Parker, October 3, 1910
This is an important year to have the assessment work done in time that is if the case is settled in our favor. If the work is not finished by the first of

the year, Mariano Sena parties may jump the claims and give you trouble again.

McNulty to Matthews, January 3, 1911

Mr. Matthews, in your letter of October the 7th 1910 you stated that you would write me shortly when to begin the assessment work. ...you have not given me instructions as yet, but in order to hold the best claims for the company I have put men to work which you will see by the pay roll. ...so far no one has tried to jump the claims as I have kept a careful watch and have several notices on the property: No Trespassing allowed: Penitentiary offense.

Matthews to McNulty, January 11, 1911

We thought you understood from my letter of October 7th last that you were to go ahead with the assessment work before the expiration of the time limit and there was no intention on our part whatever of allowing the matter to reach the point where any danger existed through lapse of time. You can go ahead and have the necessary assessment work done and send us bill of expenses, and the same will have prompt attention.

McNulty to Parker, March 3, 1911

I did think that I would have had the assessment work nearly finished in February, but owing to the stormy weather the men did not come to work the latter part of the month as there being no houses here for them to sleep in. They have to come from Cerrillos every morning which is seven miles, but I hope to get finished about the middle of the month, but it is still stormy. The cross cut in the tunnel that I am driving towards No. 1 shaft is showing up very nice colors through the hard rock, but there has not been much work done since my last letter.

McNulty to Matthews, July 1, 1911

I am sending you to day the pay roll for the month of June and also six Proofs of Labor for last year which I had recorded three days ago. I was compelled to have the Proofs of Labor recorded, as I was told by my friends that there were certain parties looking over the records in Santa Fe and from the conversation that was heard, they may yet give us trouble in court. I would advise the company to get a patent as soon as possible.

McNulty to Matthews, August 2, 1911

I am doing my utmost to have things straightened in Santa Fe about the patent; but there has been an error in the land office which you will see by the enclosed letters from attorney Easley. As General Bartlett was the attorney and agent when the last survey was made for patent the matter was all in his hands. I paid no attention to it, and now your agent, Mr. S. B. Davis of Las Vegas has got all the papers and the plat of the survey that I had posted up here for the 90 days. That included the Muniz in the group to the best of my knowledge. So you will please write Mr. Davis to send the plat to me so as I can take it to Santa Fe and have the matter looked over.

McNulty to Matthews, August 14, 1911

I had to pay nearly all my check out and shall be glad when the other comes about the first of September as you stated in your letter. ...I shall be glad for the company to come to a decision soon. As it is discourag[ing] for me here not knowing what the Company is going to do, as I have written in my former letters what is needed when we do start up. ...the time is getting short to see to it and not be leaving me in the lurch as you have done this last two years, as I want to do the work in the two tunnels. It seems to me that every one ...has an eye after the American Turquoise Co[m]pany on account of the Mariano Case.

Matthews to McNulty, September 5, 1911

We are making preparations to obtain patents on our property at an early date, and we ask that you do not proceed with the assessment work until you hear from us in the matter, as we desire to create as little expense as we can in the premises. Will you kindly let us know when the time limit is up on the assessment work so that we can be fully acquainted with such condition. Should we find that we are unable to get out our patents in time, we will give you instructions when to go on with the assessment work.

McNulty to Matthews, September 12, 1911

I trust you will send me some more money [so] I can pay some of my debts. The time limit to have the assessment work finished is the 31st day of December of each and every year. Should you get the patent at an early date, the work must be done on the Agnes P as it has not been surveyed for a patent. ...Should you not get a patent on the group, including the Muniz claim, the assessment work will have to be done on the Muniz also. That is the claim that I intend to have all of the work done on. ...it is impossible to get men to work here in order to have all the assessment work done in one month. ...I intend to do the work all on one claim ...you had better give me sufficient time to have it done in. It will take at least from two to three months to get this work done for all of the six claims.

Matthews to McNulty, September 22, 1911

With regard to the assessment work, we think you had better begin this work by October 1st. We would prefer to have waited until we could have obtained our patents before pursuing work on the property, but rather than run any risk in the matter, we think it best to act upon your advice and begin the work without further delay.

McNulty to Matthews, October 2, 1911

Your letter of Sept 22nd has been received and will start the assessment work as soon as I can get reliable men. I have talked to several miners, but they complain about the wages and no houses to live in at the mine, and the nearest town being seven miles away from here. I must have some lum-

ber to start with and I have talked to a business man in Cerrillos to get the lumber for me, and he said he would do so, as I have not the money myself to pay for the lumber and freight bill. I will have to get several things in the hardware store, powder, tools etc. Owing to the delay in getting the men and material, it may be a week or more before I can start the work. Of course the lumber and tools etc will be counted as part of the assessment work.

AMERICAN TURQUOISE COMPANY,
55 WALL STREET
NEW YORK

Matthews, throughout 1910-1911, asked for McNulty's patience since money to pay expenses consistently arrived late.

April 4, 1910.

Mr. J. P. McNulty,
    Los Cerrillos,
        New Mexico.

Dear Mr. McNulty:-

    I regret that we have not been able to send you your salary this last month, but the two gentlemen upon whom we depend for funds to run the business are absent from the city, one being in Europe and the other on the Pacific Coast. We have communicated with them and expect to hear from them in a very little while, and would therefore, ask your kind indulgence until we receive some money, when we will mail you check at once.

        Yours very truly,

        Jas. Matthews
            Treasurer.

G.

McNulty & Friends
Dialogs On Taxes
1910 - 1911

McNuty to Matthews, October 2, 1911

I was in Santa Fe last week at the [Constitutional] *Convention, and the assessor told me that the County Commissioners had raised the company's taxes for the output of ten years. Then I called up the District Attorney on the phone, I told him that I was not notified on the raise. ...to the best of my opinion I did not think that the company or the agent had been notified. ...he told me that he could not attend to it until this week. ...As I have written you after, the officials try every way to keep the American Turquoise Company in litigation.*

McNulty to Matthews, October 2, 1911

The Territory Board of Equalization met last month and not being notified I did not get a chance to appear before them. ...I think it was a scheme to put the company to more expense. ...if you had an agent in Santa Fe, he could see to these things and keep them in their place. I will do the best I can in the matter as I have always done, but your agent should be in Santa Fe.

McNulty to Matthews, October 6, 1911

You had better inform your agent, Mr. S.B. Davis, about this matter, as the district attorney says the company will have to go to court, unless my statement is accepted. ...he could do nothing himself, the Judge had the doing of it, but that he would try his best to have my statement accepted. All of this trouble could have been avoided if you would have your agent to live in Santa Fe, as I have written you many a time.

Petition from the district court in Santa Fe, October 14, 1911:

The American Turquoise Company versus Celso Lopez, Santa Fe County Treasurer and Ex-Officio Collector, October 14, 1911 J.P McNulty, being first duly sworn, upon his oath says that he is the superintendent of the mines belonging to the American Turquoise Company, located in the county of Santa Fe and Territory of New Mexico, that at a special meeting of The Board of County Commissioners of the County of Santa Fe during the month of August 1911, and without notice to the said company or to the superintendent thereof, that said commissioners assessed the net product of the mines belonging to The American Turquoise Company at $25,000.00 per annum for the years 1901 to 1911 inclusive, and that affiant had not been notified of the said raise, and that had he been he would have gone before the Territorial Board of Equalization, and to the best of affiant's knowledge neither the company nor its agent (S.B. Davis) had been notified; that there has not been any marketable stone taken out in six years, except one small cigar box of specimens or matrix that affiant had shipped this year (1911) and to the best of affiant's knowledge the output of the mines did not pay the expenses at the mine for the last ten years; that said commissioners assessed the net product of the said mines belonging to said The American Turquoise Company at $25,000 per annum, for the years 1901 to 1911 inclusive as aforesaid; the plaintiff was without any notice of the meeting called for the purpose of making said assessment, and was without any notice of the said assessment after the same had been made by the said Board of County Commissioners, and that the said assessment is unfair, without any foundation whatsoever and should be cancelled and set aside. ...petitioner prays that an Order be granted by the court directing the defendant, Celso Lopez, Treasurer and ExOfficio Collector to set the said assessment aside and to cancel the same upon the records in his office.

McNulty to Matthews, December 11, 1911

I went to Santa Fe last week and have good news to write you. The court has canceled and set aside the rate of taxes for ten years with 1911 included. So now I would advise you to pay up this years taxes as before as it becomes due on Dec 1st. inst.

McNulty & Friends
Dialogs On Finances
1910 - 1911

McNulty to Parker, April 4, 1910

Mr. Matthews has not already sent check to pay at least one month's salary to the Mexican who worked last February. I will be glad if you will please see to it as the Mexican is after me every time I go to town for his pay. I had to get the store to advance him money on his month's pay so that he could get some provisions.

Matthews to McNulty, April 4, 1910

I regret that we have not been able to send you your salary this last month, but the two gentlemen upon whom we depend for funds to run the business are absent from the city, one being in Europe and the other on the Pacific Coast.

McNulty to Matthews, September 21, 1910

Your letter of the 15th inst with check to pay my salary for the month of December 1909 has been received and many thanks for it.

McNulty to Matthews, December 4, 1911

I told my creditors that I would pay them last month, and when I was not able to do so, I had to get other securities and pay big interest for fifteen days. I also had to get security for the payment of the men I have to work, or I could not have the work done and would have to shut down.

Matthews to McNulty, December 9, 1911

We assure you it is very embarrassing to us to have placed you in this position, but, nevertheless, it is no fault of either Mr. Parker or myself that the circumstances are as they are. We are depending upon certain stockholders who are financing the company out of their private means to furnish money to meet our obligations, and we are at the point we may any day receive the necessary money to meet the expenses of the company and relieve you from further inconvenience in the premises.

Parker to McNulty, December 23, 1911

I had been in hopes of being in a position to send you a check, but some of our people have been away. However, before the end of the month, I think I will be able to send the needful.

McNulty to Parker, December 27, 1911

I was very glad to hear from you... and to know that the money will be here soon as it is surely badly needed, as I had to give my note to Mr. Delallo of Cerrillos for $69 to pay one of the men for last month (I.O. Kelly), *as he said he could not wait any longer* [for his money]. *...there is a law that no person can hold a mining claim unless the assessment work is paid for. I thought it best to pay him, so you will kindly send money as soon as possible.*

McNulty & Friends
Dialogs On the Death of His Son
1910 - 1911

John Whiteside to McNulty, July 11, 1911

In compliance with your request, I make the following statement, of your son's last illness: I arrived at the residence of your son at 5.30 P.M. Thursday the 6th, he was taken ill at 10.30 a.m. of the same day. Laura [Eddie's wife] phoned me about that time, and I told her what to do; she called me again to come out, but I was out of my office attending a patient, and did not get the call until I returned to my office, and left for there as soon as possible, and arrived there as stated above; I found him suffering greatly with pain; his heart was very weak, pulse about 180, I gave him at once a hypodermic of 14 gr morphia, and 160 gr of strychnia, repeated in 12 hour; he complained of numbness in his legs also in his hands, his abdomen was very hard, I gave him at once a large dose of salts, and repeated this in one hour; shortly after seven o'clock, the pain had subsided to a great extent, and I moved him onto a bed, about eight o'clock, I gave him an injection of soapsuds, raising his hips, this he retained 10 or 15 minutes, when this passed off quite a good deal of gas passed also, his abdomen softened up quite a good deal, and his pulse 120, which was some improvement, at this time he was without pain; he remained in this condition until about 9 o'lock, when his heart commenced to fail, at this time I gave him a hypodermic of strychnis and digitalis, from which I did not receive any favorable effect; his abdomen at this time was distended with gas, and I gave him another injection, which he passed, without any relief; I gave him a hypodermic of 130 gr of strych- and repeated it every 15 minutes, without effect; I never succeeded in stimulating the heart, and he passed away at 12.5. The cause of his death was heart failure, brought on or rather superinduced by ptomaine poisoning; just what he ate that brought it on I am not prepared to say, but am of the opinion it was more likely the ice cream; this of course is conjectural.

McNulty to Matthews, August 2, 1911

I do wish you would please send me some money as I cannot get along without it. My son who was superintendant of the Turquoise Mines in Arizona died suddenly on the 6th of July, of Potaime poisoning. I had to borrow $200 besides what I had already borrowed in order to go to his funeral and to pay a man to stay at the mines night and day with my wife while I was away. As I have not heard from the company for two months in answer to any of my letters, I am at a loss to know what the company is going to do with the property.

McNulty shows off his "town" style buggy on First Street in Cerrillos. Nellie, his white mare, is showing her age in this picture.

John Koury, who is probably the person standing at the left side of this photo, died October 20, 1904. By 1911 McNulty owned the two lots next to the old Koury store, and when he finally moved to Cerrillos from the mines in May of 1919 he probably lived in the house visible in this photo behind Nellie's head.

Chapter 9
1912 - 1915

A Telephone Might Help

I am very sorry to have to state to you that foreclosure proceedings have been instituted by the Mortgagees and the property will pass out of our hands..
                                                                Parker to McNulty

21 YEARS 7 MONTHS & A PAY CUT

The only bright spots in 1912-1913 came in the guise of visits from a mining engineer and the world-renowned Kunz, all of which raised McNulty's hopes that the mines might be restarted. The bad news for McNulty was that in return for deferred salary (running back more than two years), the ATC expected him to face down thieves, get patents, obtain legal advice, and keep notices posted on the mining claims. The company requested he play host to several visitors: Kunz, Tiffany's gemologist, and E.B. Zalenski, a mining engineer, and the superintendent of the Indian School in Santa Fe. As it stood in 1912, the mine shafts and tunnels had suffered from the lack of maintenance, the result of the lack of funds. Some had caved in; all were hazardous. McNulty's house, too, needed repair, but he didn't complain although his wife most likely had some comment. She kept the house clean, prepared the food, and kept up with many of the bookkeeping entries.

He wrote to a party who had expressed interest in his personal claims, "I am sending you today ... my own matrix as I cannot send any of the company's. ...I hope to find as good colors on my own claims ... when I have the means to go on with the work." That party expressed no further interest. McNulty continued faithfully to pursue the company's business, his optimism never flagging. He had already determined that when turquoise mining no longer paid he would return to Cerrillos to live out his days.

McNulty's roots in Cerrillos ran deep. Fannie and his grandchildren lived nearby, his mining ventures centered in the Turquoise Hill, and his friends in both Cerrillos and Santa Fe shared those interests. What he didn't have was a steady paycheck and confidence that his employment would be long-term.

McNulty took no chances in facing the turquoise thieves as they came to the dumps and the caved-in Castilian. Although he ordered the trespassers to leave the area, he did not back up his words with a gun. The marauders, far outnumbering him, confronted and ridiculed him, and the uneven standoff continued until McNulty was able to get a telephone line.

In a letter McNulty mentioned the possibility of a new telephone to the company, but he did not request that the company pay for it The ATC treasurer, Matthews, shot back that the situation didn't warrant a phone, and indeed, the company did not wish to incur any more expenses. Matthews, not accustomed to facing threatening, dangerous individuals, considered only the bottom line. How much would it cost? Valuing a little money over his safety concerned McNulty, and it was also a troubling indicator of the ATC's tenuous finances.

In 1912 Matthews wrote, "We are at a loss to understand why it should be necessary for you to get a telephone. The company is not doing any business and we see no reason for adding to our expenses."

McNulty responded, dryly noting, "I thought that the company would have been glad for me to have a telephone for our safety instead of writing me such a letter of indifference."

McNulty's approach to the Pueblo turquoise-takers consisted of a request to leave. They laughed at him, and McNulty went to the house and, using his new telephone, contacted the sheriff, Charles Clossen, to come down and round up the trespassers. Even then, when the sheriff in his noisy motor car finally arrived most of the miscreants were usually long gone. But not always. One day the

B. Altman & Co.

The Rug Department

offers exceptional values in an interesting collection of genuine

Navajo Rugs

(direct from the Indian Reservations of Arizona and New Mexico)

now on sale at unusually low prices

Beginning to-day (Wednesday)

A selected number of these choice

American Navajo Rugs

will be specially priced at

$9.75, 12.75 & 17.50 each

(Fifth Floor)

Madison Avenue - Fifth Avenue
34th and 35th Streets   New York

« *With the turquoise trade slow to non-existent, McNulty branched out to Navajo rugs. That this ad from an unidentified New York newspaper found in McNulty's papers suggests that part of this consignment of rugs may have come from him..*

True to form, McNulty wrote in his red memo book every time Pueblo Indians visited. This week, on Saturday, he successfully had three trespassers bound over for trial. Out of ten Indians, McNulty and the sheriff captured five. Out of those five, three faced trial.

≫

sheriff and the deputy did manage to corner some. Shots were fired, trespassers were captured, and the sheriff found glory in the newspaper. McNulty's deft use of the shotgun had proven useful in the arrest, and it was also left to McNulty to gather witnesses and bringing them to Santa Fe to testify.

McNulty kept the company informed as he interacted with lawyers and political leaders on behalf of the ATC. But on the business front things were quiet, as the market for turquoise remained depressed. Still, Parker, Matthews and McNulty all shared the dream, the hope of a resurgence of turquoise mining in Cerrillos. But the chief financiers — Stillman and Pinkerton — were hesitant to put more capital into those mines, instead, taking the reins of the company into their own hands so as to shed superfluous directors.

McNulty carefully controlled the expenses at the mine since he knew that he might not be reimbursed soon, if at all, and he concentrated on his personal real estate ventures and assessment work on his own claims.

The Sena Land Grant decision had paved the way for ATC to now obtain its patents, and it first pursued those patents for the Tiffany and Castilian mines. The cost of the patenting process was estimated at more then $400, and of course, McNulty carried out the details, with the help of attorneys. Getting information, helping ease the way for the patents, and making the contacts with the lawyers fell to McNulty. Legal work moved forward so slowly that by the end of 1912 McNulty had to complete yet one more year's assessment work. And then he sat, waiting for his salary. Had the patents been received in a more timely manner the mines' value would have increased and the money devoted to the assessment work could have been saved.

Since the mines had been inactive for the last ten years, Kunz arrived to assess their profitability. Kunz, now a stockholder, had a vested interest in finding marketable turquoise, but he left disappointed.

"Your opinion is beyond price," Parker wrote to Kunz. Kunz's visit, all too short, didn't produce the desired result which was restarting the mine. But the visit did pave the way for another expert, Edward Zalenski, to inspect the mines to determine what could or what needed to be done.

Zalenski expressed amazement to McNulty about the straightness of his tunnels. Such straightness was usually achieved with surveying

AMERICAN TURQUOISE COMPANY

65 Wall Street

New York, February 13, 1912

J. P. McNulty, Esq., Superintendent,
American Turquoise Company,
Cerrillos, N. M.

Dear Sir:

This will serve to introduce to you our friend, Dr. G. F. Kunz, a stockholder of the American Turquoise Co., who wishes to visit the mines in Santa Fe County. You will be kind enough to give Dr. Kunz every attention. Show him everything that belongs to the company, also affording him such information in every respect that he may desire.

Yours very truly,

R. A. Parker
President.

Form 34-A 25M-6-11
Return to
MARKET AND FULTON NATIONAL BANK,
N. Y. CITY,
If not Delivered within 5 days.

81 Fulton St

Mr. J. P. McNulty, Superintendent
American Turquoise Company,
CERRILLOS, N. M.

Introducing Dr. G. F. Kunz.

Tiffany gemologist George Kunz, now a stockholder in the American Turquoise Company, visited the area in 1912 to assess the value of the mines. McNulty required a letter of introduction from each visitor to the mine.

The return address on the envelope is Market and Fulton National Bank, a bank that eventually became part of the Bank of America.

instruments, yet McNulty had done it by eyeballing the lay of the land.

With his usual wit, McNulty commented, "I must say for a young man he is very smart as a mining surveyor and mineralogist. When he sends you a map of the workings of the property, it will give you an idea of the amount of work that is done. ...Mr. Zalenski was astonished to see the two tunnels that I had driven, without the assistance of a mining engineer, or even a compass to go by."

Another visitor to the mines, Dr. Joseph Kossuth Dixon, arrived to take pictures for his work on the Indian Memorial. Dixon, a friend to Kunz, brought his son, Major James McLaughlin, Superintendent of the Indian School of Santa Fe and the attorney for the Indians. They toured the mine areas and carried away some mementos as they prepared to build an Indian Memorial.

"They took several pictures," McNulty commented, "but having no flash light with them they could not take any inside the mine."

> Received from Mrs. Emma Mrs. Tully fifteen dollars for sinking a ten foot hole on the Progress Claim. January 3rd 1913.
>
> Juan Padilla

> Received from Mrs. Emma Mrs. Tully fifteen dollars as payment in full, for sinking a ten foot shaft on the Hawley claim. January 25th 1913.
>
> Juan Padilla

Emma kept this signed receipt from Padilla for the work he did on her claims.

Zalenski's pessimistic report wasn't enough to completely discourage the ATC. Parker continued to hold on and encourage the bond holders to keep their money invested. James Stillman and Allan Pinkerton, the major bondholders and financiers, waited for the year that would bring turquoise mining to a profitable level. That didn't happen in 1912 nor in 1913. Then in September of 1913, McNulty received news of another foreclosure proceeding. When the dust settled, two ATC bond holders had emerged, as far as McNulty knew. Those men were Allan Pinkerton and James Stillman. They had waited and waited for turquoise to rise in value. As their hopes fell so did McNulty's salary and working status, and so did the American Turquoise Company fortunes. When the takeover was completed, McNulty had already laid in the winter's wood and coal. The prohibitive cost of moving the coal and wood made it impossible to move back into Cerrillos for the winter.

After 21 years and seven months of working for the company he was asked to back-date his pay cut to July of 1912 and stay on at the mines as a guard. His notice of cut in salary was immediate, his years of service were unrecognized, and his patience was sorely tried. Towards the end of 1913 Matthews and Parker promised McNulty that he would receive all of his back salary, no matter how long it took. Through the years McNulty knew that both men had treated him in a fair and honest manner — the money arrived, although normally late — so McNulty believed his salary would be caught up, eventually.

READY TO STEP OUT

McNulty stayed with his own claims. He continued his assessment work and patented them. His wife became the bookkeeper, many times paying the workers. For the mine named after her, she paid Juan Padilla $15 for sinking a ten-foot shaft on the Hawley claim. On another of her claims, the Progress Claim, she also paid Padilla $15 for sinking a 10-foot hole.

McNulty became more cautious in his dealings with marauders — both Indians and Mexicans — and he quit approaching them directly.

Instead, he just observed, reported, and when he could he ushered the thieves into the court system. He knew that once they were released from prison he likely would become a target.

Because of the remoteness of Turquoise Hill it was clear that a telephone would help speed up communication, and possibly get law enforcement out to the mines more quickly. When a nearby rancher requested a phone line McNulty set plans into motion for the same service at Turquoise Hill. Matthews' first response to the news of this was that the company didn't want to pay for the installation, and McNulty quickly explained it was for his own protection and that the company didn't need to be worried about any additional expense.

"I am...in danger of my life at any time. If you can get anyone that will do better by the company than I have done, I will turn over everything. I am ready to step out at any moment when I am paid up in full," McNulty wrote.

Parker and Matthews ignored the letter, continuing business as usual, although at one point both Parker and Matthews thanked McNulty for his honest service. They both expressed regret at the foreclosure proceedings and promised McNulty that they would try to keep him employed by the new owners, Pinkerton and Stillman. And, McNulty responded with the hope that he could continue to work with Parker.

As Parker moved up the corporate ladder of his bank and accepted more responsibility, his contact with McNulty grew less frequent. McNulty noted this, and in one letter asked, "I have received [a letter] signed R.A. Parker, President, Gone, would like to know the meaning. Has he left the company, or gone on a vacation?"

With an increase in Parker's responsibilities came an increase in administrative assistants. Matthews said, "I will say in reply that the notation following Mr. Parker's name was the initials of the young man, G.O. Merz, who signed the letter for Mr. Parker. Mr. Parker is still connected with the company, but it happens that he is taking his annual vacation in Europe at this time. We hope it will not be long before something favorable will develop in the affairs of the company."

I RECEIVED AN EYEWITNESS SHOCK

The turquoise company business wound down and the reins of control in the company passed to a rather disinterested trustee attorney, Fredic Gilbert, while McNulty's relationship with his wife took a turn for the worse.

On the business front, all correspondence came from 55 Fulton Street, including the American Turquoise Company letters that no longer bore the preprinted heading. Now almost as an afterthought it was typed. Although the financial control of the company had passed from Parker and Matthews, Matthews continued as the signatory of the checks to McNulty. Whatever the arrangement was, it still showed that there was some hope for a resurgence of turquoise mining, and they were all waiting for that time. In September of 1915 Matthews requested that McNulty get turquoise specimens from 100-200 feet below the surface. Apparently, the treasurer had forgotten the company hadn't kept up the work in the shafts or the tunnels. The mines' mud slides had left the shafts no deeper than 45 feet. McNulty come up with some specimens, but they were necessarily from much closer to the surface.

McNulty's house deteriorated along with his marriage, but Emma and McNulty planned, rationally and carefully, how to separate and what would be best for each. They looked to dividing up the mining claims they owned, and if the claims did not sell, they determined they would lease them. McNulty offered to keep Emma's personal property until she could get around to sending for the items. Since McNulty's salary consisted of so little, he would be hard put to supply Emma any money at all.

On May 31, 1914, Emma decided that she could no longer live with McNulty because of a "shock" she had seen. (The letters don't state the exact shock.) By July of 1915, McNulty started separation proceedings and the two prepared to part ways in as friendly a manner as possible. Emma's calendar book, along with entries for purchasing sweet milk, included the understatement, "Received an eyewitness shock when I arrived at the stable." Her handwriting, neat and well ordered, belied her true emotions. Nothing would ever be the same again.

Several weeks before that event, she had followed McNulty around

The event that so shocked Emma on May 31, 1914, the nature of which she never revealed, was to haunt both of them for the rest of their lives.

Cerrillos and made several notations:

On March 22, 1914, Sunday, "9 men walked into Mr. De Lallo's Saloon through the back door."

On Wednesday, the same week, "Gambling and drinking in Mr. De Lallo's and Julian Saloons, about 10 people."

The next entry, on March 26, noted, "Gambling and drinking, the same as above."

That little "incident", never directly discussed, resulted in Emma writing to McNulty's daughter, Agnes, to explain everything about the impending separation. She also discussed an uncomplimentary letter McNulty's other daughter had sent to McNulty. The end result: McNulty filed for a separation.

Emma continued, "Papa says that I am a good housekeeper but I

TIFFANY BLUE • 267

am not a wife and companion for him and he wants a quiet separation." She noted that she was not the one to do anything wrong and that she had tried her best to be a good wife, often times seeking advice from McNulty's Mason friends about his drinking and gambling, much to McNulty's chagrin.

The couple had stayed together through Emma's mental breakdown, through tough cold winters, and through numerous Indian raids, through family fights and family visits, through times of no money,

McNulty's family was growing. Fannie had married and her two children delighted her father. James and Agnes McCraw posed for this picture sent to their grandfather.

but in 1915 the time came to part and move on. McNulty had now reached his 69th year, and Emma couldn't understand what led him to behave in such a strange matter that required their separation.

The business of paying taxes and protecting the mine slowed, and by the beginning of 1914, McNulty's back salary amounted to two years' pay. Paperwork for the foreclosure of the mines remained to be completed, and the company expected McNulty to fill in the gaps of paying past taxes, of rounding up bills, and of preparing for the current year's taxes. In the process of going over the paperwork, McNulty discovered that the taxes for 1901-1911 had been misrepresented again and essential records were missing. Thanks to the memory of Judge Abbott, the district attorney during those years, McNulty straightened things out, and showed that the taxes had been misrepresented. It seemed that the county commissioner's office and the court clerk's office had lost all pertinent paperwork important to the company. The assessor's office, however, did produce the correct paperwork, and without a lawyer, McNulty solved the problems.

With the tax problems behind him McNulty considered what the sale of the company's mines would do to his back salary. After receiving several assurances and promises that he would definitely be paid in full as part of any settlement, McNulty decided to stay on. He waited to see how the company's fortunes would progress. Apparently, the "new" owners were the only two bond holders who expressed an interest in mining and had sufficient capital to survive until the mining could prove profitable again. But at least McNulty read the handwriting on the wall and knew that his long-term position most likely was about to end. He was right. Records on file with the State Corporation Commission of New Mexico showed that the company discontinued operation November 3, 1915.

Still, that glimmer of hope that mining would start again lurked in McNulty's dream, and he offered to sell his claims to the new owners. After all, they needed the claims when work started up. As it turned out, the "new" owners were again Stillman and Allan Pinkerton. Kunz, along with the rest of the directors of the ATC, lost their positions and whatever little investment they had made.

TIFFANY BLUE • 269

McNulty & Friends
Dialogs On Finances & Taxes
1912 - 1913

Matthews to McNulty, January 11, 1912

I deeply regret, as does Mr. Parker, the delay occasioned in sending you money, but it could not be helped. ...arrangements are almost completed for financing the business of the company. You need have no further concern about your salary. We will get this money in a very few days, and a check will be sent to you for salary, and also wages for the men; at the same time, bills outstanding for merchandise purchased by you will be paid. We trust, therefore, you will bear with us just a few days longer.

McNulty to Matthews, January 25, 1912

...regretting very much that my check was so small. The check you have sent me will not pay one third of the bills and notes that I owe. ...please send me at least two month's salary. ...I have received nothing from the company for three months. ...please see to it that more money is sent to me at once to pay up my creditors. When my check came I fully expected six month's salary. ... I have finished the assessment work last week, by laying in a tramway in one of the tunnels. One man worked 10 days and the other six days.

Matthews to McNulty, January 30, 1912

I do not know from where you got the idea that we were going to send you six months salary, as I certainly did not make any such statement in my letters to you. We will send you some more money just as soon as we can obtain funds from our directors. The expenses of litigation, taxes, etc. have been met entirely from means furnished by certain gentlemen connected with this company. As you know the mines have not produced anything for over ten years. I note what you say about taking rash steps to collect your

money, but I want to say to you in a friendly
spirit that it would be absurd for you to do
anything of that sort, as it would most natu-
rally act against you, and finally do you
more harm than good. This company is not
bankrupt, but is very much alive and intends
to remain so. You will get all of your money
in due course. In the meantime, we will see
that you do not suffer for the want of things,
but it is necessary for you to exercise proper
patience until our directors have advanced
the amount needed.

McNulty to Matthews, February 5, 1912

Now, Mr. Matthews, I have written to you and Mr. Parker some months ago that I needed money to pay my debts and notes. Now, you write that you do not know by what authority I had ...that I should write for five or six month's salary. The company owes me more than twice that amount. ...Mr. Parker wrote me on Dec. 23rd 1911, that he was in hopes of being in a position to send me a check, but some of his people have been away. "However before the end of the month I think I will be able to send the needful." And this was an answer to my call for money to pay my debts and note. I have been telling my creditors that I would pay them in a few days after I received your letters. ...I am now starting on my twenty first year here, in the wilderness in charge of this property, and in danger of my life at any time. If you can get any one that will do better by the company than I have done, I will turn over everything. I am ready to step out at any moment when I am paid up in full.

McNulty to Matthews, July 4, 1912

I do wish you would please send me some money as I have borrowed $125 already to live on since you sent me the last money.

McNulty to Matthews, November 1, 1912

I have been patiently waiting to hear from you in answer to my letter of Oct. 1st and also one to Mr. Parker of Sept. the 26th, but have had no reply as yet and would like to know why you both have ignored my letters and have not sent me any money which I badly need. I request you to please give me ...some satisfactory answer by return of mail, if you have not already sent me some money.

McNulty to Matthews, November 6, 1912
Some more money will be much appreciated as I am in need of it.

Matthews to McNulty, November 7, 1912
We are in receipt of your letter of November 1st by special delivery, and have fully noted its contents. There was no desire whatever on our part to ignore your previous communications, but for reasons explained in our letter of the 30th ultimo, we were unable to answer sooner. We presume by this time you have received the check which was therein enclosed, and as promised, we now enclose the other check for $130.00, Salary for the month of Aug. 1911 which we trust will be satisfactory.

McNulty to Matthews, February 16, 1913
I wish you would please send me another check as soon as you can, as I need it.

McNulty to Matthews, August 5, 1913
I have been waiting patiently to get some remittance from the company and it is now over two months since I received any, the last check being dated May 27th and I am at a loss to know why the company does not send me my salary more regular. It will take all of four month's salary to pay up my debts, and I cannot be borrowing any more money and paying interest on same, when money is due me.

Parker to McNulty, August 11, 1913
I am in receipt of your letter to Mr. Matthews relative to your salary, and in response beg to state the matter will be given prompt attention. Before the close of

the month you will receive a substantial remittance, as I am arranging for additional money.

Parker to McNulty, September 13, 1913

We enclose herewith check for $260 to cover your salary for two months, and would ask you kindly to sign enclosed voucher and return same to us. I am very sorry to have to state to you that foreclosure proceedings have been instituted by the mortgagees and the property will pass out of our hands. I have, however, made arrangements for the payment of your salary to July 1, 1913, with the understanding that your services as superintendent will cease as of that date, and check for the remainder of your salary will be sent you in due time. The Mortgagees have decided not to operate the property for the present, but they will require the services of a watchman, and I write to ask in their behalf if you will be willing to accept the position at the salary of $60 per month, your salary as such to date back to July 1st of this year. Kindly let me know about this as soon as possible. If you are unable to accept this position, can you recommend a reliable man to take the place? We wish to say in closing that we have enjoyed the pleasant relations which have existed between us in the past, and regret very much that is has been found necessary to close up the business in this manner.

McNulty to Parker, September 21, 1913

I regret very much and am surprised at such a short notice at the change that is about to take place as I have had my coal and wood already hauled for the winter. I will say to you, Mr. Parker, your being one of the directors, Mr. Matthews, Mr. Boyert, Mr. Betts, Mr. Pinkerton and also Mr. Stillman, that I have been here in charge of this property 21 yrs and 7 mos. that I have worked honest and faithful for the company, fought their battles in court and at the mine, with the Indians and other thieves, and running the risk of my life and still in danger of the Indians, as there are two of them in the penitentiary and will be there till sometime next year, and now I receive a letter cutting my salary less than half. I have lost three good positions since you were out here, waiting for everything to be settled for the company. ...In regards to reducing my salary will say that I will attend to the property the same as I have been doing heretofore for the company at $75 per month, until you start work, or until you find a suitable man that will take less pay. Everything is so high out here, even water costs me from $5 to $6 per month. I am glad to know that my back salary will be sent to me in due time.

Parker to McNulty, October 1, 1913

We acknowledge receipt of your letter of September 21st, contents of which we have carefully noted. I am not, however, in a position to advise you at the moment whether or not the salary you name will be satisfactory to the interests which have taken over the property, but I have referred your letter to them, and as soon as I receive their answer I will at once communicate with you.

Matthews to McNulty, October 20, 1913

We have not been able to hear definitely from the parties interested as to wages from July 1st, but up to that time The American Turquoise Company is responsible, and you will receive your salary in full within a short time. We have no doubt that some satisfactory arrangement will be made for the continuance of your services from July 1st, and immediately we obtain a decision in the matter we will advise you.

McNulty to Matthews...October 28, 1913

I am very glad to hear you say that the American Turquoise Company is responsible for my back salary and that it will be paid in full within a short time, as I understand that the foreclosure of the mortgage proceedings has been started in Santa Fe, and as I have always trusted to Mr. Parker for *my salary and believe that he will see to it that I get my back salary in full, so I will not interfere with the proceedings of the mortgage as the property is worth much more than the mortgage. Hoping to hear from you soon, and that you will kindly let me know when I may be expecting my back salary in full, as it will relieve me very much.*

Matthews to McNulty, November 3, 1913

I hasten to assure you that you need have no worry whatever about your back salary. In a few days we shall send you another check and you will receive the balance at short intervals until the entire amount is paid. We not only feel that you are entitled to your salary up to July 1st, but we are also appreciative of your loyalty and faithful service to the company. We hope satisfactory arrangements can be effected that you may continue to be connected with the business indefinitely.

McNulty to Matthews, November 24, 1913

I also thank you for your letter as it gives me more encouragement to know that the company appreciated my services in the past, and that my back salary will be sent to me at short intervals.

McNulty to Matthews, January 30, 1914

Your letter of the 23rd inst. with check to pay my salary for the months of November and December 1912 has been received. ...We are having a pretty cold winter, and I expect it is the same in New York.

Matthews to McNulty, February 20, 1914

I find upon going over our tax bills that we did not receive one for the year 1911, and we should like to have you look into the matter and ascertain if there are any taxes due for that year, as in foreclosing the mortgage all charges should be known in calculating the amount to be asked for the property.

McNulty to Matthews, March 2, 1914

...in regard to the taxes for the year 1911 ...I was in Santa Fe on the 24th of February to fill out the tax blanks for the company ...after returning home, I went to Cerrillos and received your letter so I went to Santa Fe again ...to look over the matter for the taxes for the year 1911, and I found that they have on the collector's books $1200 and some odd dollars, besides the penalty against the company for the year of 1911. So I protested against the amount ...and had a talk with the district judge, (Mr. Abbott), who was district attorney in the year 1911. He said he remembered all about my making an affidavit and having set aside the raise made by the county commissioners at $25,000 per annum for the years 1901 to 1911.

Judge Abbott told me to go to the clerk of the court and have him look over the records which said clerk did so for three hours, but failed to find any record made. I also went to the county commissioners' office and I find that the $25,000 are on their books the same as on the collector's books. Then I went to the assessor's office, and I find that the tax reports in that office are just the same as I filled out for the years 1910, 1911, 1912, and 1913 at $500, so I found it correct there. As the clerk in the district court could not find his records, I went to see Judge Abbott that evening again. He said he would have the matter looked over this week as I told him that I was to write to my company.

So, Mr. Matthews, I would like very much, if there are any papers in regards to the taxes for 1911 that I may have sent you to please send them to me so I can have them with me to take to Santa Fe when I hear from you. I have a copy of the affidavit which I swore to in court in October 1911. I think I will be able to straighten out matters when I hear from you. I don't think I will need an attorney's assistance, but should I need one, I want to have permission from the company to do so.

276 • Patricia McGraw

McNulty to Matthews, March 22, 1914

I have paid the taxes in full for the year of 1911 and enclosed you will find receipt for same. ...I paid those bills so that you would have no delay in making out your report and hoping this will meet with the company's approval.

Matthews to McNulty, March 27, 1914

We thank you for adjusting this matter for us, and hand you herewith check for $23.85 to reimburse you for the amounts expended. We also enclose a check for $260 to cover your salary for the months of January and February, 1913.

McNulty to Matthews, April 2, 1914

Now, Mr. Matthews, the property is to be sold on the 15th inst, and I am somewhat worried about my back salary and would like to have some understanding from the company what they are going to do about it before the sale comes off.

Matthews to McNulty, April 6, 1914

With regard to the payment ...I assure you that you need have no anxiety whatever about it. You will be paid your salary right up to July, 1913 at the rate of $130 a month and at the rate of $75 a month from that time on. You understand that the mortgage is simply a matter of protection to them. Therefore, you are in the employ of the same interests you have been for some years, and this should be ample assurance that you will be paid according to the terms under which you are employed. Mr. Parker has made this perfectly clear to them, and they so understand it.

Matthews to McNulty, September 12, 1914

I must apologize for not sending your money sooner, but the fact is that I have been away on my vacation for the past month and the matter escaped attention during my absence. I enclose ...$130 for your salary for the month of June, 1913.

Newspaper article from the Santa Fe New Mexican, September 27, 1912 »

McNulty to Matthews, September 17, 1914

As I owed more than all the check you have sent me, I will be glad if you would please send me a few month's salary as I want to get in my winter's coal, wood, and horse feed before the roads get bad. I wish you would kindly see to this at your earliest convenience as I need the money.

McNulty & Friends Dialogs On Indians 1912 - 1913

McNulty to Matthews, July 16, 1912

Since I last wrote you the Indians have been keeping me busy, sorting in the Castilian where the mine caved in. The opening on top now is about 40 feet square and about 10 feet deep. On the 10th I saw five Indians in the hole and they ran to their horses and left. They have been coming ever since. Today I saw five more in the hole. I ordered them out and they ran.

SANTA FE NEW ME

SHERIFF CLOSSON HAS INDIAN WAR

HE FINDS INDIANS BOLDLY CARRYING OFF TURQUOISE FROM TIFFANY MINES FIVE ARE CAUGHT BY POSSE

Following a sensational roundup and the firing of a quantity of bird-shot, some of which took effect, Sheriff Charles Closson arrested five Indians yesterday evening on the charge of pilfering turquoise from the Tiffany mines, 15 miles south of Santa Fe. The prisoners gave their names as Antonio Tenorio, San Juan Corey, Juan Tecorio, Cruz Roseta and Reyes Roseta. They were brought to the city and lodged in the county jail.

From time to time for several years past, Thomas McNulty, in charge of the Tiffany mines, has been annoyed by Indians from Santo Domingo or Cochiti.

It appears that the Indians have hankered for turquoise to be used in their ceremonies and they have been slow to realize that since the purchase of the mines by the pale faces who make such fine jewelry in New York City, they have no longer the right to those "diggings". Less than two years ago, several Indians were arrested for stealing turquoise.

In former times the turquoise hunters selected moon lit nights for their operations and upon the approach of Mr. McNulty or his watchers, fled like deer. But yesterday they became bolder and carried on their work in broad daylight. To the threats of Mr. McNulty it is said they showed the utmost contempt.

Then the telephone wires were made to hum with messages and Sheriff Closson with Deputy Sheriff Seferino Baca were shortly afterward speeding in a motor to the scene of the trouble. Sheriff Closson took a shot gun with him. When he arrived the Indians fled in all directions. Seeing they would not halt the sheriff is said to have peppered them with birdshot, the Indians uttering war whoops and jumping high up in the air in a manner worthy of the wild west melodrama.

"Had I had a horse I might have rounded up a few more," said Sheriff Closson this afternoon, as he grinned at the recollection. "It is impossible to say how many Indians were in those mines. When we drove up, however, they swarmed like bees from a hive. They had been having a good time and evidently did not expect any one to interrupt them."

I will try and have an officer to catch them if I possibly can do so, if they keep coming to the mine. I would like to catch them there so as to prevent them from coming to the big mine. Two years ago I offered the telephone company $100 if they would run the telephone line to my house from the Cash Entry four miles, but they would not do it unless someone else wanted it. Now there is a ranch com-

> Memorandum for Mr. McNulty:
>
> And the purchase price of the Castilian Lode is $55.00. $ 55.
>
> The purchase price of the Gem Proof, $155.
>
> In completing these entries there may be additional costs, say $ 10.
>
> To prosecute application for patent for the Muniz Lode, you should have at least $100.
>
> And under our agreement with you we should have an advance on account of our fee for services, making a total of $100.
>   _____
> $420.00
>
> If company desires patent for the Agnes P. Lode you should have $250 to $300 to cover costs and expenses, and we would want and additional advance of $50.

To patent the ATC claims, the company needed $420 or in current terms around $20,000.

pany two miles from here, and they are also going to have the telephone line to their house. They are putting in the poles now so I expect to have the phone to my house in a few weeks, then I will be able to call the officers from Santa Fe and Cerrillos when I need them. There is seven miles of wire to be laid and about four miles of poles to be put in to get it attached to the main line.

McNulty to Matthews, August 6, 1912

    I had the mounted police out one day when they [the Indians] were in the hole and just before the mounted police arrived the Indians skipped and hid themselves. We could not find them; but I think it scared them some. The ranch man has got all his telephone poles in and wires part laid but his line will be about half a mile from here. I will have to go to Santa Fe this week and see the telephone company about putting it in my place. I do wish it was in so that I can call for assistance when needed.

McNulty to Parker, September 26, 1912

    I have written to Mr. Matthews several times about the Indians giving me trouble. For this last few weeks they have been coming steady; and today at 4:15 pm I telephoned to the sheriff in Santa Fe to come out immediately that there were fifteen Indians at the Castilian mine. He came at once with his deputy in an automobile and we finally captured five, which he has taken in to Santa Fe tonight with him. The balance of the Indians that ran away and could not be captured.

    The sheriff and deputy fired several shots at them, but don't know if any of them were wounded. The five that were captured was through my assistance with a shotgun by preventing them from running away from the sheriff. The Indians that escaped had guns with them, and one of the five that we caught had a rifle on him which the sheriff took from him.

    I have to go to Santa Fe tomorrow and be there by 9 am to prefer charges against them. I have also two witnesses, Mexicans (who live near the mine), who saw them there which I must also take in a wagon tomorrow as the sheriff said so. ...I would have taken my wife, as she is the chief witness, but I cannot leave the place alone. If they are bound over to the grand jury, she will appear as evidence against them. If it had not been for my having the telephone, we could not have caught the Indians, and I think it is worth fifty dollars, *the amount I have to pay for having it in, to myself as well as to the company. I do wish you would please send me some money as I badly need it.*

McNulty to Matthews, March 19, 1913

We went to Santa Fe on the third and as the grand jury had other cases to hear before us, we had to return home the next day and go in again on the 10th inst and got there by 12 pm. We had a hearing before the grand jury, but have not heard at this writing whether the jury indicted the Indians or not. If they have indicted them, we will both have to go to court.

New Mexican newspaper clipping, April 1913

...listing the indictments: Francisco Pacheco, Transito Romero, Manuel Tortolito, and Cruz Calabaza, Santa Domingo Pueblo Indians, for flourishing deadly weapons at J.P. McNulty, manager of the Turquoise mines, 14 miles south of Santa Fe. ...[also included in the indictments:] John Simonson and John Alter, killing a steer unlawful; George W. Armijo, obtaining a warrant by false pretense, and Cleve Woodall for killing an ass.

McNulty & Friends
Dialogs On Mining & Patents
1912-1913

Matthews to McNulty, January 23, 1912

We have instructed Messrs. Easley & Easley to proceed to obtain patents on our mines and claims at Los Cerrillos, and we trust you will render them all the assistance necessary in the matter. We have written Mr. Davis to forward all the papers in his possession relating to this matter to Messrs. Easley & Easley.

McNulty to Matthews, February 2, 1912

    I received your letter dated Jan 23rd, also a letter from Attorney Easley, which I enclose in this letter. ...To prosecute application for patent for the Muñiz Lode, there should be at least $100 and under our agreement with you, we should have an advance on account $100 of our fee for services, making a total of $420. If company desired patent for the Agnes P Lode, you should have $250 to $300 to cover costs and expenses, and we would want an additional advance of $50.

Parker to George Kunz, February 13, 1912

    I hasten to enclose herewith letter of introduction to Mr. J.P. McNulty, Superintendent of the American Turquoise Co., Cerrillos, and am very much pleased that we shall have the opportunity of having you inspect the mines in Santa Fe County of the American Turquoise Company, as your opinion is beyond price.

Parker to McNulty, February 13, 1912

    This will serve to introduce to you our friend, Dr. G. F. Kunz, a stockholder of the American Turquoise Co., who wishes to visit the mines in Santa Fe County. You will be kind enough to give Dr. Kunz every attention. Show him everything that belongs to the company, also affording him such information in every respect that he may desire.

McNulty to Matthews, March 4, 1912

    I was in Santa Fe last week and seen Mr. Easley in regards to the patent. He told me that he could not proceed any further at present, and that Mr. S.B. Davis had not sent him any of the papers in connection with it. I also had a talk with the Receiver at the Land Office in regards to the patent of the Muñiz claim I told him that the property was still in litigation at the time that the Government canceled the patent for the Muñiz claim and that he as receiver of the Land Office and his partner also objected in giving a patent to the American Turquoise Co, while the case was in litigation, and he said he would look over the matter for me when he had more time; and ...it seems to me that Mr. Easley may be able to get the patent on the Muniz on this basis. I would have written sooner only I was thinking that we would hear from you by the first of the month, as the men are anxiously waiting for their pay, although it is small they need it.

McNulty to Matthews, July 4, 1912

I have received a letter to come into Santa Fe as soon as I can for me to make an affidavit in regards to the amount of work done on the property at for the assessment before he [Easeley] can proceed further. I will go in tomorrow as requested. A few nights ago after the heavy rains, the Castilian mine caved in as the timbers have been rotten for years; now it is opened on top about 25 and 40 feet, there is still loose ground yet to fall in. I think it is about 20 feet deep to where the dirt settled.

McNulty to Matthews, August 10, 1912

I went to Santa Fe yesterday to see the telephone company and made agreement with them to run the line from the ranch man line to my house to put in poles and wires. They agreed to put the phone into my house including everything for the consideration of $50 which is a great deal cheaper than I had expected, but I have to pay $1 per month extra to Cerrillos and some extra from Cerrillos to Santa Fe. I also saw Mr. Easley and he said that he will have the survey for the Muniz claim.

Matthews to McNulty, August 16, 1912

...with reference to the telephone matter has been noted. We are at a loss to understand why it should be necessary for you to have a telephone. The company is not doing any business and we see no reason for adding to our expenses in this manner. You will, therefore, not make any contract for telephone services, unless you are willing to bear the expense of it yourself, as the company would not be at all warranted in taking on this additional expense.

McNulty to Matthews, September 3, 1912

I have got the right away to put the telephone in for my self own accommodation, and protection, as the company has never offered to protect me or the property, so the telephone is my own personal property and I am very glad of having it here and there is not one of the poles on the company's property. I have never intimated to the Company in any of my letters that I expected them to pay for it, but I thought that the company would have been glad for me to have the telephone in for our safety instead of writing me such a letter of indifference. This last ten days I have been expecting the Surveyor out to re-survey the Muniz claim, but he has not come yet. It is doubtful if the we get the patent all completed without having to do the assessment work before the first of the year, but Mr. Easley said he would try and have it done, in time to avoid doing the assessment work, but I must hurry him up. ...send me two months salary so I can pay for the phone and other bills.

George Kaseman [owner of Madrid coal mines] to McNulty, October 24, 1912.

I do not understand why you cannot buy coal from Mr. Williams. I spoke to you hurriedly this morning, but I see no reason why you should have to haul your coal three miles further. If you prefer to do so, we will sell you coal at Madrid, but you had better call up the mine office and find out whether you can get it before sending your teams. The price will be $4.25 per ton at the mines.

McNulty to Matthew, November 1, 1912

The surveyor was here on the 26th of October and surveyed the Muniz claim for patent. The notice plat may not be ready for a few weeks in the Surveyor General's Office for me to get to be posted on the claim, and it has to be posted on the claim for ninety days, before the attorney can apply for the final patent. I advise you to acquaint Mr. Parker that the assessment work must be done on the Muniz claim by the first of the year or it will be jumpable, and also on the Agnes P claim, if the Company *wants to hold it. ...there is not so much danger of the Agnes P claim being jumped by anyone as there is no turquoise in sight there, but the work must be done on the Muniz claim as it is the principle claim that we have turquoise in.*

Matthews to McNulty, November 7, 1912

With reference to the assessment work, we had hoped that the patenting of our claims would be effected in ample time to save the necessity of doing any assessment work, but inasmuch as we cannot obtain the patent on the Muniz claim for sometime, we will have to go ahead and have the assessment work done on that claim, and you may proceed at once. So far as the Agnes P. claim is concerned, we prefer not to have that done at present. It can be taken care of later.

McNulty to Matthews, November 14, 1912

I will start the assessment work as soon as I can get a good man, as they are all at work, and it is very hard to get a good miner. In regards to the Agnes P claim if you intend to hold it, it could be done in the tunnel of the Muñiz claim before we get the Muñiz patented, but not afterwards, as it would have to be done on the Agnes P claim by itself.

McNulty to Matthews, December 2, 1912

Your letters of the 14th and 23rd of November came promptly to hand. We note what you say with reference to the assessment work on the Agnes P claim. If you can have the assessment work on the Agnes P done at the same time as that on the Muniz claim, without any cost other than what it costs to do the Muniz claim alone, you may go ahead and have it done, but we do not wish to create any additional expense at the present time, and would prefer to have the assessment work on the Agnes P claim remain for a later date than to incur any expense in connection with it at this time.

McNulty to Matthews, February 4, 1913

I have finished the assessment work on the Muniz claim and laid off the man.

Zalenski to McNulty, November 18, 1912

At Mr. J.A. Stillman's request, I have arranged to make an examination of the American Turquoise Company's property and am writing to ask how to reach you from Los Cerrillos. I expect to leave here between Dec. 5th. and 10th., but will let you know as soon as possible the exact date. Can I arrange to stay with you at the property? This would probably save time, instead of driving back and forth from Cerrillos.

McNulty to Zalenski, November 23, 1912

I am glad to hear that Mr. J.A. Stillman is going to take some interest in the property, in having you to come out here and examine it. In answer to your inquiry about staying here at the mine while inspecting it, will say that we will try and accommodate you the best we can do. As there is very poor accommodation at Cerrillos, I would suggest that you come to Santa Fe, and stop at the Palace Hotel, and if you will let me know the day that you intend to arrive in Santa Fe I will meet you there with my single buggy and we can drive out here, which is seventeen miles.

I would like you to please let me know about five days before hand, as I do not go to Cerrillos every day for my mail it being seven miles from here. I do not mistrust you, on account of past troubles, you will need a letter of introduction from Mr. R.A. Parker, President of the American Turquoise Co. I regret very much that you will not be able to examine all of the workings of the property owing to the rotten timbers and ladders, etc, but I think you will be able to see sufficient to warrant the company to proceed with the work.

Zalenski to McNulty, November 26, 1912

...have your letter of Nov.23, and thank you for the information regarding accommodations etc. I will be glad to stay with you at the property. I note what you say in regard to a letter of introduction from Mr. R.A. Parker, president of the company, and have written to get this, or a letter from Mr. Stillman. I will get off at Santa Fe as you suggest, and stop at the Palace Hotel. ...will be glad to have you meet me with your buggy to drive out to the property.

Parker to McNulty, November 27, 1912

In order that we may be in a position to know what the prospects are for the mining properties owned by the American Turquoise Co., we have instructed Mr. Edward R. Zalenski, who is an expert, to make an examination, both in Santa Fe and Grant Counties. I have given him a letter of introduction to you and I hope you will do everything in your power to make his examination easy and complete. Our future operations will devolve largely on the basis of his report.

Zalenski to McNulty, November 30, 1912

Am leaving here Monday, Dec.2, and will arrive in Santa Fe Wednesday, Dec.4, about five or six p.m. Will stop at the Palace Hotel, as you suggest. I will be glad to have you meet me Thursday morning, if possible, or if not please send word how I can get out to the property. I have a letter to you from Mr. Parker.

McNulty to Matthews, December 7, 1912

...am sending you today the pay roll for the Month of November, but the hardware bill, powder etc, will send next time. I met Mr. Zalenski in Santa Fe on the 4th, and we went to the Land Office and Surveyor General Office on the 5th to see about the patent. and also to the Corporation Commissioners to see about other matters, and then drove home in the afternoon. I have been showing him around the property yesterday and today. We do not know exactly how long it will take to examine all the inside of the property; but he will not be able to see one half of the workings in the big mine on ac-

count of the timbers and ladders being rotten. Everything is moving along all O.K.

McNulty to Matthews, December 15, 1912

I met Mr. Zalenski on the 4th inst in Santa Fe and we drove out in the afternoon of the 5th inst and he has been examining the property every day up to noon of the 13th inst, then I drove him to Cerrillos and he went to Grant County. Very true, turquoise mining is new to him, which I could see, as he had to take all the information from me on the Turquoise bearing rock, but I must say for a young man he is very smart as a mining surveyor and mineralogist, and when he sends you a map of the workings of the property, it will give you an idea of the amount of work that is done. ...Mr. Zalenski was astonished to see the two tunnels that I had driven, without the assistance of a mining engineer, or even a compass to go by. By him examining this property first it will help him considerably in Grant County on the Turquoise bearing rock, and I gave him all the information I knew about the Grant County property before he left here. I am very glad that he came here to examine the property as it will give the company a better idea what they have got here, and I hope his report will be satisfactory.

McNulty to Parker, February 27, 1913

I would like to know if Mr. Zalenski had sent in his report on the property to Mr. Stillman yet, and also if he has shipped all the turquoise matrix that he took away from here with him for Mr. Stillman.

Parker to McNulty, March 4, 1913

```
     Yes, Mr. Zalenski did send to Mr. Stillman
with his report samples of stone taken from
the different mines in Santa Fe and Grant
Counties.  His report is very complete and
interesting although it may not be as en-
couraging as we would like to see it.  At any
rate, Mr. Zalenski is an expert, we think,
in his line.
```

Easley [McNulty's patent lawyer], February 11, 1914

We have to advise you that patent for the Blue Gem group [McNulty's claims] of lode mining claims has been received at the local land office and is ready for delivery.

McNulty to Matthews, October 23, 1914

Am also glad to know that the company have bought in the property, and hope that work on the property will be started soon.

McNulty to Matthews, January 8, 1915

The weather has been so severe here that we could not go to Cerrillos for 5 days. ...You may be wondering why I get short of money. It is because I have claims that I have to have the assessment work done on and as one of my notes will be due on the 14th inst. I am very glad that you sent me as much as you have. These claims that I have had the assessment work done on are joining the Castilian one on each side, running parallel which my wife bought from a party three years ago, and am having the assessment work done as the company may need them if they should start up to work on the Castilian. The other claims I have had patented which takes in two thirds of the two hills where the Muniz and Morning Star claims are. There are 31 acres in the group I have patented. I told Mr. Zalinsky (the expert) who was here that I would not sell them to anyone else if the Company wanted them, which I expect he put in his report about the hills when he was here to examine the property. I write you this so that when you reorganize you will know all about this property and that you will acquaint Mr. Parker about it.

McNulty to Matthews, June 1, 1915

As I have not heard from you for some time, I am writing to know what is the matter? I am badly in need of money as I have to borrow and run credit and wish you would please see to it that I will get more than one month's salary at a time. The unusual heavy rains these last two months has damaged the house considerably. The walls are giving away, and I have 4 big timbers bracing the walls outside to keep them from falling as it is a dirt roof on the top. It is too heavy for the walls and last month it leaked all over the house and all bedding, mattresses, and carpets; everything was saturated through. We had to keep mopping up the water for 24 hours. The only remedy to save the house will be to put rubber slate roofing as the walls will not stand a shingle roof, the timbers would be too heavy. The house needs plastering on the outside as the rains washed the adobes away, and it has not been plastered since it was built 14 years ago. I wish you would please notify Mr. Gilbert about this before the rainy season starts in or we will have the same experience and perhaps the walls will fall out.

Matthews to McNulty, June 15, 1915

I will see that you get some more money very soon. I have taken up with Mr. Parker the question of roofing your house, of which he approves, and have put the matter up to Mr. Gilbert for final decision, at the same time urging him to have the thing done. No doubt you will hear from him very shortly. I am sure everything will work out all right.

Gilbert to McNulty, June 17, 1915

Mr. James Matthews has turned over to me your letter to him of the 1st instant. Will you kindly procure several estimates for the necessary rubber slate roofing and for the plastering on the outside of the house. I am willing to pay, as Trustee of the American Turquoise Company, a nominal sum for such repairs but must insist that the repairs be made for as small a sum as possible. You can have this work done and send the bill to me for payment, which should not exceed, in my estimation, more than $100.

McNulty to Gilbert, July 18, 1916

I went to Santa Fe and made several inquiries and got the material as cheap as possible which *you will see from the itemized bill, and I hired cheap help and put it on myself. All the plastering I have done on the house is the top of the walls on the building and around the foundation where it was giving way with cement and sand and the remainder of the house is still unplastered, which may take about $20 to finish it. I did not want to finish it till I heard from you, and I also thought it better not to do it for a month or so till the rainy season is over...*

Gilbert to McNulty, July 23, 1915

You are also authorized to complete the plastering, but let it not exceed $20.

Matthews to McNulty, July 28, 1915

Our esteemed friend, Dr. George F. Kunz, is desirous of obtaining some small specimens of turquoise rock taken 100 and 200 feet from the mine, and also at the point of contact between the turquoise and the other rock. I ask therefore, if you will be kind enough to send to Dr. Kunz, in care of Tiffany and Company, 401 Fifth Avenue, New York City, two or three pounds of each by mail, and to make a sketch of where they came from.

McNulty to Gilbert, August 2, 1915

Your letter of July 23rd with checks to pay for labor and material for finishing the house has been received and many thanks for it. Enclosed you will please find receipts for same. Am glad to have permission to plaster the house when the weather permits. It is a good thing the roof was fixed as we had the heaviest storm here in eleven years and as some of the holes are full of water, it will save much for the hauling of water to do the plastering with. I will be glad if you will kindly see that I get some remittance soon as I am badly in need of it.

McNulty to Matthews, August 2, 1915

...in regards to George K. Kunz ...will say it is impossible to go that depth as no one can go below

the 45 feet in depth in either of No. 1 or No. 2 shafts, as the timbers in No. 2 shaft are all rotten which is the main shaft. I cannot obtain any turquoise specimens from there until it is retimbered and the No. 2 shaft, the timbering and the dirt of No. 2 shaft has fallen in and filled the shaft to about 40 feet from the top.

I explained this to Kunz when he was here and showed him the only place where I could get out some specimens or turquoise in No. 2 shaft in the tunnel and crosscut at 45 feet from the surface where I went through some of the old Spanish workings. I will ship to Dr. Kunz in about a week from now some specimens I took from there as soon as I get them trimmed for shipment, the same kind of blue as the last ones I shipped to the company. Only in one place where I put a ladder in the main way, about 16 feet, the other report below this depth was taken from what I told him.

You will find in Mr. Zalinski's report that he did not go any deeper in the mine than 45 feet from the surface on account of the rotten timbers. I wish the company would have some work done where I have taken out these specimens, as it is at the bottom where the Spaniards finished working. I don't know what is under till some work is done there, and I would like to sink a winze or shaft to ascertain what is under.

McNulty to Gilbert, September 25, 1915

...it has taken me some time to get a party to take the contract at my price of $16 but I got two men, father and son, and it has taken them five and one half days to do it. They hauled three loads of sand three miles and hauled water every day in their wagon when they came to work. I think they will not take a contract again like this one; some parties wanted $30 to do it. ...I have had a hard time to hold the walls. I had two timbers bracing one end and I hand to put one more against it yesterday.

McNulty to Gilbert, October 6, 1915

My wife and I have separated and divided everything up on the 26th of August last. So I am down to bedrock and in debt. So if you will please send me some money as soon as you can as I need it.

McNulty to Matthews, November 25, 1915

You will please see to it that I get some money soon as you can if you have not already sent it as I am in debt and need some money to pay some of my debts. I have written to Mr. Gilbert on October 6th that I was down to bedrock and in debt but have not heard from him as yet.

Annual Report to the State Corporation Commission of New Mexico, 1915

The Corporation herein named, organized under the laws of new Jersey, does hereby make the following report in compliance with the provisions of Sec. 48, Chap. 79, Laws of 1905, entitled, "An Act to Regulate the Formation and Government of Corporation for Mining, Manufacturing, Industrial and other Pursuits." [Listing of officers], Robert A. Parker, President, James Matthews, Secretary, Courtland Betts, Director, Wm. A. Pinkerton, Director, W.. Bogart, Director; Noted: James Matthews is also shown as treasurer of the company. This report was filed Nov. 2, 1914. Nothing has been filed since but there is a letter in the files dated November 3, 1915, and signed by Shearman & Sterling, 55 Wall Street, New York City, which states that the company is no longer in business and had abandoned its charter. Evidently these attorneys represent the new owners.

Chapter 10
1916 - 1921

The Protection of the Law

We are instructed by the present owners of the Turquoise Mines that they have decided to dispense with the services of a superintendent, and they have asked us to inform you that your services will therefore not be required after September 1, 1917.
     Shearman & Sterling [lawyers for defunct company] to McNulty,
August 9, 1917

SICK TO BED

Although McNulty owned a lot of land in 1916, he had little cash on hand. His meager salary along with his rental properties paid his expenses, but his health deteriorated to the point that he fell heavily in debt. Since he needed to hospitalized, McNulty shot off multiple letters to the new trustee of the company, Fredric Gilbert, but the miner's request for back payment of salary went unnoticed. Finally in desperation, McNulty sent a letter to Parker asking for help. His letter stated, "Sick to bed. Three weeks under doctor's care." McNulty termed his illness The Grip.

Gilbert received the letter from Parker, and the trustee reacted immediately by sending $525 to McNulty by special delivery. Of course, a letter arrived later and noted that the company paid McNulty's salary from September 1914 through March of 1915. That meant McNulty's salary was only one year behind. "We hope that you will have a speedy recovery," Gilbert's letter stated.

In spite of the company's inability to pay for McNulty's salary, Gilbert ever so politely asked him to keep watch on the mines. No matter how many foreclosures, no matter how many times the Pinkertons and Stillman wrestled for control of the company, they still hoped for the best. So did Gilbert.

By April of 1916 McNulty's health improved enough so that he could carry on letter writing. At that time, Gilbert asked about the possibility of finding copper or gold on the Muñiz and Morning Star claims. McNulty dryly responded that the trustee should look at a previous report completed by Zalenski that described the situation. McNulty said that the Muñiz, the Morning Star and the Castilian mines contained some copper, gold, silver, and turquoise, but the other claims showed nothing. With that pronouncement, Gilbert lost interest in mining and the taxes for the claims went unpaid. McNulty took it upon himself to pay the taxes. Then he sat, waiting for reimbursement, which eventually arrived.

He sent many letters back East, and just as many went unanswered. He reminded Gilbert that he stayed on the claims because they were too good to abandon, and some day things might change.

With things shut down, McNulty turned to his own claims and tried to sell them or at the very least find a partner to help finance mining operations. He still believed riches lay below the surface in the form of gold or silver. Should the price of turquoise rise, he knew a fortune could be made. One of McNulty's friends commented that the miner must have believed the riches of King Solomon's legendary mines were within reach. McNulty thought that if properly funded, his mines could produce $20,000 per year in turquoise, copper, or silver. He found no takers, no partners, no lessees, and no buyers.

The mining near Cerrillos had pretty much played out for the turquoise company, but McNulty worked his own claims. The company clearly had no intention of investing any more money into mining ventures. Months went by without word from the trustee. More months went by without any of his watchman's salary arriving.

McNulty's earlier illness had slowed him down. He felt old. "I am one month on the twenty sixth year here, and I am getting old and would like to see the company do something..." McNulty commented.

Suddenly, August 9, 1917, the company, through its lawyers, sent McNulty $900 to pay up his entire salary, and he received a notice that his services were no longer required. The 71 year-old took the news

McNulty was a guiding force in the Scottish Rite organization and he enjoyed his time interacting in the Masonic circles. He was instrumental in establishing the Masonic Lodge #19 in Cerrillos, which for many years met in this Cerrillos building.

in stride. After all, he had been considering moving back to Cerrillos, and now, with his salary completely paid he had enough to move or stay and hire people to help him work his own claims. The only problem was that McNulty had already determined he would spend the winter in the Turquoise Hill and with all his winter supplies laid in, he would have to bear the expense of taking it back to Cerrillos. But he could get it done. Then he asked who was to replace him. The answer: no one. The company decided to abandon the property and leave it unprotected, including the dumps and the mine shafts and tunnels. This McNulty could not fathom. Too much to be risked — thieves would steal from the dumps. They would dismantle the house. They would work the dumps and the mines, and they would remove all the tools.

    A flurry of letters flew back and forth between New York and New Mexico. Gilbert wanted McNulty gone, then he decided to let McNulty stay rent-free for his guard services. McNulty at first declined the offer, but eventually he decided to stay. McNulty again pointed out that copper lay in the mines at about 60 feet below the surface —

native copper that could coat a knife in less than one minute. However, once the copper was evaluated it was virtually worthless.

"I have made up my mind to stay here while I have one dollar to buy things with rather than leave the property vacant," McNulty said in 1917. He offered to work the property for his salary, an offer ultimately accepted.

One of the brighter moments for McNulty in 1917 occurred when he bragged about winning a bet from the U.S. Senator Thomas Catron. McNulty had bet $200 to Catron's $100 that Charley Clossen would be defeated as sheriff. Clossen lost and McNulty won. The miner smugly reminded his daughter of the times that Clossen had refused to protect his house from robberies and had indeed declined to investigate many of the Indian incidents. Catron paid up, then a few months later, McNulty wrote to the senator and requested a pension from the United States Infantry which Catron expedited.

With more time on his hands since he didn't have to complete assessment work for the company, McNulty engaged in civic activism, organizing for various causes. For 1917, McNulty and the business owners of Cerrillos decided that the postmaster needed a raise, and they set about getting Congress to raise the third class postmaster's salary to $150 per year or a whopping $12.50 per month.

With mining activity stopped, the trustee determined that the mines would be held for sale, with their dollar value in land and not in turquoise, gold, silver or copper. To that end, Gilbert controlled every cent, yet at the same time he expected McNulty to take care of tax issues and offer a modicum of protection for the buildings and perhaps the dumps.

Every day that McNulty's business took him off the property, thieves would come and sort the dumps. If his stay extended over any length of time, the thieves blasted, carried away stones, and removed timbers and tools. Just as in the past, the sheriff slowly responded, but eventually he managed to capture one family of thieves, who subsequently were never prosecuted. The evidence they had left behind were their horses with prominent brands proclaiming their ownership.

By March of 1918, Shearman and Sterling, representatives of Gilbert, remarked that they had hired attorneys to settle the increased tax issue. After all, they were being taxed more than any other mineral property in the state. McNulty answered that they should have

JOHN W. STERLING
JOHN A. GARVER
CHAUNCEY B. GARVER
CORTLAND BETTS
CARL A. MEAD
HARRY W. FORBES
FREDERIC N. GILBERT
FREDERICK W. JACKSON

CABLE ADDRESS,"NUMLATUS"

LAW OFFICES
SHEARMAN & STERLING
55 WALL STREET, NEW YORK
NATIONAL CITY BANK BUILDING

March 11, 1918.

James P. McNulty, Esq.,
  Cerrillos,
  New Mexico.

Dear Sir:

    We are in receipt of your letter of March 2, enclosing bill for the 1917 taxes on the Turquoise Mines, and have sent a check in payment of the same to the County Treasurer. As you know, the taxes for 1917 are nearly four times what they have been in previous years. We took up the matter with Messrs. Easley & Easley, at the time the assessment was raised last Spring, but they assured us that while the valuations were increased, the rate would be correspondingly reduced, and that therefore the amount of the taxes would be approximately the same. Replying upon their advice, we did not prosecute an appeal from the assessment. Since we learned the amount of the taxes for 1917 we have written several letters to Messrs. Easley & Easley for an explanation, but have received no reply from them. We certainly hope that the taxes for this year will be reduced to the amount previously paid, in view of the fact that there is no income from the property.

Sherman & Sterling, lawyers for Fredric Gilbert, conceded that McNulty should take care of the tax problems since the money they sent to lawyers had accomplished nothing.

hired him instead of the lawyers since the elder lawyer of the firm had died and the younger one was in a hospital in California. It was no wonder that the taxes had not been properly attended to. McNulty got the taxes reduced. Maybe the commissioners and assessor agreed with him when he offered to sell all the improvements for $250. No one took him up on the offer.

    October 10, 1918, McNulty faced reality. The mines produced no profit in turquoise. He had spent $900 prospecting, tunneling, and hiring workers, and he only managed to sell $360 worth of stone. Even facing that reality, McNulty's loyalty lay with the land. He still paid the taxes and still requested Gilbert have some samples assayed for gold or silver. Gilbert did not share McNulty's dream.

McNulty wrote in 1919 that he was too old to live at the Turquoise Hill any more, especially since he lived alone. He told Gilbert that the time had come to find someone to stay on the property or to let the capital improvements and mining equipment fall to thieves. Even the dumps and the mines would be fully worked once he left.

GRATITUDE & TAXES

Gilbert asked McNulty one more time in 1919 to see to the taxes since the trustee had not received a tax bill. This McNulty agreed to do. Unfortunately, this time the tax assessment remained in place, and Gilbert had to pay substantially more for the non-producing mine.

Even though McNulty had left the mines and didn't "go up very often", when he did arrive on the claims he noted all the stolen property and the work that had been done. He moved a little more slowly now than he used to since he was more than 71 years old, and in his life he had seen a lot of hard action. To get to the mines he had to take roads by buggy. By the time he got out of the buggy, tied his horse, and retrieved his rifle, the thieves usually had enough time to run off. On one visit, he noted that the people had taken doors, windows, cellar doors, mop boards and started to take up the floor from the house. He pretty much knew who had taken the items, and if they could be found he could identify them. He could even identify accurately turquoise taken from his dumps and his mines, but that evidence never did stand up in a court of law.

Finally in 1920, Shearman and Sterling remarked that they appreciated McNulty taking an interest in the property and assured him of Gilbert's gratitude. "We are, however, grateful to you and trust that the future may have in store something worth while for the property on which you spent so many years...", their letter commented.

Ever the optimist, McNulty determined that he would sell the Turquoise Company mines and maybe his own mines. He set about doing just that in spite of the fact Gilbert declined to state the amount

INDIAN WARS.   *Act of March 4, 1917.*

3-645

Certificate Division.

Notice of Issue and Fees To Claimants

DEPARTMENT OF THE INTERIOR
BUREAU OF PENSIONS

Washington, D. C., MAR 23 1918

James McNulty,

Sir:-

Herewith is transmitted a certificate No. 7799 for Orig pension, issued in your favor. No one is recognized as attorney in this case and No fee is payable by the Disbursing Clerk for the payment of pensions.

You should not pay any fee yourself to any person for services as agent or attorney in the prosecution of this claim.

Very respectfully,

Acting Commissioner.

McNulty began receiving a pension from the government for his service in the army. He was approaching 70 years of age and had occasional bouts of sickness. He tried to stay on the claims, but he knew he would need to move closer to civilization.

he wanted for the mines. If and when the final deal was made, the Pinkertons and the Stillman estates had to agree to the terms, since they were the only two bond holders left. Throughout the years other bond holders had been forced out through foreclosure proceedings.

When McNulty reached 75 years of age, he felt a need for assistance from his daughter, and he granted her power of attorney.

Cerrillos N. Mex.
Dec. 21, 1919

Shearman & Sterling,
55 Wall St.,
New York.

Gentlemen:

I have been up to see the property today and found that it is in terrible shape. Parties are working the mine and also sorting the dump. There was a party of six (two women and the rest men) on the dump and as soon as they saw me they ran. Before I could get out of the buggy and get the horse tied they got over the hill and out of reach although I had a rifle with me.

They have taken doors, windows, cellar doors, and mop boards and have started to take up the floor from the house.

I am going in to Santa Fe tomorrow to see if I can get the sheriff to come out with me

---

McNulty's life had been the mines, and he struggled against those who stole from them. Left without a guard, the mines were open to anyone. They took turquoise from the dump and even hauled off the doors and windows.

TIFFANY BLUE • 301

LAPIDARY WORK
A SPECIALTY

FOREIGN OFFICE AND WORKSHOP
DIETZENSTRASSE 49
IDAR, GERMANY

DENVER, COLO., Sept. 13 191 8

Mr J. P. McNulty
Cerrillos N. Mex.

Dear Sir: Received the parcel with 30 ounces rough Turq. for which I enclose Check for $100.00.

There seem to be quiet a few very light colored pieces in, which stones after they are cut do not sell. But we will try it out and cut them all and I shall see whether we could use more or not for that price. As I said in my last letter, no price is too high for the rough material, as long as we can get enough for the finished goods. But people are used to buy Turq. very cheap, and therefore it will be hard to educate them to the point, that they are willing to pay more for nice goods. But I shall let you know and if we can make it go, I will order some more of that material.

Very truly yours
Wm. Kley.

In 1918 McNulty sent a parcel of turquoise to a lapidary in Germany, but that lapidary declined additional Tiffany turquoise. Worldwide, all turquoise was so inexpensive that people wouldn't pay more for the better quality stone.

McNulty & Friends
Mining Business & Finances
1916 - 1921

McNulty to Parker, January 5, 1916

Please see to it that the trustee or someone of the company send me some money, at least one year's salary. Sick to bed. Three weeks under doctor's care. May have to go to hospital. Have man here with me and no money to pay. I owe $600. Please answer and take for this message out of my salary.

302 • Patricia McGraw

Telegram, Gilbert to McNulty, January 6, 1916

Sending check for $525 by special delivery.

Shearman & Sterling to McNulty, January 6, 1916

Mr. R.A. Parker has turned over to us a telegram you sent him on January 5th. We enclose herewith Mr. Gilbert's check as Trustee of the American Turquoise Company for $525 to cover salary for the months of September, October, November, and December 1914, and January, February and March, 1915. We also enclose a receipt for salary paid to you on August 4, 1915, of $225 covering salary for the months of June, July, and August 1914. ...We are extremely sorry to hear that you have been ill for the past three weeks and hope that you will have a speedy recovery.

Gilbert to McNulty, April 20, 1916

I should be pleased to know what prospects there are for finding any copper or gold on the Muniz and Morning Star claims. Will you write me fully on this subject.

McNulty to Gilbert, April 28, 1916

All turquoise mines in New Mexico are copper mines after a certain depth from 40-100 feet. When Mr. E.A. Zalenski, the mining engineer, was here, I have shown him everything and have told him all about the bottom as we could not go down. He had taken several hundred samples. So if you see his report to Mr. J.A. Stillman in the year 1913. You will know more about the property, the Muniz, the Morning Star, and Castilian claims, are all right for copper, gold, silver and turquoise, but the Gem and the Sky Blue claims are not. ...the Phillip [Phelps] *Dodge Company has bought all the turquoise property in the southern counties and are working them for copper.*

McNulty to Shearman and Sterling, September 13, 1916

I have not got a reply from Mr. Gilbert to my let-

ter of August 25. I now write you, gentlemen, and ask you to please send me some money as I need it. If you will send me one year's salary, it will pay my debts and keep me for the winter.

McNulty to Shearman and Sterling, November 13, 1916
We enclose herewith a check to your order for $300, covering your salary for December 1915, January, February and March 1916.

McNulty to Shearman and Sterling, November 21, 1916
Gentlemen, if it were not for the back salary that the company had owed me, I could not live on the $75 per month as it takes all of one hundred dollars per month as everything is three times as dear as they were two years ago.

For many years McNulty conducted his banking business at the First National Bank of Santa Fe.

McNulty to Shearman and Sterling, November 25, 1916
I have paid the first half of the American Turquoise Company taxes for the year 1916 and enclosed you will find receipt for same, $14.70. The last half will be due next May.

McNulty to Shearman & Sterling, March 4, 1917
As I have not heard from the American Turquoise Company for some time, I expect you have forgotten all about me, but I am still here after a hard winter so far. I had to go to Santa Fe last week to fill out the blanks for this year's taxes. Which will be the same as last year if they do not raise it.

304 • Patricia McGraw

The First National Bank
of Santa Fe, New Mexico

Capital, Surplus and Net Undivided Profits
$225,000.00

OFFICERS
LEVI A. HUGHES, President
ARTHUR SELIGMAN, Vice President
JAMES B. READ, Cashier
CHAS. J. ECKERT, Asst. Cashier.

DIRECTORS
LEVI A. HUGHES   PAUL A. F. WALTER
ARTHUR SELIGMAN   SALAMON SPITZ
BENJ. F. PANKEY   JOHN PFLUEGER

ORGANIZED DECEMBER 3, 1870

MEMBER FEDERAL RESERVE SYSTEM OF
THE UNITED STATES
DISTRICT No. 10

No deposit too large for SAFETY. None too small for COURTESY.

The Flag!

IT speaks sublimity, and every part has a voice. Its stripes of alternate red and white proclaim the original union of thirteen states to maintain the declaration of independence. White is purity; red, for valor; blue, for justice.
—*Charles Sumner (1873)*

McNulty's bank showed off the assets of the bank and rewarded depositors with a patriotic flag.

McNulty to Shearman and Sterling, March 15, 1917

I would like to hear from you if the company will do some work soon. I am one month on the twenty sixth year here and I am getting old and would like to see the company do something.

Shearman and Sterling to McNulty, August 9, 1917

We enclose herewith a check to your order for $900, covering your salary in full to September 1, 1917. ...We are instructed by the present owners of the Turquoise Mines that they have decided to dispense with the services of a superintendent, and they have asked us to inform you that your services will therefore not be required after September 1, 1917.

McNulty to Shearman and Sterling, August 15, 1917

Your letter August 9 inst with check to pay my salary to September 1st has been received and

*many thanks for it as it is the first time in 25 years and six months that I have been paid up in full.
...in regards to me being discharged I will say that I will turn over everything belonging to the company to the man that you send here and show him all the property on the first. All except the house. It may take a week or 10 days for me to get all of my things moved to Cerrillos as I have to give 30 days notice to get my house. I have $30 worth of coal and wood and two tons of hay I must take to Cerrillos if the man that comes here does not buy the coal and wood. If you had given me notice sooner, I could have everything moved by the first. I got the coal, wood, and hay last week. I would like it very much if the company would send me a recommendation for the many years I have been in charge of their property.*

Shearman & Sterling to McNulty, August 21, 1917

```
     It was not the intention of the American
Turquoise Company to supplant you by having
another man take your place.  The property,
as you know, has not produced anything for
the stockholders for a long time, and it was
their desire that further expenses for car-
rying the property be reduced to a minimum.
They had, however, intended to leave the
property without any superintendant or care-
taker.  But this would not apply to any per-
sonal or movable property there might be on
the land, which we think should be disposed
of.  We shall be glad to have you advise us
as to the best manner for handling such prop-
erty.  The persons interested in the prop-
erty have long relied on you to look after
their interests and they have never desired
to employ anyone in your place.  If, there-
fore, you find it convenient to remain on
the property, we are sure the owners would
be glad to have you do so, for an indefinite
length of time, provided that in case of a
sale of the property your being there would
not interfere with the purchasers taking full
possession when they desire to do so.  On
behalf of the American Turquoise Company, we
desire to express appreciation for your long
```

continued interest in the property and, although we have been dealing at long range, our clients never had any reason to suspect that you were not serving their interests to the best of your ability.

Easley to McNulty, September 2, 1917

We are in receipt of a wire this morning from Shearman & Sterling, lawyers in New York, stating that you have wired that you are leaving next week and that tools, appliances and other property need protection. They also state that they have wired you to remain temporarily and ask us to arrange with you to remain till this property can be sold. Please do so and by no means leave without placing some responsible party in charge of things. Upon receipt of this letter tomorrow, please wire us what you are willing to do in the matter. We are writing to these gentlemen telling them that we have written you and believe you will stay till some arrangement is made. We have also said to them, that in our opinion, the buildings, mine etc., need protection and that you have been there for years and have always taken proper care of things.

Shearman and Sterling to McNulty, September 4, 1917

We have received your telegram as follows; "Will move to Cerrillos next week. Send someone here so I can turn everything over to him. The property is too good to leave without a watchman. Tools, timbers, springs, etc. Will be stolen by Indians and Mexicans. Please answer." And have telegraphed you as follows: "Telegram received. If watchman necessary to protect movable property would appreciate it if you would remain until such property can be disposed of." It is the intention of owners to save expenses by having no watchman for the mines or to protect minerals. We are telegraphing Easley and Easley. We enclose a letter which was drafted on the day of its date but the mailing of which was overlooked because of the vacation of the gentleman in our office who had it in charge. We sincerely trust you will give this matter your best attention and wish you could find it convenient to continue to live on the property. Since dictating our letter of August 21, the persons interested in the property have also expressed the wish that you would continue to live there without payment of rent under the terms stated in our letter.

McNulty to Shearman and Sterling, September 6, 1917

I told Mr. Easely that I would stay here although I had part of my things moved to Cerrillos until the American Turquoise Company could get rid of certain personal property which I will say will be a sad mistake for the company to do so. The property will be ruined by Indians, Mexicans, and Americans. Very true, you can sell a lease for the dumps as there is a lot of turquoise and specimens in them but if there is no watch man, they would work the mine also. Now, gentlemen, do not think for one moment that I am writing you this for you to keep me here. I will say right here that I do not want to stay here as I have property of my own that will pay to work for gold, silver, and copper and have the turquoise for a side issue.

McNulty to Shearman and Sterling, September 12, 1917

I know that the property has not produced much in 12 years and I will say that it is the company's own fault as there is a big body of gold and copper ore in the Muniz mine No. 1 on the east side of the shaft in the drift and crosscuts for 70 feet in length. The copper is coming through the rock and to wet a knife and put some of this copper on it, it will coat the knife with copper in one minute. I have written to the company about the copper for a great many years. Experts if they see free gold and native copper, they will make a favorable report. This copper is about 60 feet from the surface now in the No. 2 mine while doing the assessment work about 6 years ago. I broke into an old Spanish workings with a crosscut from the tunnel and shipped some specimens and turquoise from it.

308 • Patricia McGraw

Easley to McNulty, September 20, 1917

We have to advise you that we have heard from the attorneys for the owners of the property of the American Turquoise Company. They have decided to no longer keep a custodian at the property of the company in this county. Therefore, you will please arrange to move the personal property of said company to Cerrillos, to be stored in your building in accordance with our former understanding, not later than the 1st day of October, 1917. The storage charge to be agreed upon between you and the said attorneys, Messrs, Shearman and Sterling. ...The owners are willing to allow you to use and occupy the buildings free of charge for your services in looking after the property, but you today verbally declined this offer. I have written to the company to start work on this old Spanish shaft but it has not been done as yet.

McNulty to Shearman and Sterling, September 22, 1917

I have been in to Santa Fe on the 19th as Mr. Easely had written me. He gave me orders to move the moveable property to Cerrillos by the 1st of October and as I think it will not pay the company even to do that and leave the property to ruin. As I have worked for the company for over 25 years, I have made up my mind to stay here while I have one dollar to buy things with rather than to leave the property vacant. Now, gentleman, the company does not care for the specimens and matrix, etc. ...Why not let me work it and get some out and it may pay my salary. The man or men I would need to work it and I would keep the property in good shape.

Shearman and Sterling to McNulty, March 11, 1918

...enclosing bill for the 1917 taxes on the Turquoise mines, and have sent a check in payment of the same to the county treasurer. As you know, the taxes for 1917 are nearly four times what they have been in previous years. We took up the matter with Messrs. Easley & Easley, at the time the assessment was raised last spring, but they assured us that while the valuations were increased, the rate would be correspondingly reduced, and that therefore the amount of the taxes would be approximately the same. Relying upon their advice, we did not prosecute an appeal from the assessment. Since we learned the amount of the taxes for 1917, we have written several letters to Messrs, Easley & Easley for an explanation, but have received no reply from them. We certainly hope that the taxes for this year will be reduced to the amount previously paid, in view of the fact that there is no income from the property. We note that you are still living on the property and looking after it, in a general way, and we hope that you will find it convenient to continue to do so.

McNulty to Shearman and Sterling, March 29, 1918

I will see to it that the taxes are not raised this year. I protested last year, but you left it to Mr. Easley. Politics had something to do with it. Old Mr. Easley died last October and young Easley is in a hospital in California this last four months. I will show your letter to the commissioners if they raise the taxes and take an appeal. I have been sick for three weeks with the grip so I went to Santa Fe on the 18th to see a doctor.

I stayed there five days, and when I came back, I found that there had been a lot of stuff stolen by some parties who I think were Mexicans. They broke into the tool house or sorting cabin and stole some tools, one can of oil I had for the whim and cable, and a box of a lot of specimens and small turquoise that was not good enough to ship to New York. I had them in the cabin. They also dug up the dump. There must be four or five of them by all the damage that is done, but they did not break into the tunnels where I have most of the things locked in.

I found the lock that was on the cabin with a key they used broken in it. The key was stuck tight. They could not get it out. I got it out with pliers so I will keep it. It will help in court if I catch them.

Now, gentlemen, if the company will give me permission as I have written you before to take out some stone or specimens, I will have a man here with me. I will see that the property will not be ruined until the company sends someone here to look after it.

Shearman and Sterling to McNulty, April 27, 1918

We duly received your letter ...in which you request permission to take out some stones or specimens from the turquoise mines, offering in return to keep an eye on the property, so that it will not be destroyed or injured by trespassers. We think it will be all right for you to do this, and you may consider that you have permission to take out specimens from the mines.

McNulty to Shearman and Sterling, May 8, 1918

I thank you very much for giving me the permission to take out turquoise from the American Turquoise Company property to pay my salary if I can find the stone and market to sell them. I have not been able to find a man as yet to go to work for me; the first work I will have to do is to repair the house which is in very bad shape and I can assure you that the property will be taken good care of.

McNulty to Shearman and Sterling, June 27, 1918

I find that the assessor has raised the taxes on the personal property at the mine and I have taken an appeal for the assessors and have turned the papers over to the county commissioners who will meet as a board of equalization next week, and if they can't come to my terms I will take an appeal to the state board. I offered to sell the improvements at the mine to the assessor or county commissioners for two hundred and fifty dollars. I started working on the mine about three weeks ago and have not yet found anything to pay expenses so far but hope to find better stone. I have also repaired the house a little.

TIFFANY BLUE • 311

Shearman and Sterling to McNulty, July 30, 1918

    We ...note with great satisfaction that you have been able to obtain a reduction of the assessed valuation of the Turquoise Mines. We quite agree with you that it would have been much better had we put the matter of last year's assessment in your hands instead of retaining Messrs. Easley & Easley.

Wm Kleg [lapidary work] to McNulty, September 13, 1918

    Received the parcel with 30 ounces rough turquoise for which I enclose check for $100. There seems to be quite a few very light colored pieces in which stones after they are cut do not sell. But we will try it out and cut them all and I shall see whether or not we could use more or not for that price. As I said in my last letter, no price is too high for rough material as long as we can get enough for the finished goods. But people are used to buying turquoise very cheap, and therefore it will be hard to educate them to the point that they are willing to pay more for nice goods. But, I shall let you know and if we can make it go, I will order some more of that material.

McNulty to Shearman and Sterling, October 10, 1918...

    This is to let you know that I am still here at the mine. I have been prospecting in the mine for turquoise and also have done some sorting in the dump but that did not prove satisfactory. I have spent over $900 already prospecting for stone and have sold $360 worth but I am still in hopes that I may be able to make it pay enough to pay me what I have been enduring this winter. The party you recommended to me for stone from Arizona wrote me to send samples. I shipped some at $16 per pound and they returned saying they could not handle it. I thank you for helping me get customers. And should I get some of good quality will send a few samples to you. I hope you are well at this time. We are having the "Spanish Influenza" out west. I see by the papers that there are a great many cases in New York.

McNulty to Gilbert, February 21, 1919

I have put the company's property in for taxes this week the same as last year. I told the assessor to let me know if it was raised and he said he would. I made it out as acting agent. Well, Mr. Gilbert, I had to quit working in the mine some time ago as I cannot make it pay. I have not sold but three dollars worth since last October. I opened up some new ground but got nothing that was good. I had my man to clear things down in the mine a 100 foot or more from the surface. So if you send anyone here, they can go down 100 foot and go 200 foot from one mine to the other at 85 foot from the surface. I am sending you today by parcel post a box with some turquoise in it for you and your family and Mr. Shearman and Mr. Sterling and families as I promised in my letter of October 1918. You will find a salt sack in the box full of turquoise rock taken out 100 foot from the surface that was close to the copper rock. I wish you will have it assayed or analyzed for gold and copper. I would like to hear the results. I always said there is a big body of copper in the hill.

Gilbert to McNulty, March 12, 1919

I ...duly received the specimens of turquoise rock ...for which please accept my thanks. I note your suggestion that the rock should be analyzed for gold and copper, and will give the matter consideration.

McNulty to Gilbert, April 30, 1919

I will move from the property to Cerrillos in a week or ten days from now as I cannot live here any longer by myself. But will come to see the property often as long as I can feed and keep a horse or until you get some one to look after it. I will put all the things in the tunnels and lock the tunnels. I expect the windows and doors will be stolen from the house soon after I leave here. They will perhaps ruin the property also as I will be 7 miles away from the property. I think you should have someone on the property. I can get a man for about

$50 per month to look after it. I have been here in charge of the property 27 years and three months and no vacation in all that time nor a pension. I am [too] old to live here any longer by myself. I would like to hear from you soon.

Shearman and Sterling to McNulty, May 28, 1919

We have received from M.A. Ortiz, assessor, a notice dated March 21, 1919, but post marked May 19, 1919, to the effect that the turquoise mines have been assessed for the year 1919, at the sum of $6,250, of which $1250 is in the nature of a penalty. We recall with pleasure that you were able to obtain a reduction last year of the assessment from $5,000 to $1955, and would be glad to pay you a reasonable amount for your services if you will undertake to obtain a reduction of this year's assessment. We note that it was your intention at the date of your last letter to move from the mines to Cerrillos shortly after the letter was written. While we regret to have you go, we could not, of course, expect you to stay on without compensation if you desired to leave. We will be glad to hear from you, from time to time, as to the condition of the property in general.

McNulty to Shearman and Sterling, June 6, 1919

...referring to the taxes on the turquoise mine, I wish to say that the county commissions have been in session this week as a board of equalization so I went to Santa Fe two days ago and have taken an appeal from the assessor's raise on taxes and have presented the papers before the county commission to see to have the taxes reduced. They took no action but have taken the matter under advisement and will notify me later. They told me to employ an attorney to advise me but I said to them that it is too simple a matter and I would plead my own case. For the assessor has raised the valuation of the land from $30 per acre to $90 per acre. If the county commissioners do not reduce the assessor's valuation, I may have to go before the state board in July. I moved to Cerrillos on May 10, but frequently go to the mine.

McNulty to Shearman and Sterling, June 18, 1919
I received this notice [denying change in valuation of property] which you will please find enclosed and I would like to know your instructions of taking an appeal to the state board.

Shearman and Sterling to McNulty, June 25, 1919
As this assessment seems very unjust, we would be glad to have you take an appeal to the State Board, which we note will meet in July, and keep us advised of the result of your efforts to obtain a reduction of the assessment.

McNulty to George Armijo, sheriff, August 22, 1919
I wish to inform you that some party or parties have broken into the American Turquoise Company's mines and are doing great damage to the property by mining and blasting. It appears to me that it is not the work of Indians for the doors and windows have been carried away from the house and the locks and staples on the mine have been broken. As the American Turquoise Company are taxpayers, they claim protection of the law.

McNulty to Shearman and Sterling, October 19, 1919
I wish to inform you that parties have again broken into the mine and are working it even after I put new locks and staples on. I have not sold my horse yet so I go to the mine twice a week. There has been a great deal of damage done, and windows and doors have been carried away from the house. I went to the Santa Fe on the eighteenth of August and informed the sheriff of the damage done to the property. He told me to write to him so that he might have some grounds to work upon, saying that he would capture the offenders, but he has done nothing yet. In regard to the taxes, I went to Santa Fe last week but they have not got their books straightened out yet. I gave them notice that if

> Cerrillos, N. Mex.
> April 4, 1921.
>
> Mr. Frederick H. Gilbert. (Care Shearman &
> New York City. Sterling)
>
> Dear Mr. Gilbert
> As court started last month and as I told you in a previous letter that I would fight the case to a finish I went to Santa Fe ten days ago. The district attorney told me that the Judge said that he thought there would be no cases tried except two murder cases this term of court, and that if my case came up he would notify me, if I could
> I saw the sheriff to find out what he would about getting the parties that was robbing the property. He said that he had answered your letter and was waiting for a reply before he could do anything.
> Since I last wrote to you, the two heavy

McNulty wrote to Gilbert about the trouble he was having with trespassers and vowed to take the thieves to court.

the company's tax were not reduced, I would take an appeal to the court.

McNulty to Shearman and Sterling, November 29, 1919
    I have been waiting for the decision of the state board of equalization but I found a notice in the New Mexican which you will find enclosed. If you wish to take an appeal to the court I believe you

can have the valuation of the land reduced to about $13 per or perhaps lower as the property is not worked and it is assessed higher than any mineral land in the state and there are no improvements now for everything has been stolen. I do not go up very often now.

McNulty to Shearman and Sterling, December 21, 1919

I have been up to see the property today and found that it is in terrible shape. Parties are working the mine and also sorting the dump. There was a party of six (two women and the rest men) on the dump and as soon as they saw me they ran. Before I could get out of the buggy and get the horse tied, they got out of reach, although I had a rifle with me. They have taken doors, windows, cellar doors, and mop boards and have started to take up the floor from the house. I am going in to Santa Fe tomorrow to see if I can get the sheriff to come out with me and make a thorough search for the doors and windows and also search for the stolen turquoise, as I have a suspicion of certain parties and I can swear to the doors if we find them. Enclosed you will please find the card for the taxes which was dated December first and I received it today, the 21st.

McNulty to Shearman and Sterling, December 25, 1919

I have been to Santa Fe since I wrote to you, and the deputy sheriff and myself went to the mine on Monday last. When we got in sight of the property, there were five men (four of whose names you will see in the enclosed clippings) sorting on the dump. They got away but left their horses, which were identified as the property of Padilla. So I swore out warrants for him. He is now held under five hundred bond to await the action of the grand jury. The other three were this man's father and his two uncles. They have always been stealing lumber and things from the property while I was living there, but I could never catch them. I shall try very hard to have them indicted when the grand jury meets.

Shearman and Sterling to McNulty, December 29, 1919
   ...note with satisfaction that you have succeeded in obtaining the arrest of one of the persons who had been stealing and destroying property at the turquoise mine. We trust that you will be able to obtain an indictment and conviction and that the prosecution of Padilla will serve as a warning to others. The taxes for the year 1919 have been paid, as it was thought inadvisable to incur the expense of taking the matter of the assessment to court.

Shearman and Sterling to McNulty, March 12, 1920
   We are in receipt of your letter of the 7th instant, advising us of the indictment of the turquoise thieves. We thank you for this kind interest you are taking in the property and assure you of our appreciation. As you know, the property is no longer in the hands of the American Turquoise Company but is being held for the benefit of the stockholders of that company. You also know that the investment was a disastrous one and the stockholders long ago decided not to put any more money in it. We are hopeful that some day an opportunity to sell it may come along. In view of the fact that there is no money with which to pay any expenses, we have hesitated to call upon you for anything; we are, however, grateful to you and trust that the future may have in store something worth while for the property on which you spent so many years.

Shearman and Sterling to McNulty, September 15, 1920
   We ...note what you say in regard to the tax assessment and the punishment of the parties who have been guilty of depredations at the mines. The title to the property formerly owned by the American Turquoise Company now stands in the name of Mr. Frederic N. Gilbert, who acquired title some years ago at a sale in foreclosure of a mortgage on the property. Mr. Gilbert will be glad to consider any reasonable offer for the same

but does not wish at the present time to set a price on the same.

McNulty to Gilbert, December 9, 1920

The Mexicans are still working the property off and on. I have not been up to the mine for about six weeks as I have no way of going up there. I wrote you some time ago in regard to setting a price

CAPT. CHAS. H. COOK
DEALER IN
Precious and Semi-Precious Gems
GEMS RE-CUT AND POLISHED
LAPIDARY WORK OF ALL KINDS

New Milford Ct
Jan 20 1921

Mr J. P. McNulty
Cerrillas
N Mexico

Dear Sir
I would be pleased for you to submit samples of nuggets & matrix turquois as that is my only assurance you is you know what there are any of and let me know an any other gem stock how of past garnets Thanking you for answering I remain yours to do business from Capt Chas H Cook
New Milford Conn
Best of luck to you

Throughout the years, people contacted McNulty for samples of turquoise, but no one wanted to invest anything in the mining operation since the price of turquoise remained so low.

on the property. As a Boston party has bought all the copper property in this district about a month ago, I had a talk with the man who bought it about your property but I could not tell him what price you wanted and as your property is out on the prairie all by itself three miles from other minerals and the land all around it is taken up for homesteads as close as a hundred yards to American Turquoise Company if there is not an advertisement put in the paper or someone looking after it, it will be a thing of the past. If you will give me some idea of the price you would ask, I will have the Boston party to look over the property when he comes out. I would suggest to ask twenty to thirty thousand though you may have to sell for less.

Capt. Chas Cook, dealer in precious and semi-precious gems, to McNulty, January 30, 1921

I would be pleased for you to submit samples of nuggets and matrix turquoise. Are there any mines around you if you know where there are any opals? Let me know. Or any other gem stock? How about garnets?

Criminal Complaint: May 3, 1921

J.P. McNulty, being first duly sworn on his oath says, that John Doe, late of the County of Santa Fe aforesaid, did unlawfully and feloniously, on the 10th day of February, 1921, in Santa Fe County, steal, take and carry away off the property of J.P. McNulty lumber of the value of $150, contrary to the form of the statute in such case and provided, and against the peace and dignity of the State of New Mexico. Wherefore, affiant prays that warrant may issue directing that the said John Doe be arrested and dealt with according to law...

McNulty to Gilbert, April 4, 1921

I went to Santa Fe ten days ago. The district attorney told me that the judge said that he thought there would be no cases except two murder cases tried this term of court and that if my case [Padilla theft case] *came up, he would notify me. I saw the sheriff to see if I could find out what he would do about getting the parties that are robbing the property. He said that he had answered our letter and was waiting for a reply before he could do anything.*

Since I last wrote to you the two heavy doors have been carried away from the tunnels and they have torn down the adobe building in which I used to live, and they are carrying away the lumber from the building. There are still at the mine a tram car and about 120 ft iron track and an old whim with 2 buckets which I think should be taken away before they are stolen. I shall remove them if you give me the authority, providing they are still there when I hear from you, so they may be of value if you ever sell the property or decide to do any work there.

Gilbert to McNulty, April 8, 1921

After the receipt of your last letter, I telegraphed the sheriff requesting that he give proper protection to the property. I have not heard from him since the telegram was sent and I have not received the letter from him to which you refer in your letter. I think it would be advisable to remove the tram-car, iron track and whim with two buckets to Cerrillos as you suggest, and hereby authorize you to do so.

Shearman and Sterling to McNulty, December 2, 1921

When we telephoned you yesterday, we forgot that it was necessary to obtain the consent of the Pinkertons to our arrangement. Before writing you, therefore, giving you authority to sell, we are waiting to receive advice from the Pinkerton Estate. Mr. Pinkerton is on the coast, so it will probably take two weeks before we receive final word about the matter.

TIFFANY BLUE • 321

№ 26253   **RECEIPT FOR SUBSCRIBER**

OCTOBER _Oct. 11_ 1918

GIVE THIS RECEIPT TO SUBSCRIBER

RECEIPT IS HEREBY ACKNOWLEDGED OF SUBSCRIPTION FOR $ _100 00_ _____ PAR VALUE OF THE

4TH LIBERTY LOAN 4¼% BONDS   COUPON OR REGISTERED (PLEASE INDICATE)

THROUGH _First National Bank of Santa Fe_
(NAME AND ADDRESS OF BANK OR TRUST COMPANY THROUGH WHICH PAYMENTS ARE TO BE MADE)

Receipt of the first payment of $_____ is also acknowledged.
Balance with accrued interest from October 24th, 1918 at 4½%, payable as indicated below.

☐ In full, on or before October 24, 1918.
☐ In Installments in accordance with Treasury Department circular No. 121. 20% Nov. 21, 1918; 20% Dec. 19, 1918; 20% Jan'y 16, 1919; 30% Jan'y 30, 1919, all payments with accrued interest.
☐ In Installments to be arranged with the Bank designated.

LIBERTY LOAN COMMITTEE

By _Mrs. Thos. De Lallo_
VOLUNTEER WORKER

THIS RECEIPT IS TO BE GIVEN BY WORKER TO SUBSCRIBER, WHO SHOULD PROMPTLY GO TO THE BANK OR TRUST COMPANY INDICATED ABOVE AND ARRANGE FOR PAYMENT

McNulty invested in liberty bonds, this receipt signed by the wife of the man in the photo on page 184.

McNulty & Friends Personal Dialogs

Charles R. Galbrath [potential mining financier and nephew] to McNulty, January 30, 1918

    I was more than pleased ...to learn that you are enjoying good health. Note carefully what you say regarding the turquoise property and your claim of thirty acres, and beg to advise that at present I do not know a single prospect who would likely be inclined to take a venture of that kind. However, have no doubt if you would make the same known to your many friends out in that section that you would not have any trouble in disposing of the interest that you name. Would add however, if I ever do run across anyone who would want to make an investment of that kind, nothing would afford me more pleasure than to put him in touch with you and tell him all the nice things of the many years acquaintance I have had with you.

322 • Patricia McGraw

Alpheus Keen [Ancient Free and Accepted Masons Grand Secretary] to McNulty, February 1919

> Brother Dwire, our Grand Chaplain, will be in Santa Fe on Saturday, March 8, at which time Brother Hanna will install him into the office of Grand Chaplain, and I am writing you upon the request of Judge Hanna, to see if it is possible for you to arrange to be in Santa Fe on the same date, when he hopes to install you as Grand Sword Bearer of this Grand lodge.

Peter Cameron, Grand Patron of the Order of the Eastern Star, to cNulty, August 3, 1920

> If you think it possible to organize a successful chapter at Cerrillos, will you kindly give the matter what attention you are able and advise the writer what may be expected in this line? If there is anything we can do to help the matter along, do not hesitate to ask for assistance.

Peter Cameron, Grand Patron, to McNulty, October 29, 1920

> Up to present have had no advice from you or any action in the matter [instituting a chapter of the Order of the Eastern Star], and as time is getting very short in which chapters may be instituted, this being allowed only to within sixty days of the meeting of the Grand Chapter, am getting a little anxious in regard to Cerrillos. What appears to be the matter? If those whom should be interested are not anxious to have it carried through, it would probably be advisable to drop the matter, but do not wish to do this if there is any possibility of establishing a healthy chapter. It may be that you have not got the time to devote to this matter. If such is the case can you suggest the name of anyone who would take it up, and if so will you kindly turn the matter over to them and urge them to take prompt action

McNulty's living will, October 19, 1921

> *It is my desire that in case of accident or other eventually, that my daughter Fannie McNulty*

The First National Bank of Santa Fe
1750

OFFICERS:
L. A. HUGHES, PRESIDENT
ARTHUR SELIGMAN, VICE PRESIDENT
PAUL A. F. WALTER, VICE PRESIDENT
F. L. WARDLAW, CASHIER
CHAS. J. ECKERT, ASS'T CASHIER
WALTER L. KEGEL, AUDITOR

SANTA FE, N. M.
October 19, 1921.

DIRECTORS:
L. A. HUGHES,
ARTHUR SELIGMAN,
PAUL A. F. WALTER,
BENJ. F. PANKEY,
JOHN PFLUEGER
SALAMON SPITZ

To whom it may concern:

It is my desire that in case of accident or other eventually, that my daughter Fannie McNulty McCraw, shall act as my business agent or administrator with power to act in the administration or management of my real estate and personal property.

James P. McNulty

Witness / Signed in presence of witnesses.
Marguerite Dumbauld
Paul A. F. Walter.

McNulty, at age 75, arranged that his daughter, Fannie McNulty McCraw, might take charge of his affairs should something happen to him.

McCraw, shall act as my business agent or administrator with power to act in the administration or management of my real estate and personal property.

Parker to McNulty, March 4, 1916
I am no longer connected with the American Turquoise Company and in future kindly address your communications to Mr. F.N. Gil-

bert, co Shearman and Sterling, 55 Wall Street, New York, N.Y.

McNulty to his children & their husbands, November 30, 1916
I am in good health and hope this will find all of the McCraw family in good health. I have been cleaning house for 2 days. I did not go to town today but will tomorrow. No, Fannie, I did not lose one bet, but won good money, a seal skin cap, a Stetson derby, I already got and some more I will not get. I won $100 dollars from Mr. Tom Catron. I bet him $200 to one that Charley Closson would be defeated so I got that money and $30 in Cerrillos I got. So I got square with Closson when he did not come when my house was robbed. There is $30 more to come to me in Santa Fe which I am sure of. As Mr. Catron is the stakeholder. I have not bought a hat in 20 years. ...I will be 74 my next birthday.

McNulty to Thomas B. Catron, U.S. Senator, December 1, 1916
Enclosed you will please find all the papers I can find and also my discharge which you will please return in due time. All the papers that I have sworn to are in Washington.

Catron to McNulty, December 16, 1916
I have your letter ...with your application to receive a pension for services in the U.S. Army. I infer from looking through all the papers that it is impossible for you to get a pension under the law, and I am therefore this day introducing a bill in Congress to grant you a pension, and will do all that is possible to have early action taken thereon.

McMahon [McNulty's nephew], January 23, 1917
Mother [McNulty's sister] not expected to live.

McNulty to Dr. J.J. DePraslin [potential mining financier], October 18, 1917
I was pleased to hear that you made a large deal in Albuquerque and hope you will have luck with it. In regards to my property, I have written to the

other party before I got your letter that I gave you a verbal option for a certain length of time. I would like to hear from you again. As I am confident that your company could make at least twenty thousand inside of year and this property will pay from the start. But I have not got the means to work it. That is why I want some party with a little money to take an interest with me and work the property. There is a mill site and a town site that can be taken up alongside of the property.

United States Bureau of Pensions, March 18, 1917 for the Indian Wars, Act of March 4, 1917

James McNulty who was a private Co. D 27 Regiment United States infantry is entitled to a pension at the rate of twenty dollars per month to commence March 4, 1917.

A.A. Jones, United States Senator on Committee on Finance to McNulty, August 29, 1919

I am in receipt of your favor of August 23rd, together with other letters and a petition from the people of Cerrillos in reference to an increase of salary for the postmaster at Cerrillos. There is a resolution now pending in the House of Representatives entitled "H.J.R. 151" which will increase the pay of third class postmasters $150 per year, and a ten per cent increase for fourth class postmasters. There is a committee now investigating as to what should be done with reference to raising the pay of all post office employees, and a report will probably be made at the next session of Congress, but the resolution above mentioned is for temporary relief. I assure you, it will be a pleasure to assist you people in anyway possible. Will you please advise Mr. Palmer and the others who have written me of the contents of this letter.

Senate Bill 7413, 64th Congress, 2nd Session

A bill granting a pension to James McNulty. Be it enacted by the Senate and House of Representatives of the United States of

326 • Patricia McCraw

America in Congress assembled, that the Secretary of the Interior be, and he is hereby, authorized and directed to place on the pension roll, subject to the provisions and limitations of the pension laws, the name of James McNulty, late of Company D. Thirty seventh Regiment, United States Volunteer Infantry, and pay him a pension at the rate of $30 per month.

Fannie McNulty McCraw

Chapter 11
1922 - 1933

The End of The Turquoise Trail

We have received the consent of the Messrs. Pinkerton to permit you to sell the Tiffany Turquoise mines on terms that give you one-third of the net selling price.
        Shearman & Sterling to McNulty, January 17, 1922

PERSERVERANCE PAYS OFF

The seventy-six year old Irishman from Sligo decided in 1922 that he would sell his own claims along with the Tiffany mines. He had spent too much time on the grounds, too many hours chipping out turquoise, struggling against all who came to let the claims fall for back taxes. It had been one heck of a thirty-year ride. Surviving the demands of New York, snowstorms, raids, and politicians, McNulty outlasted them all and saved the mines. He believed that turquoise would make a great comeback, and he knew what lay below the surface of Turquoise Hill could again produce handsome profits if only the right person would cross his path.

Even though retired, McNulty received requests from across the nation and as far away as Europe for information on mining in general, and turquoise mining in particular. Some writers expressed interest in the turquoise mines and they looked to McNulty as the expert.

One man was L.I. Fletcher, a fast-talker with nationwide connections who engaged in real estate transactions. While Fletcher carefully

> Cerrillos N. Mex
> Jan. 4. 1922
>
> Mr. Frederick N. Sterling
> New York, N.Y.
>
> Dear Sir,
> I arrived home all right and found your letter here, which stated that you had to await the Pinkerton's reports as to how to dispose of the property.
> I would have written sooner but was waiting to receive the tax report to send you. They have been late in sending out the notice which I just received today and which you will find inclosed. Please see to it. I hope to receive an early reply. Best wishes for a happy and prosperous New Year.

Fannie carried on most of the major correspondence for her father. The Pinkertons were required to approve any mine sale, and McNulty received their nod that he could have one half of the selling price the mines.

guarded his secrets, he cautioned McNulty to watch what he told to others. Fletcher said he had multiple buyers for McNulty's properties, but no deal materialized.

Fletcher wanted to know about the gold and copper potential of the mines. He asked questions about how turquoise was sold and how a person guaranteed his assets were not stolen. Even though his buyer wanted McNulty's mines, the buyer also wanted to know how much turquoise came out of the Tiffany mine as well as the color of the stones. The Tiffany name possessed a mystique that attracted all sorts of interest. Of course, McNulty had to assure the potential buyer that the mine claims had been patented and assessment work was no longer required.

CABLE ADDRESS,"NUMLATUS"

JOHN A. GARVER
RALPH CREWS
GUY CARY
PHILIP A. CARROLL
CHAUNCEY B. GARVER
CORTLAND BETTS
CARL A. MEAD
HARRY W. FORBES
FREDERIC N. GILBERT
FREDERICK W. JACKSON
WALTER K. EARLE
JOSEPH F. DEMPSEY

SHEARMAN & STERLING
ATTORNEYS AND COUNSELORS AT LAW
NATIONAL CITY BANK BUILDING
55 WALL STREET

NEW YORK   January 17, 1922.

J. P. McNulty, Esq.,
    Cerrillos,
        Santa Fe County,
            New Mexico.

Dear Sir:

      Thank you for your favor of January 4, 1922, enclosing tax bill for $48.59, the amount of which we are remitting direct to the Treasurer.

      We have received the consent of the Messrs. Pinkerton to permitting you to sell the Tiffany Turquoise Mines, on terms that give you one-third of the net selling price. Of course, this applies only in case the sale is the direct result of your efforts and would have no application to a sale which we might effect, not instigated by you. Therefore, you may now proceed to see what you can do toward securing a purchaser for the Mines. We are, of course, to be free to accept or reject any offer you secure. The foregoing division of the net selling price applies to a sale not exceeding $20,000. Above such figure, as agreed with you when you were here, we will arrange upon a different basis of compensation.

Yours very truly,
Shearman & Sterling

In 1922, McNulty traveled to New York City to set the terms he desired should he sell the Tiffany mines. The address of Shearman and Sterling, 55 Wall Street, was the First National Bank of New York City. From 1892 to 1918 FNB was run by James A. Stillman, and upon his death, by his son James A. Stillman, Jr. The Stillmans were among the richest men in the United States, and the chief financiers of the Tiffany mine operation.

Fletcher commented, "They [the buyers] sure ask a lot of questions, and it is best to humor them. It is next to impossible now-a-days to get a mining man to go and examine a property unless he has the data to read over, study over and consider whether it has real merit and is worth while."

The deal hinged on McNulty's answers, which were apparently not to the buyers' satisfaction.

Every year from 1922 to 1925 McNulty paid the taxes on the property since Gilbert, the trustee for the remaining bond holders, failed to do so. The mines no longer produced any marketable turquoise, but the tax assessor acted as if they did. That, and other inaccuracies, and late tax bills, had to be constantly protested and corrected. Sometimes, even after McNulty requested them, tax bills never arrived. One check sent to the assessor disappeared before it could be credited to the proper account. McNulty paid that bill, too.

The few times that Gilbert tried to pay the taxes he was unable to get a bill, and he finally turned to McNulty take care of it. Sometimes Gilbert reimbursed McNulty, and sometimes he did not.

The continuing problem of theft at the mines forced McNulty to swear out John Doe warrants and become a deputy sheriff himself. Many a time he took his horse and buggy to the mines only to see numbers of people working inside the partially filled-in tunnels and picking through the dumps. Finally, the sheriff of the county caught seven men, and they were bound over for trial. But due to "politics", the men were let go. After all, the sheriff could use their vote in the upcoming election and so could the judge. The judge dismissed the case because McNulty couldn't identify the turquoise found in the men's homes — even though the sheriff had captured the thieves on the scene!

Just a few months past his 79th birthday, on March 16, 1925, McNulty received a telegram from one of his New Mexico mining friends, W.C. Porterfield, who had found a buyer for the mines. The price: $18,000. This belated birthday present cheered McNulty and kept his dream alive. The buyer, Chester H. Smith of Boston, had great plans for the mine, but those plans did not include the services of the elderly and sometimes ill McNulty.

Through a flurry of telegrams and finally a visit from Smith, the mines sold with an agreement that McNulty would get one-half of the selling price. Porterfield received $100 per month out of each pay-

> OFFICE OF
>
> ## TOMAS P. DELGADO, SHERIFF
>
> STATE OF NEW MEXICO,)
>)ss
> County of Santa Fe.)
>
> I, Tomas P. Delgado, Sheriff of the County of Santa Fe, do hereby appoint *J. P. Mc. Nulty* ....a deputy sheriff within and for the county of Santa Fe, in the State of New Mexico. Given under my hand this *7th* day of *May*.....A. D. 19*23*
>
> *Tomas P. Delgado*
> Sheriff of the County of Santa Fe, in the State of New Mexico.
>
> ### OATH OF OFFICE
>
> STATE OF NEW MEXICO,) *Copy.*
>)ss
> County of Santa Fe.)
>
> I,................................do solemnly swear that I am a citizen of the United States, and a resident of the County of Santa Fe, in the State of New Mexico, and that I will faithfully support the Constitution of the United States and the Constitution of the State of New Mexico and that I will faithfully discharge the duties of deputy sheriff to which I have been appointed, to the best of my ability, and that I am not the holder of any moneys due the State of New Mexico nor any county thereof. SO HELP ME GOD.
>
> Subscribed and sworn to before me this..................day of.......................A. D. 19......
>
> ....
> Notary Public.

In spite of his advanced age, McNulty asked to be appointed a deputy with arrest power so he could arrest thieves when he found them on the mining claims.

ment received for a finder's fee. Each month, beginning in June, 1925, the First National Bank of Santa Fe received a wire of $2,000 for eight months. An original payment of $2,000 also arrived. Documents showed that Gilbert received 50,000 shares of stock in the new mining venture, now known as Chesterfield's Turquoise Deposit and Mfg. Co. Total capital stock turned out to be $250,000. McNulty, too, took part of his commission in $2,000 worth of stock.

With the paperwork done, Smith started up the mines and hired a watchman as well as six miners to clear out the tunnels and shafts. He had told the McNulty that due to his age he was no longer needed on the site. Smith's enthusiasm carried the venture as he promoted

```
                                              Pittston Pa.
Dear Uncle James:                             Oct. 25 1924
              Just a line to let you know what is doing in and around
Pittston and just like before I never have very pleasant news.
Aunt Mary McMahon died in New York Wednesday Oct 22 at 5 A.M. with her
family all with her she was sick about 6 months with gall-stones and a
heart condition and has been almost at deaths door at any time during
that time but finaly passed away after suffering all that time. on
Thursday they had a Mass for her in New York with Father Munley as celabre
celebrent and then took the body to my home where we kept it Thursday
night when all the family and friend s spent the night with it on
Friday morning the funeral was held with services at St Johns Church
and was buried in St Johns Cemetery the Nephews of Aunt acted as
pallbeares all her family Mart and wife,Mary and husband, Will and his
wife and familywere here Aunt Ann was able to attend but My Mother
could not we had a very large funeral about twenty auto's and quite a
number walked which was a very nice sight for us as funerals nowdays
are not very large only relatives taking part on Thursday night our house
was filled with people which added to the high esteem that the people
had for Aunty.the family all went back to New York right after the funeral
was over I am inclosing some newspaper clippings about the funeral so you
can see none of John McMahons was here as the distance was so great and
time so short Aunt Ann and Mother was all broke up on account of Auntys
death and you was mentioned a great deal during the time she was here but
today they feel pretty good . We received Fannies letter and was very glad
to hear from you sorry you dont get very good health and hope and pray
that you and yours will live for some time to come.
              Will close with best love to all from all,I am as ever.
                                 James L. Callahan
```

McNulty's sisters back East were considered pioneers, and their communities held them in high esteem. Throughout the 1920s McNulty received news of family members' deaths. Mary died at 5 a.m. on October 22, 1924.

turquoise manufacturing throughout the nation. From May 7 to October 24, 1925, Smith kept ownership of the mines, but by the end of October, Smith had acquired a partner: Los Cerrillos Turquoise Gem Corporation, which completed the payments for the mines.

While in New Mexico Smith suffered a setback that put him in the hospital in Santa Fe. At first McNulty thought Smith would recover, but in the end an infected carbuncle killed the new mine owner. For McNulty, the loss of this new-found friend hit hard. No longer involved in the Tiffany mine and no longer consulted for his expertise, McNulty let the Los Cerrillos Turquoise Gem Corporation carry on the business of turquoise mining.

After Smith's death the Turquoise Gem Corporation discovered a small problem with the title to the Tiffany mining claims. During the first foreclosure in 1899 one person was accidentally left out of the proceedings. The Gem Corporation wanted to file a suit to quiet title, and they expected McNulty to pay for it. The miner in turn wrote to Gilbert in 1926. The trustee figured that McNulty had been "amply" rewarded for his sale of the American Turquoise Mines, and Gilbert left it up to McNulty to get the money from the purchasers to clear the title. The trustee had washed his hands of the mines, and he had garnered money for the estates of Stillman and the Pinkertons, who had virtually abandoned their interests in the mines. The trustee fulfilled his duties and showed little further interest. Gilbert told McNulty that this turn of events was likely an effort to shakedown the New Yorkers again for money, and he would not be a part of it, nor would he supply any more money. McNulty took care of the matter.

STILL VISITING THE MINES

McNulty's attention turned away from mining and to his aging, ailing sisters whose health prevented them from writing. Writing chores were taken on by McNulty's nieces and nephews. Even McNulty's return letters to the family back East grew infrequent. Fannie, his daughter, took up his writing when time permitted.

McNulty's health had its ups and downs. His sharp marksman's eyes required stronger spectacles, his steps had slowed considerably, and he stumbled more often. His ulcer acted up and McNulty spent more time now in Albuquerque getting medical tests. One stumble broke several ribs and almost put him in the hospital. He had difficulty recovering

NOTICE OF SALE

NOTICE IS HEREBY GIVEN that the undersigned has a lien upon the personal property of Dan Lopez described as follows, to-wit:

1 Range
1 Iron Bed-stead
1 Mattress
Tables, Dishes and Miscellaneous Household Articles

now located in the house Number 6 Block 79 in Cerrillos, New Mexico, to secure the payment of $40.80 due me under a lease of date June 21, 1931.

I will sell the above described property at public auction to the highest bidder for cash on April 29, 1932, in front of the said house Number 6 Block 79 at the hour of 4 o'clock P.M.

JAMES P. MC NULTY

Although McNulty had multiple real estate holdings, he sometimes had trouble getting rent payments. He had to evict Dan Lopez and sell off items in order to get his rent payments.

He spent his time managing his real estate holdings, which were mostly centered in Cerrillos. Daily walks around town kept him in touch with mining news, too. When his health and the weather permitted it, McNulty traveled to the mines to see how the work progressed. He couldn't stay away, and he still hoped to sell his own mines some day.

Through his requests for an increase in his $30 per month pension, McNulty told the story of his early years in the army. Fannie collected these stories in her notes.

Back in 1868 McNulty's battalion was dispatched to help find Indians who had recently broken away from reservations. On one protracted action his company ran low on food, their only rations being

HOLM O. BURSUM, N. MEX., CHAIRMAN
PORTER J. MCCUMBER, N. DAK.   THOMAS J. WALSH, MONT.
REED SMOOT, UTAH.   WILLIAM H. KING, UTAH.
DAVIS ELKINS, W. VA.   DAVID I. WALSH, MASS.
CHARLES E. TOWNSEND, MICH.   PETER G. GERRY, R. I.
LE BARON B. COLT, R. I.
OVINGTON E. WELLER, MD.
  GEORGE CURRY, CLERK.

United States Senate,

COMMITTEE ON PENSIONS.

Oct. 21st, 1922.

Mr. James McNulty,
Cerrillos, New Mexico.

My dear Mr. McNulty:

    I am advised under date of Oct. 20th by the Commissioner, Bureau of Pensions, that you are to receive a pension of $50. per month from Sept. 18, 1922. Certificate covering this matter will be forwarded you at an early date.

    I am pleased to have been of this slight service to you.

Very truly yours,

H. O. Bursum

The chairman of the United States Senate on the Committee on Pensions informed McNulty about the success of getting his pension increased to $50 per month.

one ounce of pork and hard tack. This did not fill their stomachs. At one point some of the soldiers drank from brackish water and immediately became sick. The horses and mules, no longer able to carry supplies, ate cottonwood leaves and bark. McNulty attributed this time of trial and bad food for the subsequent loss of most of his teeth.

    One of his favorite stories concerned the time he sat with territorial Governor Bent in Taos, New Mexico. While sitting there on the porch the two came under attack by Indians, and as both dived under the table, an arrow removed a portion of McNulty's ear as well as a chunk out of his thumb. He told his daughter about the Indians who could accurately aim and shoot arrows under the necks of their horses while at full gallop. The governor came out unscathed this time. Another story McNulty repeated covered the time he and several other "young men" decided to liberate some dynamite from the army and send it to Canada to be shipped to Ireland — a long way from New Mexico. Too long, in fact. As McNulty put it, they had a discussion with U.S. cavalry leaders, and the young men saw the error of their ways and decided to stay employed rather than run off with the dynamite. All agreed: the original plan was a bad idea.

McNulty now had time to enjoy his friends and personal activities that included Masonic meetings. His Masonic brothers held him in high esteem, and they sought his advice and help establishing new lodges. McNulty never missed a lodge meeting for over 32 years.

NOW TIME FOR FAMILY

As McNulty entered his twilight years, he never gave up on daring to dream of profitable mining activity on the Turquoise Hill, and he never lost his spunk. He still took a buggy trip out to the hills. Life, in general, had been good to him, and the mining business, most interesting. His adventure in the turquoise search covered more than 30 years, and he survived Indian attacks, raging snow storms, extreme heat, unscrupulous, double-dealing business people, and politicians with hidden agendas. Among his friends he could count governors, sheriffs, Wall Street investors, old Spanish families, and local Indians.

As for his home life, he had plenty of nieces, nephews, grandchildren, and great grandchildren. His two daughters, along with their children, made his life complete. It was Fannie, his daughter, who kept an eye on her father, helping him out when necessary. She and her son James McCraw saved all of his records; the McNulty papers.

The only news of Emma Hawley came in 1922. She had found her way to California. She also said she forgave McNulty for his injustice to her. After that no more news from her arrived.

McNulty received regular news about his family in Pittstown, Pennsylvania, in 1923. It was rarely good. One time he received word of his sister and her family becoming victims of coal gas in their house. McNulty's sister and her husband died, and the rest of the family fell gravely ill. McNulty's sisters Ann and Mary couldn't attend the funerals because their health too was fragile.

His extended family sent a constant stream of letters along with requests for help, usually in the form of money or jobs, and McNulty obliged when he could. For those nieces and nephews who seemed unemployable, McNulty checked around New Mexico for potential jobs, and many times he came up with job offers for them. When his relatives needed money for car repairs, college, or doctor's bills, McNulty sent what he could. And sometimes, he found himself short of money.

"As I have been under heavy expense for the last month having two doctor bills to pay, I should appreciate it very much if you would send me the eighty-five dollars of mine which you have. About fourteen

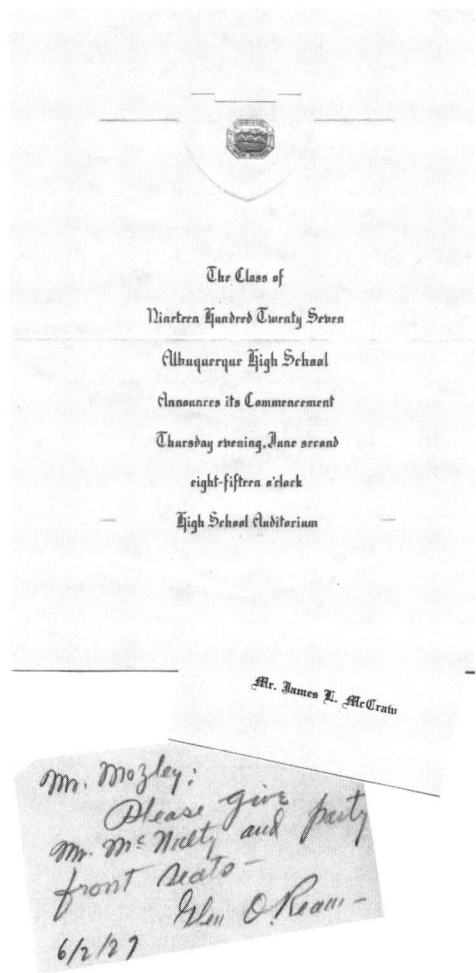

McNulty attended the graduation of James McCraw, his grandson, from Albuquerque High School in Albuquerque, New Mexico. McNulty received special treatment since he was seated up front where he could see and hear the celebration.

days ago as I was coming home with some groceries, I caught my foot in a wire, fell, injuring my chest and breaking several ribs. I could not go to the hospital for lack of funds although I may have to go yet as I do not improve," he told one of his property managers.

Still, McNulty enjoyed hearing of the adventures of his relatives back east.

One of his nieces started up a boarding house/restaurant business outside of New York on five acres. Her 14 room house contained a dining room, a dance hall, and five private tables. Suitably located near a gas station, she expected, after she modernized the building with electric light, hot and cold running water, to attract tourists. The initial price of the home: $11,000. Once it was fixed up, she planned to sell it for $50,000. She anticipated that McNulty would visit her sometime in 1927.

For his grandson, Johnnie, the son of Eddie, McNulty gave the gift of education at St. Michael's College in Santa Fe. When Johnnie became ill, his grandfather paid the hospital bill. In 1929, Johnnie was rushed to St. Vincent Sanatorium in Santa Fe by Dr. C.A. Rising who operated an ambulance service as well as a funeral service. The cost for the ambulance ride: $5, the cost for the nine-day hospital stay: $51.65, the cost for the doctor: $40. Although Johnnie wasn't the best student at college and he had difficulty keeping a job, he had no qualms about asking his 84 year-old grandfather for money.

"I know I haven't written to you for a long time and I had to rush to get to write this. This is a dun. Can you spare me $17.50 as soon as possible?" Johnnie asked in 1930. And, no matter the conditions under which he helped his family members, McNulty expected to receive a thank-you note, or a visit in person.

In 1926, the Free Masons asked McNulty for his help in protesting "in the strongest terms against the condition existing in some European countries, wherein masons individually, and Masonic bodies as an institution are being subjected to persecution."

McNulty became such an honored character of the Masonic Lodge in Cerrillos that in 1932 when it appeared that he would miss an important lodge meeting in Las Cruces, New Mexico, due to his ill health, the meeting was moved to Cerrillos so that he could count 32 years of continuous service, and never miss a meeting. The August 12, 1932 *New Mexico State Record* Newspaper recorded the event:

THE GRAND LODGE
OF
ANCIENT, FREE AND ACCEPTED MASONS
OF
NEW MEXICO

ALPHEUS A. KEEN, GRAND SECRETARY
P. O. BOX 535
ALBUQUERQUE

March 26, 1932.

At the Fifty-fourth Annual Communication of the Grand Lodge of Ancient, Free and Accepted Masons of New Mexico, held at Las Cruces, March 21, 22 and 23, 1932, the following officers were elected and appointed:

Thomas J. Hall	Roswell	Grand Master
John Milne	Albuquerque	Deputy Grand Master
William H. Duckworth	Clovis	Senior Grand Warden
Reuben Perry	Albuquerque	Junior Grand Warden
Edward R. Paul	Santa Fe	Grand Treasurer
Alpheus A. Keen	Albuquerque	Grand Secretary
George L. Machen	Albuquerque	Grand Lecturer
John J. Kelly	Douglas, Arizona	Grand Lecturer Emeritus
Charles C. Hill	Roswell	Grand Chaplain
Ira L. Pennington	Clayton	Senior Grand Deacon
Raymond E. A. Drolet	Farmington	Junior Grand Deacon
Joseph Wertheim	Carlsbad	Grand Marshal
Alva L. Hamilton	Tucumcari	Senior Grand Steward
William M. Bickel	Gallup	Junior Grand Steward
James P. McNulty	Cerrillos	Grand Sword Bearer
Arthur C. Culver	Albuquerque	Grand Tyler

The Fifty-fifth Annual Communication will be held at Roswell on Monday, March 20, 1933, at ten o'clock A. M.

Alpheus A. Keen,
Grand Secretary.

McNulty was installed as Grand Sword Bearer for the Free Masons in 1932. Although he couldn't attend the meeting in Las Cruces, the lodge held a special ceremony in Cerrillos for the aging Irishman.

Patricia McGraw

The New Mexico State Record renders the account of the Grand Lodge of Masonic Order's visit to McNulty in Cerrillos. This extended his service in the Masonic Order to 32 years without interruption.

[continuation of newsclipping at right]

Indian War Veteran:

Mr. McNulty, now 86 years of age, is a veteran of the Indian wars. He is a charter member of the Cerrillos lodge, which was instituted in 1890, and a member of the first class of the Scottish Rite in Santa Fe 1909. He has served several terms as master of the lodge at Cerrillos. Those who were present report Mr. McNulty was very happy, and deeply touched by the tribute. This is a story about the Masonic order and one of its grand old men. But perhaps it will not be out of place to add that Mr. McNulty has been a life member of the Santa Fe lodge of B.P.O.E for a quarter of a century. It would be wholly superfluous to add that Elks hold him just as high in their esteem.

Throughout the years of 1932 and 1933, the Free Masons, the Scottish Rite, the Benevolent Protective Order of Elks kept tabs on McNulty, sending visitors, letters, and honoring him. When he slipped on the ice going to his mailbox in Cerrillos and suffered a broken hip, the Masons sent him a note, one that arrived on the day of his death:

GRAND LODGE OF MASONIC ORDER HONORS MCNULTY

James P. McNulty of Cerrillos, a member of the grand lodge of Masons of New Mexico for 31 years, was unable to attend the session of the grand lodge which was held at Las Cruces some weeks ago. But the grand lodge stretched the veteran's years of continuous service to thirty-two by re-electing him grand sword bearer.

And the grand lodge did more than that. It decided that if Mr. McNulty could not come to the grand lodge, the grand lodge ought to go to Mr. McNulty. So it did just that. And in honoring its venerable and faithful member, the grand lodge highly honored itself.

Monday Night

The extraordinary pilgrimage to the home of Mr. McNulty was made Monday night, led by Thomas J. Hall of Roswell, grand master. Other officers of the grand lodge in the caravan were:

Reuben Perry, Albuquerque, grand junior warden; A. A. Kean, Albuquerque, grand secretary; Edward R. Paul, Santa Fe, grand treasurer. The last three named hold the rank of the thirty-third degree, honorary, of the Scottish Rite. Mr. Kean is the dean of grand secretaries of the United States. He has held the office for 47 years. Other Masons from Santa Fe, Albuquerque and Cerrillos swelled the number in attendance to more than fifty. Following the session of the grand lodge, when Mr. McNulty was installed as grand sword bearer for his thirty-second term, a banquet was served at the Lamb hotel in Madrid.

Indian Was Veteran

Mr. McNulty, now 86 years of age, is a veteran of the Indian wars. He is a charter member of the Cerrillos lodge, which was instituted in 1890, and a member of the first class of

From the Grand Lodge of Ancient, Free and Accepted Masons of New Mexico: Grand Master Thomas Hall to McNulty, January 25, 1933.
...have just received the information thru Brother Edward R. Paul of your unfortunate accident of several days ago. The Grand Master hastens to extend the sympathy and wishes for a speedy recovery from the bottom of seven thousand Masonic hearts. I am sure that they appreciate the long and valuable service you have rendered to your fellowmen and brethren during the time when men had to be men, and Masons had to stand together. I am notifying all Constituent Lodges thru my monthly letter of February 1st of your ill fortune and no doubt you will hear from them direct. With the sincere hope that you will soon be able to take your place among the good brethren of Cerrillos.

Health issues plagued McNulty in his later years, everything from broken ribs to an ulcer to a broken hip. To treat his ulcer, McNulty's prescription included soda bicarbonate, bismuth subuit, maganes [sic.] carbonate, and aqua mint jip. But it was the broken hip combined with pneumonia that killed McNulty on January 25, 1933, at the age of 87. Many obituaries hit the New Mexico papers. The *Albuquerque Journal* and the *New Mexican* in Santa Fe ran multiple stories on his death. The Santa Fe paper ran the most extensive obituary, full of many mistakes. Rumors had swirled around McNulty's life; and so it was with his death, with many people making up "facts" to fill his life story. McNulty's daughter took the time to correct the article:

The *New Mexican*, Thursday January 26, 1933...

James P. McNulty, Civil War Veteran and Mining Man of Cerrillos, Dies Aged 84 [should have been 87] **Years:**

The funeral of James P. McNulty, New Mexico's veteran mining man, and Civil war veteran, who died last night, aged 84 [87] years, at St. Vincent's hospital, will be held in Santa Fe. The arrangements and day of the funeral will be announced tomorrow. The body will rest in the drawing room of C.A. Rising and Company. A week ago McNulty slipped on the ice as he was going to the Cerrillos post office for his mail, and broke his hip. He was brought to the hospital here, where he died, all efforts of physicians and surgeons to save him being of no avail owing to his advanced age. McNulty was a native of Central City, Colo., "the little Kingdom of Gold", and nearly all of his life he dreamed of the two precious metals, gold and silver, which had produced such enormous fortunes. McNulty was regarded as a successful mining man, having had the nerve and courage to stick it out, despite failures of others in the southwest. He owned many mining claims in Cerrillos and around Albuquerque and Magdalena.

Another Old Timer Gone

In his death New Mexico and the Southwest lost one of its oldest miners, prospectors, ex-soldiers, Masons and picturesque characters. It was said of him by the late Clinton J. Crandall that McNulty for years believed that King Solomon's original and unparalleled mines were located near Cerrillos, N.M. He was custodian for many years of the famous Tiffany turquoise mines near Cerrillos, and later became owner when the Tiffanys abandoned their holdings [He never owned the mines]

The Tiffany Mines

Joseph Byrne of Cerrillos and Santa Fe, said today that the Tiffany mines probably covered an area of 200 acres, and were acquired by the famous New York jewelers 40 or 50 years ago. According to legend, Mr. Byrne said, the turquoise mines were known to the Spanish conquistadores over three centuries ago, and were rediscovered about a half century ago.

Trouble With Indians

The taking over of these mines by the Tiffany firm led to intermittent troubles with the Santo Domingo Indians and more than once McNulty, as custodian of the mines, had groups of these Indians hauled into the state courts to prosecute them for trespassing. McNulty charged that Indians were taking out the turquoise for their jewelry work, and that they sent bands of turquoise hunters to the mines to work in the moonlight. It was the late George Volney Howard, lawyer of Santa Fe and later of El Paso, also a picturesque character, who defended the Indians in one of his matchless addresses to the jury, in which he referred to the Indians as the "poor horny-handed sons of toil." The Indians got off.

Came Here in 1880

Mr. Byrne said today that McNulty was one of the group of early miners, who had known Haw Tabor and other magnates of the Colorado field, and who had tried to develop silver mines in this region. Silver then was worth $1.25 an ounce and lured countless people from all over the country, from various parts of the world, to Colorado and New Mexico. Silver then was found at the grass roots, but the next deposit turned out to be lead, then zinc and then water at 100 feet.

Silk Hatted Brigade

"When McNulty was down at Cerrillos, prospecting the silk-hatted, frock-coated brigade of professional men from the east could be seen passing over the hills," said Mr. Byrne today. "They came because they had heard of the great strikes at Leadville and around Denver and other parts of Colorado. They were lured to stay and spend money in New Mexico when silver was found at the grass roots. Little did they know how much silver would be found, however. This section never was really drilled or mined; it was only prospected. It always has needed capital for a diamond drill. McNulty and ONeill and other mining men of the 1880 period saw possibilities but, so far, only a few holes have been dug. We do not know what these mines might produce."

Sold To C.I. Smith

Mr. Byrne says that McNulty's biggest deal, perhaps, was the sale of the Tiffany mines to Col. Chester I. Smith, Boston promoter, who came out here a few years ago and interested local and eastern capital in the turquoise mines. The demand for turquoise in jewelry fell off two decades ago, but there was a revival and Col. Smith saw vast possibilities in the mine. His venture, however, was not an instantaneous success and he died soon afterward in a hospital in this city. McNulty is said to have made $18,000 [the mines sold for $18,000 total] on the transaction of finding a purchaser for the mines. Mr. Byrne says the Tiffanys allowed the mines to fall to McNulty in payment of his $2,000 a year salary as custodian. [Totally incorrect statement; mines were sold to Smith.]

Organized Masonic Lodge

McNulty and the late Mike O'Neill, his mining companion, organized the branch of the Masonic lodge No. 19, at Cerrillos and for over 32 years McNulty served as an officer of the grant lodge and was a faithful attendant at all meetings in Santa Fe. He was a familiar figure on the streets of the Ancient City, his snowy white mustache contrasting with his ruddy countenance. He was always cheerful and hopeful of "big developments" in the mining industry of New Mexico.

Leaves Two Daughters

McNulty is survived by two daughters, Mrs. Fannie McCraw of Cerrillos, and Mrs. Sarah [Agnes] Kohler of Tucson, Arizona. Many grandchildren also survive him.

McNulty & Friends
Selling a Mine Or Two
1922 - 1933

McNulty to Sterling, January 4, 1922

I ...found your letter here which states that you had to await the Pinkerton's report as to how to dispose of the property. I would have written sooner but was waiting to receive the tax report to send you. They have been late in sending out the notice which I received today.

Shearman & Sterling to McNulty, January 16, 1922

We have received the enclosed form of return to be made by the owner of mining property for the year 1922. Will you kindly attend to the matter of having it filled out, executed and filed, keeping in mind the fact that the legal title to the property now stands in the name of Frederic N. Gilbert.

Shearman & Sterling to McNulty, January 17, 1922

We have received the consent of the Messrs. Pinkerton to permit you to sell the Tiffany Turquoise mines on terms that give you one-third of the net selling price. ...The foregoing division of the net selling price applies to a sale not exceeding $20,000. Above such figure, as agreed with you when you were here, we will arrange upon a different basis of compensation.

Shearman & Sterling to McNulty, February 11, 1922

Sometime ago we wrote to the county treasurer of Santa Fe County at Santa Fe, New Mexico, asking him to send us the bill for the tax for the year 1921, on the property in Santa Fe County, formerly owned by the American Turquoise Company, but we have not yet received the bill from him. Will you be good enough to obtain the tax bill and send it to us for payment?

McNulty to Gilbert, February 26, 1922

Answering your favor of the 11th inst. in which you state that you did not receive the tax bill. I wish to say that after writing twice to the county treasurer and receiving no reply, and as the time was up for the payment, I went to Santa Fe yesterday and paid the tax myself. ...I wish to call your attention to your letter of January 17 written by FNG stating that you had received the tax bill which I sent you and saying that you were then remitting $48.59 direct to the treasurer which the treasurer says he never received. Hereafter, the property will be in your name instead of the American Turquoise Company.

Gilbert to McNulty, March 6, 1922

Are you making any progress toward the disposition of the property?

McNulty to Gilbert, April 12, 1922

I have not been able to do anything as yet towards selling the property. It is getting more ruined every day. Some people are working it steadily and I have not the means to prosecute them. I put an ad in the Santa Fe paper for the last ten days but have had no results yet.

John Doe [blank] Warrant for turquoise thieves, May 2, 1923

J.P. McNulty being first duly sworn, on his oath says that at the county of Santa Fe, State of New Mexico, on the 1st day of May, 1923, John Doe, whose true name is to affiant unknown, did unlawfully and feloniously break and sever, with intent to steal, ore and mineral from that certain mine, lode, ledge, or deposit in the county of Santa Fe, State of New Mexico, known as the Tiffany Turquoise Mine and did take, remove, and conceal the ore and mineral therefrom with intent to defraud one Frederic Gilbert, who is the person rightfully entitled to the same; all contrary to the Statute in such case made and provided, and against the peace and dignity of the State of New Mexico. Wherefore, affiant prays that warrant issue against the said John Doe, so that he may be arrested and dealt with according to law.

Appointment of McNulty to Deputy Sheriff, May 2, 1923

I, Tomas P. Delgado, Sheriff of the County of Santa Fe, do hereby appoint J.P. McNulty a deputy sheriff within and for the county of Santa Fe, in the State of New Mexico. Given under my hand this 2nd day of May A.D. 1923 Tomas P. Delgado

McNulty to Gilbert, July 8, 1923

I am writing you to let you know that I am still looking after your property. I had the taxes reduced on the property last year and this year. I paid last year's taxes on February 26, 1923, and have mailed you the receipt but I have not heard from you as yet. I would like to know if you received it or not. The property is in very bad shape. The shafts are all filled in, the sides blacked in so that it is impossible to get into the mines now. I swore out John Doe warrants on May 2nd last; the deputy sheriff in Santa Fe has one and also the deputy sheriff in Cerrillos, but they have not caught any of the parties yet. I have offered a reward of $5 for every one caught at the mine.

I am enclosing the sworn complaint which you will please return to me again as I may have to get out more warrants in Cerrillos as this complaint will hold good for three years. I have an ad in the Albuquerque Journal for the sale of the property. I shall put it in some Eastern papers as I have not had any answer except but one answer from this and I believe that I have held the price too high. I should like you to let me know the very lowest price you would take. It is almost impossible to sell it in the shape the mine is in now. I should appreciate an early reply and the return of the enclosed copy. I am enclosing the advertisement and should like very much to have you publish it in a Boston or a New York paper or any good Journal you know.

Tucked right under a "Strawberries for Sale" ad sat the Tiffany Mine for sale ad. McNulty eventually managed to sell those claims although he never sold his own.

Gilbert to McNulty, July 18, 1923

I appreciate your kindness in looking after the turquoise mine. I return you herewith the complaint, as you request. But, as we told you when you were here, we have practically abandoned our interest in the property. If you can make anything out of it for yourself by making a sale, we will undoubtedly let it go for whatever price you can obtain for it and recognize your efforts in the matter.

FOR SALE MISCELLANEOUS

STRAWBERRY PLANTS, Progressive Everbearing, are now for sale. $2.00 a hundred. Jensen, U. S. Indian School. 4-15

FOR SALE—The American Turquoise Company mine, better known as the Tiffany Turquoise Mine, in the Cerrillos Mining District. This property is a valuable copper and gold proposition, in which the turquoise alone should pay cost of operation. Claim consists of about 50 acres. For terms and further information, address J. P. McNulty, Cerrillos, N. M. 4-12

BOARDERS WANTED.

GOOD TABLE BOARD, by week. 115 Cerrillos Road. Phone 166-W.
 4-8tf

MALE AND FEMALE

McNulty to Gilbert, January 9, 1924

This is to let you know that I have made every effort possible to sell the mine during the past year but have not succeeded because the copper is no good. I had an advertisement in several western papers and some eastern ones but with no results. Several parties came to examine the property and had tests made which showed that what copper there is of low grade which cannot be treated to advantage in the smelter. I do not like to give up entirely since looking after the place for thirty two years as I paid last year's taxes and shall continue to do so.

In your last letter you stated that the company gave up all claim to the property and that I could go ahead and make what I could out of it. But the only way I could make anything out of it would be if you could give me a deed to the property, which would be as good as a pension for me..as I would lease or rent it to some one who might work it for the turquoise and trade with the Indians. I shall stand all costs of making out the papers if you decide to let me have the deed. The only payment I would offer you would be some nice Indian rugs which I have. I shall not forget you if I get anything out of it.

McNulty to Gilbert, January 25, 1924

The Sheriff of Santa Fe with three deputies was here yesterday to notify me that he arrested seven Mexicans whom he caught at work in the mine. The time for the hearing is set for tomorrow at 2 P.M. and I shall have to be there early to see my attorney. The sheriff is anxious to have them prosecuted and advised me to get my own attorney and not to trust to the office of district attorney. This I intended to do anyway for they did not prosecute the men the last time when I had them indicted. As that party can poll fifty votes for the district attorney I fear he would not prosecute them. I shall fight them to a finish and I intend to get a good attorney. Of course it will cost some money to do so, and as I offered a reward of $5- each for all they would catch. I shall have to pay $35- to the sheriff.

McNulty to Gilbert, January 30, 1924

Since I wrote you last I went to Santa Fe on Saturday for the hearing of the seven men the Sheriff caught at the mine. They are bound over to the Grand Jury under $1000 bond. That same day I had thirteen search warrants made to search their houses etc. and the sheriff went to their houses on Monday with some deputies. They found five and half pounds of turquoise with matrix and so I had to go again to Santa Fe yesterday as they were tried before the Justice of the Peace.

I swore that the stone was stolen from your property but three of them swore it came from their own property. I had my attorney and they had one and the justice said there was not enough evidence to show on my side that it came from the mine and so he returned the stone to the Mexican again. My attorney said we could not take an appeal as the justice had the power to settle it and he will do no more about that case but he will see that they are prosecuted if they are indicted. Of course it has cost me a good deal of money so far but as I stated in my last letter that I shall fight it to a finish.

R. R. EXPRESS OFFICE, HOLBROOK, ARIZONA

WHITE CONE TRADING CO.
E. E. NELSON, PROP'R
LICENSED U. S. INDIAN TRADER
NAVAJO BLANKETS AND SILVERWARE
A SPECIALTY

——— DEALER IN ———
WOOL, HIDES AND PELTS
SHEEP AND CATTLE

NA-AH-TEE CANYON, ARIZONA

Nov. 18, 1924.

Mr. McNulty,
Cerillos, New Mexico.

My dear Mr. McNulty:--
    Please send me, by return Parcel Post, C. O. D., twenty ($20.00)dollars worth of your very best quality of slab turquoise.
    Perhaps you will remember the kind that Mr. Joe Hatch of Fruitland got of you this summer. The blue was at least 3/8ths of an inch with just a tiny little bit of rock on each side--no waste at all. It was the prettiest blue I ever saw.
    If you will get this off to me at once, it will be a great favor.
    Thanking you for your courtesy, I am

Very truly yours,
Mrs. E. E. Nelson -

McNulty constantly received requests for information on turquoise in the Cerrillos area. Even though the big mining days had past, people around the world dreamed of finding those nuggets that had escaped notice. Demand for the sky blue stone returned slowly.

McNulty to Gilbert, March 19, 1924

As I have had no reply to my two last letters I wish to write again to inform you that I have filled out the tax blanks on the property for this year in February. Also to let you know that there is not to be any grand jury this spring as it is another election year. I shall have to wait till next fall to have the parties who robbed the mine prosecuted. I am still trying to dispose of the property but can get no buyer.

McNulty to Gilbert, November, 1924

I writing to let you know that I am still trying to sell the property but can not sell it. I have offered to one party for a 1000 dollars but they said it would cost more for taxes then the property was worth. But I will pay the taxes for this year and then I may throw up my hands and say good bye. Very true it has cost me quite a bit of money this last nine years. Now in regards to the men that the sheriff caught in the mine — there was no court nor jury this year. But they say there will be after election. That is politics to catch votes. But as I have written you before I will fight it to a finish if I have to mortgage the house I live in. Very true my life is in danger not safe with that crowd.

Gilbert to Edwards [local attorney for McNulty], February 18, 1925

I am inclined to execute this power of attorney but inasmuch as the Pinkerton estate has an interest in a part of this property, I desire to inform them of my action and obtain their approval thereof. I am endeavoring to locate the present representatives of the Pinkerton estate hoping to interest them in this matter. ...but this search has already consumed some time, and will, of necessity, take some further time. Therefore, I suggest that Mr. McNulty let this matter rest until I can get the Pinkertons to approve my action in signing this power of attorney.

W.C. Porterfield [agent selling mines] to McNulty in telegram, April 30, 1925

Have party here from New York. Wants turquoise mines. Can you on your property make a showing of turquoise in place of your mines how many patented claims. Wire me immediately collect. Price, and if you can give title. Party waiting for answer.

McNulty to Gilbert, telegram, May 4, 1925

Subject your approval. Have sold turquoise property to reliable Boston parties for eighteen thousand dollars. Payable mntly in nine months payments to be made in bank here. Wire me instruc-

tions here immediately as parties are waiting. I have been working hard and will expect half of sale which I hope you will do.

Porterfiled to McNulty, May 5, 1925

This agreement made this date by and between J.P. McNulty and W.C. Porterfield provides that in event of closing deal now pending with Chester H. Smith for purchase of the Cerrillos Turquoise property, provides that W.C. Porterfield is to recover $100 out of each payment received monthly by J.P. McNulty for the first eight monthly payments and the 9th monthly payment to be $200.

Gilbert to McNulty, telegram, May 6, 1925

Yr Fourth Gilbert SGD McNulty receipt acknowledge. Answer soon possible.

WESTERN UNION TELEGRAM

Form 1207 A

CLASS OF SERVICE DESIRED
TELEGRAM
DAY LETTER XXXX
NIGHT MESSAGE
NIGHT LETTER

Patrons should mark an X opposite the class of service desired; OTHERWISE THE MESSAGE WILL BE TRANSMITTED AS A FULL RATE TELEGRAM

NEWCOMB CARLTON, PRESIDENT   GEORGE W. E. ATKINS, FIRST VICE-PRESIDENT

Send the following message, subject to the terms on back hereof, which are hereby agreed to

May 4, 1925.

To   Mr. Frederic N. Gilbert,

Street and No. (or Telephone Number)   C/o Shearman & Sterling,

Place   55 Wall Street, New York City, N. Y.

Subject your approval have sold turquoise property to reliable Boston parties for eighteen thousand dollars payable monthly in nine months payments to be made in bank here Wire me instructions here immediately as parties are waiting I hope been working hard and will expect half of sale which I hope you will do

J. P. McNulty

McNulty wired Gilbert about the potential sale of the mines and set off a storm of wires and letters between Cerrillos and New York City.

352 • Patricia McGraw

Gilbert to McNulty, telegram, May 7, 1925

    Referring telegrams McNulty May fourth yours May fifth. Will sell at price stated. Cannot give McNulty more than one third of price without consent of interested parties. Stop. Will endeavor obtain their consent to giving them one half and trust we can.

Agreement between McNulty and Chester Smith [purchaser of the property], May 7, 1925

    This agreement, made in duplicate, this 7th day of May, 1925, between James P. McNulty, representing the owners of the herinafter described mining property of Cerrillos, New Mexico, of the first part, and Chester H. Smith, of Boston, Massachusetts, of the second part, Witnesseth: That in consideration of the sum of One Dollar to him in hand paid, the receipt whereof is hereby acknowledged, and performed by the second party as hereinafter set out, the first party covenants and agrees as follows:

    1. On or before June 15th, 1925, to place in escrow in the First National Bank of Santa Fe, New Mexico, good and sufficient mining deeds, conveying to the second party, free from all liens and encumbrances, the following described five patented lode mining claims in the Cerrillos Mining District, Santa Fe County, New Mexico: The Gem, Muniz, Morning Star, and Sky Blue, constituting what is known as the Gem Groups; and the Old Castilian; containing fifty (50) acres, more or less.

    2. To place in escrow with said deeds, an abstract of title of the said property, showing merchantable title.

    3. To instruct said bank to deliver the said deeds and abstract to the second part upon the payment of the sum of Eighteen Thousand Dollars ($18,000) and the delivery of certain stock, as hereinafter provided.

    The second party covenants and agrees, upon the placing in escrow of the said papers by the first party as aforesaid, to pay to the credit of the first party of the said Bank, the sum of Two Thousand Dollars ($2,000) on or before June 15th, 1925; and to pay the further sum of Two Thousand Dollars ($2,000) on or before the 15th day of each calendar month thereafter for a period of eight (8) successive months. The second party further agrees within sixty (60) days from this date, to cause to be issued to the first party fifty thousand (50,000)

TIFFANY BLUE • 353

June 29, 1935.

Mr. Chester H. Smith,
100 Boylston St.,
Boston, Mass.

Dear Mr. Smith:-

      I am returning to you, as agreed, Certificates Nos. 2 and 3 for 2,000 shares each of the capital stock of Los Cerrillos Turquoise Gem Corporation, endorsed in blank and witnessed.

      Mr. Gilbert came to my terms, and I have today received one-half of the first payment made by you. Mr. Edwards is writing to you about the title.

                                Yours very truly,

                                McNulty

McNulty accepted some of his commission in the form of shares in the turquoise mines. He still believed that riches could be found there especially since Chester Smith planned to start the mines in a big way.

shares of the capital stock, full paid and non-assessable, par value one Dollar ($1), of a corporation with a total authorized capital of not to exceed two hundred and fifty thousand dollars ($250,000), to be organized by the second party to take over from the said second party the above described mining property and to develop the same, said corporation to be known as Chesterfields's Turquoise Deposit & Mfg. Co.

354 • Patricia McGraw

McNulty to Gilbert, May 11, 1925

I am writing to let you know how I came to sell the property through the Porterfiled Bros, one in Boston and one in Grant County, New Mexico. I had written Mr. Porterfield last year that I would sell it for $15,000, but when he got here with the Boston man, I raised it to $18,000 so Mr. Smith agreed to the price and I have to pay Porterfield Bro. $1,000 out of what I will get out of the deal. That is if the Boston people will make the payments and Mr. C. Smith told me to put a watchman at $60 per month which I have done.

If they do not send the money I must pay the man myself but I trust they will for it has cost me over a thousand dollars in money this last seven or eight years beside by time to protect the property. I have been honest and true to the company and now Mr. Gilbert, I trust to you to see to it that I will get more than one third of the purchase price and that you will write me as I should like to hear from you. My attorney wanted to know who would pay for the drawing up the plat and abstracts of property and I told him that I should pay it as soon as he has them made out. This is another bill I shall have to pay. I hope this deal doesn't fall through for it may take many years to dispose of such property again for it would be a hard thing to sell it as the property is in bad shape.

Gilbert to McNulty, May 16, 1925

I have your favor of the 11th inst. and appreciate all you say therein. The Stillmans, who have a one-half interest in the property, will gladly give you one-half of what they receive and I am now endeavoring to get the consent of the Pinkerton estate to do likewise. I realize your pitiable condition and would like to do everything I can to help you. As the property has been abandoned by the owners, who had even refused to pay the taxes accruing thereon, this selling price comes as a complete surprise and has been due entirely to your efforts and I trust, in view of your many years of service, that I shall be able to obtain the consent of the Pinkerton estate to deal with you as generously as the Stillman estate is willing to do.

Smith to McNulty, telegram, May 29, 1925
    Wire received and believe it advisable to retain man. My understanding he payable once a month. Mailing check to you today. Everything progressing nicely here.

McNulty to Smith, June 2, 1925
    Watchman working. No check yet. Ship turquoise and rugs this week.

Smith to McNulty, telegram, June 12, 1925
    Wired two thousand dollars today. First National Bank Santa Fe per purchase agreement. When did you ship rugs. Best regards. Mailing check thirty dollars.

Gilbert to McNulty, telegram, June 18, 1925
    Forwarded deed to bank today with instructions to pay you one third of each installment. Stop. Letter follows.

Deputy sheriff appointment, June 15, 1925
    I, Isaisas Alarid, sheriff of the county of Santa Fe, do herby appoint J.P. McNulty a deputy sheriff within and for the county of Santa Fe, in thd State of New Mexico. Given under my hand this 15 day of June, A.D. 1925. Oath of office: I, J.P. McNulty do solemnly swear that I am a citizen of the United States, a resident of the County of Santa Fe, in the State of New Mexico, and that I will faithfully support the Constitution of the United States and the Constitution of the State of New Mexico and that I will faithfully discharge the duties of deputy sheriff to which I have been appointed, to the best of my ability, and that I am not the holder of any monies due the State of New Mexico nor any county thereof. So help me God.

McNulty to Smith, June 27, 1925
    My dear Mr. Smith, your registered letter received and in reply will say that the deed is in the bank, but the trustee has cut me down to one third. So I

gave him notice that I will put a lien on the property, but Mr. Edwards, my attorney, has not heard from him yet. I can not see that me doing so will interfere with your company as you can work my property cheaper and to better advantage. I shall go to Santa Fe the 29th. You said in your telegram 2 weeks ago that you mailed me a check to pay the watchman. It did not come as yet. See to it. The 4 rugs are worth 200 dollars but you can have them for 150.

McNulty to Smith, June 29, 1925

I am returning to you, as agreed, Certificates Nos. 2 and 3 for 2,000 shares each of the capital stock of Los Cerrillos Turquoise Gem Corporation, endorsed in blank and witnessed. Mr. Gilbert came to my terms, and I have today received one-half of the first payment made by you. Mr. Edwards is writing to you about the title.

Porterfield to McNulty, July 2, 1925

I am duly in receipt of yours of June 30th with check $100 covering part commission on the sale of the Turquoise mines. I thank you for this and hope that the deal may be consummated to the satisfaction of all. My brother, M.W. saw Mr. Smith in Boston and he seems still enthusiastic over his acquisition of a fine turquoise mine.

Porterfield to McNulty, July 21, 1925

It is difficult to understand why they do not keep the watchman paid. In fact, Mr. Smith is quite an enigma to me, but from what my brother writes me from Boston they have big plans for the promotion of a big turquoise manufacturing and selling proposition and a determination to carry it to completion and of course, we all wish them success.

Smith to McNulty, July 31, 1925

On account of your age and all your own affairs you have to look after, it seemed advisable for me to engage Apolonio Marez to stay on the property and guard it until my arrival. I have so notified him by letter today. Matters are progressing nicely here, and I expect to leave Boston within the next week or ten days for New Mexico. Upon my arrival we can go over all matters to your satisfaction.

Smith to McNulty, August 14, 1925

I wired Mr. Edwards today to notify you that $2,000 was on deposit at the First National Bank to your credit, as per contract for the third payment.

Porterfield to McNulty, August 22, 1925

A recent letter from my brother in Boston stated that he had seen Smith who stated that he was leaving in a few days for New Mexico to start work, but from what you state, it appears that he has not yet arrived. Sometimes you can't tell what some people mean when they say something. But I suppose he is rustling and possibly doing the best he can, and I hope, for the sake of all concerned that they may be able to keep up the payments until it is completed. I can't understand why they don't provide pay for the Mexican watchman. I had recommended to Smith that he ought to keep you on his pay roll and in his employ, that you knew more than anyone about the property, how to mine in the most economical way to sort and take care on the production, etc. but he seems to have his own ideas and to insist on his own way, however impractical they seem to be.

Porterfield to Smith, August 22, 1925

You have, I think, the best Turquoise Property in the U.S. and it should be properly worked by experienced turquoise miners.

Porterfield to McNulty, September 20, 1925

I am pleased to have yours of 17th enclosing check $100 covering fourth payment account of turquoise deal. I note that you state that Mr. Smith is at the mines working 5 or 6 men, but you say nothing about his conferring with you regarding methods or manner of operations, but from what you state it appears that he is depending on his own ideas as to methods etc. Well, that is perhaps his own business and we might just as well not give ourselves any undue concern so long as they keep up the payments. However, I do not understand why he does not see fit to avail himself of your years of experience and knowledge of the business. All is going well here, good rains, grass growing fine, cattle getting fat, beef getting tender, lots of good fruit and melons you better come down during your vacation and we will take some joy trips.

Edwards to Gilbert, October 24, 1925

The Los Cerrillos Turquoise Gem Corporation which as taken over Mr. McNulty's contract with Colonel Smith for the purchase of the five turquoise claims, and which company has been making the payments under the contract, has had the title to the property examined, and it found that in 1893, the American Turquoise Company entered into a contract with one Herbert A. Thomas. ...Mr Thomas assigned one-half of his rights under this contract to a man by the name of Harry Wood, of Springfiled, Green County, Missouri. ...In the foreclosure proceedings brought by the Farmer's Loan & Trust Company, Thomas was joined as a defendant but Harry Wood was not. ...There is a possiblity that Harry Wood might come in and claim a lien upon one-half of the gross proceeds from the sale of turquoise made by the successors of the American Turquoise Company. In order to clear the property of this cloud, it will be necessary to bring a suit to quiet the title against any claim of Mr. Wood. The makers of the deed have been requested to remove this cloud, and I am writing both to you and Mr. McNulty concerning the matter.

McNulty to Gilbert, October 26, 1925

    Mr. Smith that bought the property from me is in the hospital these last 3 weeks sick. He is some better. They are clearing out the mines with eight men working. I will be 80 years next March. Please write me.

Porterfiled to McNulty, October 27, 1925

    I am pleased to acknowledge receipt of yours on recent date enclosing your check $100 as commission of the turquoise deal. Hope they keep it up, and also I hope Mr. Smith has recovered from the affliction of carbuncle which you mention.

Paul Walter [vice president First National Bank] to McNulty, December 12, 1925

    We are in receipt of telegraphic orders to pay $2,000 on the Turquoise Gem Corporation's escrow, less the charges for telegram, or other expenses.

McNulty to Gilbert, December 17, 1925

    I have written you October 26 about certain matters but have not heard from you as yet. I have been to Santa Fe on December 15. I have signed for $1,000 one thousand dollars to be sent to you. And the attorney told me that he thinks the two last payments will be held back until matters are straightened out. So now it is up to you to see to it. I have paid out over seven hundred dollars these last five years to lawyers, rewards, search warrants and trips to Santa Fe and paying the taxes for five years. I have also paid this year's taxes in full. I have worked hard to save the property for you or you would never get one dollar for it, so I think that you should pay me some of the expenses. But I will not pay any more.

McNulty's Letter Collection 1926-1933 Mining Business

Geo. B. McFadden, mining engineer, to McNulty, February 18, 1926

Your name has been given me as one to whom I might write for information about the Cash Entry and Bottom Dollar lode claims and also for information regarding what is locally called "The Four Sans" group, consisting of the San Juan, San Rosa, San Marcus and San Miguel lode claims, all being in the Los Cerrillos Mining District, Santa Fe County, N.M. I shall appreciate it very much if you will give me the names and addresses of the owner or owners of all of these claims. Are all of them being worked now and if so are they worked under bond and lease or on straight lease or by owners? If any of them are idle please say which ones are idle. If any of them are held by lease, is the lease for sale? Or are any of the claims for sale?

Leonard Grant, General Land Investment Corporation, to McNulty, July 11, 1927

Your ad in the Albuquerque Journal noted, for 30 acres patented mining claims, and mines. Can you furnish an engineer's report, giving prospective tonnage of the various mines, and the forms and occurrence of the different ores? Also please give details as to developments already made, distances to nearest R.R. and towns, size and conditions of veins or deposits, etc. If you want to sell outright, please name price that will cover our commission, of ten per cent, also the same commission, if you prefer to lease. We are in a position to interest eastern capital in a few sound propositions.

McNulty to Grant, July 16, 1927

I formerly worked this property for turquoise, when market for same was good, but I have never worked it for gold or copper. There is over eight thousand dollars worth of development done on the property. One prospect shaft was sunk sixty-five foot in depth the ore of which assayed ten dollars in gold. The property has not been worked for sixteen years.

There is one shaft, twenty six foot in depth that has parities of copper 5 ft. wide, which, I think, will turn into a big body of ore. As I am a man over eighty years of age I can not look after the property. As to getting samples, I think it advisable for you to send an expert or engineer to examine the property. ...I sold the Tiffany Turquoise Mine to a Boston Syndicate, two years ago. They made me an offer, eighteen months ago, of twenty-five thousand dollars, for my property which I turned down. I hold my property for at least thirty thousand dollars.

My property is worth three times as much as the property I sold them for eighteen thousand. I tell you, truthfully, that the other company can do nothing without my property, as I own two thirds of the hill, and you may be able to make a good deal with that company. If you think you can handle this please answer by return mail as I have other people interested in buying.

Fletcher to McNulty, October 3, 1929

I have a party in the market for a Turquoise property and have been informed that there is Turquoise in your section of N.M. Any assistance you will kindly give me in getting in touch with owners of Turquoise properties will be appreciated very much.

Fletcher to McNulty, October 10, 1929

I have a buyer but he insists that I must get complete data of the property so he can get a good idea of what it is like so he will consider whether it will interest him enough to go to the expense of going and examining it. I ...note you have an old friend in Prescott, John Mahoney; he is an old prospector and mining man. ...I will go and see him tomorrow [to] let him know I heard from you. Now I have one buyer for a Turquoise property and two parties that are dealers in precious gem stones. It is possible I may get you a buyer for your Turquoise. ...Turquoise Questions: Where situated. How many Claims. Ground patented. Title Perfect. How far from nearest R.R. Point. Size of ledge. Is it well defined and good sized outcrop. How much development work done. Condition of road. Value in Gold. Value in Copper Value in Silver. Give best description of how the turquoise occurs and value of the turquoise found in adjoining property. Give the best idea of the value of Turquoise that has been mined from Tiffany property. Also amount of gold-Silver-Copper mined. Has any Turquoise been mined from your property? How large bunches of Turquoise was ever found in the Tiffany or in your property? Give all the information about your property that you believe a buyer would want to know and would interest him. It is important to give complete data presenting a property to a prospective buyer. ...Now about your turquoise that you have for sale, what quantity have you and give me an idea of value per pound, or whatever way the value is judged. In what manner is turquoise sold. Do you ship it to buyers. If so, how are you protected so you get a square deal.

Fletcher to McNulty

I believe you have a good property and if you will give an short option on it, time enough say 90 days as I have to do it all by correspondence and the parties that want to buy are in New York. ...I have one buyer in New York and another in California. I met and had a long talk with our friend Mahoney; he said he was going to write you and tell you of the big time he had at the old Indian Veterans reunion in Las Angeles.

Samuel Nuehauser to McNulty, May 8, 1930 [from Rheinland]

I heard that you are the proprietor of a turquoise mine and wrote to ask you, if you would send me samples of your stones in order to see, if they are suitable for the want here. I write you these lines in the same intention and hope you will forward me a small quantity, sufficient to see the quality, with your lowest quotation. If the quality is satisfactory, ...I should like to have the sale of your stones for this country.

SIEGFRIED KAHN, PRESIDENT
MRS. KATHERYN GOLDFLAN, VICE-PRES.

MRS. ELSA KAHN, SECY. & TREAS.
SAM GOLDFLAN, MANAGING DIRECTOR

Southwest Theatres, Inc.

CAPITAL STOCK $250,000.00
EXECUTIVE OFFICE
ALBUQUERQUE, NEW MEXICO

SAN FELIPE THEATRE
OLD ALBUQUERQUE

March 3rd. 1930.

James Patric McNulty:-
Cerrillos, N.M.

Dear Sir:-

Inclosed find two copies of lease sighn them and return one copy to me.

Say Mr. McNulty I went up and looked the place over in day light the next day and the Kalsomining looked terrible. I had the whole place Kalsomined and will pay half of it.

There was a back water bill of 6.85 on the place up there and I paid that, also pipe was broken off in bath room I had to have that replaced too for water was all over the place, and I had to put window glass in the front and back doors also in one window on the east side of the house.

Also had to buy new grate for Kitchen stove but I will pay for that.

I am sorry that this all had to be done Mr. McNulty but it just had to, to make the place livable. I hope that this will be all that has to be done.
The following is list and amount of repairs with attached receipts for same which I deducted from rent payable.
Window Glass 2Doors 1 window, $7.00
Back Water Bill   6.85
Kalsomining Kitchen 1,room   11.00
                              $ 24.85

Hoping that this is satisfactory with you, I am,

Very truly yours,

J.R./Smith

"WHERE THE SUN SHINES EVERY DAY"

P.S I think I have a job for that nephew of yours...

McNulty's Albuquerque rentals required constant fix ups. And many times his renters were nice. Here, J.R. Smith offered McNulty's nephew a job in 1930.

364 • Patricia McGraw

McNulty's Personal Notes & Letters
1925 - 1933

In McNulty's own handwriting as he applied for an increase in his pension: Undated Questionnaire:

1. The 16th day March 1846 or 1847 in County Sligo Ireland. Records burned. Co D. 37, U.S. Infantry, had been the 3rd Battalion of the 19th. [Question: Where and when were you born & where did you serve.]

2. Pittston, Pa. [Where did you live.]

3. in the latter part of May 1866 [When did you join the infantry.]

4. in New York City [Where did you sign up.]

5. in Pittston, Pa. [Where did you live.]

6. Pittston Pa. [Where did you begin duty.]

7. Farmer and miner [What is your occupation]

8. The later part of May1869 Forgot date [When did you receive your discharge]

9. at Camp Trinadad, Colorado [Where were you discharged.]

10 Pittson Pa. in 1870 and 1871. Chicago, Illinois 1872 and 1873. Pittston, Pa, 1874, 1875, 1876; Colorado 1877, 1878, and 1879; and balance of years to the present in New Mexico. [Where have you lived.]

11. No occupation now. [What is you current occupation.]

12. Five feet 6 inches; 175 lbs, blue, white, fair, scar on right ear by Indian arrow 1868. Also scar on my left thumb by an arrow. [Describe yourself.]

13. James Patrick McNulty. I had Patrick added to my name in the year 1875 by the Catholic bishop in Pittston, Pa. [What is your name.]

2nd page of personal history:

3. Emma McNulty maiden name, Hawley. [Who is your wife.]

4. December 18th, 1898 by Catholic priest in Santa Fe, NM. [When did you marry]

5. Yes, in Guadalupe Church, Santa Fe, NM. [Where did you marry.]

6..Yes. My first wife, Agnes Dunn, married, April 1873 in Chicago, Ill. Died August 1882 in Leadville, Colorado. Married twice only. [Did you have another wife or how many times were you married.]

7. Have no knowledge if married before. [Has your current, living wife been married before.]

8. Got separation in August 1915. [What is status of your current married situation.]

9. Edward James, born the 9th day of February 1874 at Pittston, Pa., died in 1912; Fannie, born October 31, 1876 at Pittstown, Pa. Sara Agnes Born the 15th day of April, 1879 at Central City, Colorado. [List your living children and birth dates.]

McNulty to Daniel Lopez, [renter], January 11, 1922

You are hereby notified that under the terms of my lease with you beginning June 21, 1921, upon the building in Cerrillos, you have defaulted in payment of the rent due on November 21, 1921. You are therefore, given notice that said lease is terminated, and that I hold all personal property of yours on said premises under a lien for the amount of rent now due, to-wit: $25.

McNulty to Lopez, May 2, 1922

Enclosed you will please find a list of the things I have sold at the sale on the 29th of April for the rent and windows broken and you can see that I have done very good to get that price for things I sold as I had a man there to bid so as to get as much as could be got for them. Now the other things you had better sell them as soon as you can or take them away as you will have to pay storage and there is certain parties will try to get them for money you owe them. There is a little stove not much good, 2 tables and 1 wash stand, 2 lamps not much good, dishes. Do not know how much money. Say what you will take for them. ...you said the blankets and 2 pillows belonged to May. She can get them.

Note stating what McNulty sold, April 29, 1922

The following goods were sold. ...1 range to Mrs. Martinez, $17; 1 table to Mr. MacNety, $4; 1 bed & mattress to Mrs. Martinez, $13; 4 chairs to Mrs. Martinez, $6; sold by Jose Gonzalez.

McNulty to H.C. Bursum, Senator from New Mexico, April 6, 1922

I am now receiving $30 per month. I am past 76 years of age and was disabled while in the service. I shall greatly appreciate it if you will take *this matter up and send me the necessary papers, upon which to apply for this increase of pension.*

Bursum to McNulty, October 21, 1922

I am advised under the date of October 20th by the Commissioner, Bureau of Pensions, that you are to receive a pension of $50 per month from September 18, 1922.

Callahan [nephew] to McNulty, February 5, 1923

Well it is sad news I have for you this time Aunt Catherine has passed away. While she had received Communion that very morning. I will never forget Sunday night when a neighbor called me, my sister, Kathryn and myself went to aunt's house and found them all unconscious from coal gas. The chimney was filled with suet and all the fumes from a new fire was going through the house and the entire family in a serious condition. Aunt died two hours after Uncle John and Kathryn and Agnes while still very sick are recovering nicely but Uncle and Agnes are not entirely out of danger as the shock of telling them

DEATHS

MISS ANNA M'NULTY DIES

Miss Anna McNulty, daughter of Mr. and Mrs. Nicholas McNulty of 33 Pine street, died Saturday evening at 9 o'clock in St. Mary-Keller Hospital, South Scranton, after a brief illness of heart trouble. Deceased was an amiable young woman and her death has caused wide sorrow throughout the community, many of her friends being unaware of her illness.

Miss McNulty was a student nurse at St. Mary-Keller Hospital, and had been well until a few days ago when she was taken suddenly ill. On Thursday evening her condition became alarming and her family was called to her bedside. She lingered until Saturday evening when she passed peacefully away.

The sympathy of the community is extended to the bereaved parents on their irreparable loss. Deceased was a brilliant young woman whose lovable disposition and sterling character won the respect and friendship of all with whom she came in contact. She was born and reared in this community and for several years had been an operator at the local exchange of the Bell Telephone Co. Two years ago she entered St. Mary-Keller Hospital as a student nurse and would have completed her course next year, had she been spared.

Miss McNulty was a faithful communicant of St. John's R. C. Church and a member of the Blessed Virgin Sodality. Besides her parents she leaves the following brothers and sisters, Mrs. Merle Finnan, Joseph, Edward, Walter and Francis, all of this city.

Her funeral will be held Wednesday morning at 9 o'clock from the home, 33 Pine street. A solemn requiem mass will be sung in St. John's Church at 9:30 and burial will be in St. John's Cemetery.

Misfortune has fallen heavily on Mr. and Mrs. Nicholas McNulty within the past three weeks. On November 16, their son, Walter, had his left collar bone broken while playing at Coxton yards. Two days afterward Mr. McNulty, a veteran engineer on the Lehigh Valley Railroad, had his leg broken when a lever accidently slipped and struck his leg with terrific force. He is now at Pittston Hospital recovering from the accident. About two years ago another, daughter, Catherine, a student in the sophomore class of Pittston high school, died following short illness.

Another obituary arrived in Cerrillos for McNulty. This time it was his young niece, Anna.

about Aunt Kate's death may have its effect. They told them last night while they received it pretty good. The reaction has not started in yet. Aunt Ann and Mother are all broke up over the affair. Neither them or Aunt Mary will be able to attend the funeral which will be held Wednesday at 10:15 from St. Johns. I was told last night that aunt was preparing to move to Bayonne, N.J., to live near her son John. But, poor soul, her preparation was cut short she certainly was cut off without any ceremony at all just in the midst of her planning. Loretta her other daughter tried all day to get a phone call through from Williamsport but could not for some reason or another. She is all broke up and she has the nicest pair of twins here with her. They are 11 months old. Aunt Ann and mother are not well. Together with this shock they are not good at all. Well, Uncle, next Monday, I will be married and had a trip planned to Florida.

Emma to McNulty, September 22, 1922

Though I may never see you again ...give my love to Fannie, Agnes, Laura and their families. God bless you.

Callahan to McNulty, October 25, 1924

Just a line to let you know what is doing in and around Pittstown and just like before I never have very pleasant news. Aunt Mary McMahon died in New York Wednesday Oct 22 at 5 A.M. with her family all with her. She was sick about 6 months with gall-stones and a heart condition and has been almost at death's door at any time during that time but finally passed away after suffering all that time. On Thursday they had a Mass for her in New York with Father Munley as celebrant and then took the body to my home where we kept it Thursday night when all the family and friends spent the night with it. On Friday morning, the funeral was held with services at St John Church and was buried in St. Johns Cemetery. The nephews of Aunt acted as pallbearers all her family Mark and wife, Mary and husband, Will and his wife and family were here. Aunt Ann was able to attend but my Mother could not. We had a very large funeral about twenty autos and quite a number walked which was a very nice sight for us as funerals nowadays are not very large only relatives taking part. On Thursday night our house was filled with people which added to the high esteem that the people had for Aunty. The family all went back to New York right after the funeral was over. I am enclosing some newspaper clippings about the funeral so you can see none of John McMahons was here as the distance was so great and time so short Aunt Ann and Mother was all broke up on account of Aunty's death and you was mentioned a great deal during the time she was here but today they feel pretty good. We received Fannies letter and was very glad to hear from you sorry you don't get very good health and hope and pray that you and yours will live for some time to come.

Yesterday's Funerals

The respect in which Catherine McNulty was held by her numerous friends and schoolmates was shown by the large number present at her funeral, held yesterday morning at 9:45 from the home of her parents, Mr. and Mrs. Nicholas McNulty, 32 Pine street. At 10:30 a requiem mass was celebrated in St. John's Church by Rev. C.A. Murray. St. John's choir sang the responses, and at the offertory Prof. M.E. Golden sang an "Ave Maria." As the remains were born from the church the choir sang, "Face to Face." There was a beautiful array of floral tributes. They were carried by Misses Jeanette and Grace Tierney, Alice Jeanette and Grace Curley, and Anna Walker. The casket was borne by Peter Curley, John and Gregory Loughney, Elmer Hoffman, Oswald English and James Linnen. Burial was in St. John's cemetery.

Callahan [nephew] to McNulty, March 4, 1925

Aunt Ann is not getting very good health but is still able to get around the house and does quite a lot of work. John is now living with her with his wife and two sons. She still has her little nephew Ward with her. Aunt Ann was to a funeral of her grand-daughter Nick and Katie McNulty, a 15 year old girl who died of kidney trouble and was buried last Wednesday. She was buried last Wednesday. Aunty was able to go but I thought she shouldn't because it wasn't a very nice day, but she is none the worse for it.

Callahan to McNulty, August 12, 1925

Well here we are very close to your old home. I suppose it will be a great surprise to you to know I am here. We are going to Dramore West tomorrow by automobile; Sligo is a very quaint old place. I suppose all the buildings are hundreds of years old and they look the part, well Uncle, you will hear from us later.

A Generation Passes
Dialogues of 1926 - 1933
Personal

Agnes [grand-daughter] to McNulty, July 22, 1926

Dear Grandpa — Just a line to thank you for your gift: it is lovely. I am going to have a black velvet dress trimmed with the buckles.

James Callahan [McNulty's nephew] to McNulty, December 6, 1927

Just a few lines to tell you the latest news about your friends. I don't expect you to write me every time I write you so once in a while will do or when you are in a writing mood. In my last letter I told you of Nick McNulty. ...they have another terrible affliction their daughter died Saturday night after a very short sickness. On Thursday, they had at the hospital where she was learning the nursing profession a supper that included frankfurters "hot-dogs" they call them here. ...after lunch the girls, four in number, went to church to confession to receive the first Friday. ...on their way home they stopped in a lunch room and had a chicken sandwich ...at one, Anna woke up and started to vomit. The roommate, a nurse, called others and the doctor and they tried to do all they could for her, but it seems that when she vomited she strained her heart. ...it also affected the liver. The doctors said right along she would be alright but she never rallied enough to realize that she was so bad. ...she was in a coma state ...until Saturday night about nine o'clock she died; it was certainly a sad affair. Aunt Ann was to the house to see her Sunday. ...she is keeping fine, but all broke up over the death like all people when they see the young go so quickly and themselves left. ...but we must all wait for our time.

Mary Flood [McNulty's sister-in-law] to McNulty, April 2, 1929

Jim I am so heart broken over losing my dear husband. Oh how, I miss him. I can't hardly write but I just seem to want to write to my people, and poor Fannie I am so sorry to hear of her losing her husband also.

Mahoney to McNulty, December 22, 1929

I tried to find some of our old comrades who served at Sumner or Union but have not heard of any. ...I doubt if there are any of them living now. At the Convention at Los Angeles there were over 300 and I found none who were in the Army in my time. All served after I had been discharged in 1870 so you see they are few of us left of that time. We had the best lot of people at the convention I ever met. ...[the next convention] will be held in San Francisco, September 1930 and I will be there if alive then.

Frances [grand-daughter] to McNulty, January 12, 1930

We certainly enjoyed hearing from you all during the Xmas Holidays. We would so love to have sent you all something, but it seems as if each year around Xmas times get hard. This Xmas was not such a pleasant one as

P.S. You are a Charter member of
Gen Geo Crook Camp No 3 U.S.W. Veterans

Prescott
Sept 11th 1929

Mr Jas P McNulty
  Cerrillos N.M.

Dear old Comrade I just received your most welcome letter this morning and am real glad to hear from you I was of the same idea as you were about myself. I often thought that there was something the reason I did not hear from you but better late than never. I am going to Los Angeles tomorrow to attend the Convention and will send you an account of the whole doings. I had a letter from an old 37th Inft man by name of Edward Shultz who served in Co E at Fort Wingate in 1867 to 1869 he is in Hartford Conn his adress is 26 Brownell Av. he is one of the good old timers there are very few of us left. I hope that this will find you as well as it leaves me and hope to hear from you often. Yours with kindest regards

J F Mahoney
Prescott Arizona

J.F. Mahoney, one of McNulty's old army buddies, kept in touch with McNulty and even helped direct interested miners to McNulty.

Papa had one of his drunken spells and left us. Mother is going to get a divorce. She has it in the hands of a lawyer. I am afraid that it will have to go to court as Papa won't agree to Mother's terms. We want the home and about $100 a month but he only wants to give her the home and $50 for four years. This would make a hardship on her. ..of course Mother will have no trouble getting a divorce as Papa has been drinking excessively and running around having a good time.

...Papa threatens to quit his position in order that Mother will be unable to collect alimony. ...This last time on December 13, Papa came in a raised a racket, kicked Mother, then left us. Mother just wanted you all to know how things are as she knew you would like to know. ...Poor Mother hates to take it to Court as it will probably be a fight as Papa has quite a few drunken Elk friends that will no doubt help him. Please do write to her soon as it will make her feel much better a little moral support always helps.

Agnes [daughter] to McNulty, February 28, 1930

Dear Papa, Just a note to tell you that I got my divorce on Tuesday. They were very nice to me. ...I got the home and just $50- per month but clear of debts. People think it is a terrible settlement but my lawyer thought it best to keep the home.

Loretta Scott [niece] to McNulty, May 30, 1930

Dear Uncle James, Well, Uncle you and Aunt Ann are the only ones left out of the McNulty family. My Poor Mother had to be among the ones to be chosen. Well, God is just. Uncle James I am up against it. ...I have had hard luck all the time; now my husband is laid off, no work. I wonder if you could get him a job out there. ...We have nothing, Uncle James. ...I am here in Williamsport. No work here. ...and get him [my husband] a job. He is a chef or cook you all call it. ...I am down and out.

Johnnie [grandson] to McNulty, June 6, 1930

Dear Grandfather: I know I haven't written to you for a long time and I had to rush to get to write this. This is a dun. Can you spare me $17.50 as soon as possible. I had a wreck and broke the top and wind shield and I will have to pay for it by Sunday, day after tomorrow or I will lose my job. I could pay for it this week but I had to pay for my room rent. I bought some underwear so that leaves me 2.50 to eat on for next week. I have been going to work at eight in the morning and working till about two o'clock the next morning or about eigh-

teen hours a day. Last week we hired a new man and am getting off earlier. I am still getting fifteen dollars a week. I hope you can spare that money now as I have to have it by Sunday. I was not hurt at all.

John Callahan [nephew] to McNulty, July 30, 1931

It is some time since I wrote you but it is just a hard thing for me to do is write. ...I hope this will find you all well. You know you said you expected to make us a visit this spring or summer but it won't be long now until the cold weather is on us. Wish you could make us another visit. I talk about you many times how you and Mother would sit and talk about your kiddy days and how you would run away from school. ...What makes it better, I saw the school in Drumore, West Ireland County, Sligo. I don't know whether I told you, but I was there about six years ago. Dear Aunt Ann [McNulty's sister] is very low. In fact, her death is expected any day. She told Katie with whom she lives that she would not speak any more. That was Thursday, but today I thought she was just the same as for the past few days. The doctor said he could not do anything for her [and] that she was just like a piece of machinery just wearing out and nothing could be done. So it is just a case of wait until her time comes. ...Things are very slow here in the mines and shops where I work. We haven't done a thing since May 29 and only worked about forty days this year so you can see how that is. And the shops are only working about one fourth time, so this old town is pretty hard hit. ...I know it is just about the same all over the country and it is so hard to figure what is the cause. If Al Smith was the President, every one would blame him but that is not the case for which I am glad. Well, Uncle, I will ...write you in case aunt dies as I know you will want to hear I know.

Callahan to McNulty, August 21, 1931

Aunt Ann has passed away. She died Tues-

374 • Patricia McGraw

```
day night at 10:20 having been in coma since
last Friday noon.   ...I am enclosing an ac-
count of her death.
```

Newspaper Tributes to McNulty
1933

James McNulty, Cerrillos Mine Owner, is Dead

Had Been Officer of New Mexico Masonic Grand Lodge for 30 Years; Owned Property Here

Santa Fe, Jan. 25 (AP) — James P. McNulty, 84 [really 87], a prominent mining man of Cerrillos, died in St. Vincent's hospital here Wednesday night. McNulty suffered a fractured hip when he slipped and fell on an icy sidewalk near his home in Cerrillos last Wednesday and his death was the result of complications following the injury. For more than 30 years Mr. McNulty had served as an officer of the grand lodge of the Masonic order in the state. He was the owner of several mining claims and real estate at Cerrillos and also held property in Albuquerque. He is survived by a daughter, Mrs. Fannie McCraw, a teacher at Cerrillos, and by another daughter who lives in Arizona. Funeral arrangements have not been completed.

Albuquerque Journal January 26, 1933:

Masons Going to Santa Fe For Funeral, Scottish Rite, Shrine and Grand Lodge Officers and Members Will Honor James McNulty Albuquerque members of the Scottish Rite and Ballut Abyad Temple of Shriners headed by Jack Linn, Shrine recorder, and A.A. Keen, secretary of the Grand Lodge of Masons, will leave for Santa Fe Sunday morning to attend the funeral services of James P. McNulty. McNulty, 83 [really 87], prominent mining man, died at Santa Fe from complications following a fractured hip sustained in a fall on an icy pavement near his home in Cerrillos. Thomas J. Hall, Roswell, grand master of the grand lodge, arrived in Albuquerque Friday night to join the Albuquerque delegation to Santa Fe. The funeral services will be held at the Scottish Rite cathedral at 2 o'clock Sunday afternoon. The Scottish Rite will have charge of the service at the cathedral and the grand lodge at the grave. The grand

James P. McNulty, Civil War Veteran and Mining Man of Cerrillos, Dies Aged 84 Years

The funeral of James P. McNulty, New Mexico's veteran mining man, and Civil war veteran, who died last night, aged 84 years, at St. Vincent's hospital, will be held in Santa Fe. The arrangements and day of the funeral will be announced tomorrow. The body will rest in the drawing room of C. A. Rising and company.

A week ago McNulty slipped on the ice as he was going to the Cerrillos post office for his mail, and broke his hip. He was brought to the hospital here, where he died, all efforts of physicians and surgeons to save him being of no avail, owing to his advanced age. McNulty was a native of Central City, Colo., "the little Kingdom of Gold" and nearly all of his life he dreamed of the two precious metals, gold and silver, which had produced such enormous fortunes. McNulty was regarded as a successful mining man, having had the nerve and courage to stick it out, despite failures of others in the southwest. He owned many mining claims in Cerrillos and around Albuquerque and Magdalena.

ANOTHER OLD TIMER GONE

In his death New Mexico and the southwest lose one of its oldtime miners, prospectors, ex-soldiers, Masons and picturesque characters. It was said of him by the late Clinton J. Crandall that McNulty for years believed that King Solomon's original and unparalleled mines were located near Cerrillos, N. M. He was custodian for many years of the famous Tiffany turquoise mines near Cerrillos, later when the Tiffanys their holdings.

THE TIFFANY MINES

Joseph Byrne of Cerrillos and Santa Fe, said today that the Tiffany mines probably covered an area of 200 acres, and were acquired by the famous New York jewelers 40 or 50 years ago.

According to legend, Mr. Byrne said, the turquoise mines were known to the Spanish conquistadores over three centuries ago, and were rediscovered about a half century ago.

TROUBLE WITH INDIANS

The taking over of these mines by the Tiffany firm led to intermittent troubles with the Santo Domingo Indians and more than once McNulty, as custodian of the mines, had groups of these Indians hauled into the state courts to prosecute them for trespassing. McNulty charged that Indians were taking out the turquoise for their jewelry work, and that they sent bands of turquoise hunters to the mines to work in the moonlight.

It was the late George Volney Howard, lawyer of Santa Fe and later of El Paso, also a picturesque character, who defended the Indians in one of his matchless addresses to the jury, in whch he referred to the Indians as the "poor horny-handed sons of toil." The Indians got off.

CAME HERE IN 1880

Mr. Byrne said today that McNulty was one of the group of early miners, who had known Haw Tabor and other magnates of the Colorado field, and who had tried to develop silver mines in this region. Silver then was worth $1.25 an ounce and lured countless people from all over the country, from various parts of the world, to Colorado and New Mexico.

Silver then was found at the grass roots, but the next deposit turned out to be lead, then zinc and then water at 100 feet.

SILK HATTED BRIGADE

"When McNulty was down at Cerrillos, prospecting, the silk-hatted, frock-coated brigade of pro-

---

NERVOUS WOMEN
Lydia E. Pinkham's Vegetable Compound

n so nervous it seems as though I fly" . . . "My nerves are all on . . "I wish I were dead" . . . 'em have we heard these expressom some woman who has become and run-down that her nerves onger stand the strain.
oman should allow herself to this condition if she can help She should give Lydia E. Pinkgetable Compound a trial. For ty years women have taken this tonic to give them renewed ind vigor.
f every 100 women who report that they are benefited by this Buy a bottle from your drug- . . . and watch the results.

lodge will convene at the Montezuma lodge prior to the service. McNulty was born in Ireland. He was a member of the Cerrillos Lodge No. 19, A.F. and A.M., a member of the Scottish Rite bodies of New Mexico, a member of the Ballut Abyad temple and a grand sword bearer of the grand lodge of the state since October, 1900.

Albuquerque Journal January 27, 1933

Pioneer Passes

With the death of J. P. McNulty of Cerrillos, the state loses one of its earliest living pioneers. He fought the Indians in 1866 marching from Kansas through Oklahoma Indian Territory and Texas to New Mexico where he was on detached duty between Ft. Sumner and Ft. Union, being sent out in pursuit of Indians raiding whenever stages or caravans were held up. Mr. Mc was associated the Custer before he went to ___. Mr. McNulty's discharge papers were signed in Santa Fe in 1869 giving him the honorable discharge with the words: "honest, brave and faithful soldier." He had to go to Denver for his pay where he remained several years during which time he organized the Ancient Order of Hibernians. He lived in Central City, Colorado, where he was in business for some years. After the death of his wife in 1882 he returned to New Mexico where he has remained till his death. For 30 years Mr. McNulty was Superintendent of the Turquoise mines near Cerrillos owned by the American Turquoise Co. He was the first one to get turquoise for commercial use shipping it to Tiffany's in NY. who handled the output of that time.

JAMES P. McNULTY

SUPT. OF TURQUOISE MINES

CERRILLOS

NEW MEXICO

PAST MASTER CERRILLOS LODGE, NO. 19. A. F. & A. M.
SANTA FE CHAPTER NO. 1, R. A. M.
SANTA FE COMMANDERY NO. 1, K. T.
NEW MEXICO CONSISTORY NO. 1, A. A. S. R.
BALLUT ABYAD TEMPLE, A. A. O. N. M. S.

McNulty's business card listed his achievements in the Masonic world. But clearly, that of which he was most proud, was the title of Superintendent of the Turquoise Mines.

ABOUT THE AUTHOR

Patricia McCraw lives in the South Valley outside of the city of Albuquerque, New Mexico, with her husband, Arnold Brown, three horses, a donkey, and six dogs. A former English/Journalism teacher, she currently runs her own small newspaper. She may be reached at PatMcCraw@aol.com.

As a small child she played in the streets of Cerrillos without ever realizing the historical richness of that town. *Tiffany Blue* is a celebration of that heritage.

A portion of the proceeds from the sale of this book will be donated to the Cerrillos Hills Park Coalition, to keep the *Tiffany Blue* story alive. A complete transcription on CD of the original McNulty Papers is also available from the Coalition. See www.CerrillosHills.org for more information.